RACE AND POLITICS IN SOUTH AFRICA

RACE AND POLITICS IN SOUTH AFRICA

Edited by

Ian Robertson
and
Phillip Whitten

Transaction Books
New Brunswick, New Jersey

Library of Congress Catalog Number: 76-50334
ISBN: 0-87855-137-9 (cloth)
Printed in the United States of America.

Library of Congress Cataloging in Publication Data

Main entry under title:

Race and politics in South Africa.

    1. South Africa—Race relations—Addresses, essays,
lectures. I. Robertson, Ian.   II. Whitten, Phillip.
DT763.R27   301.45'1'0968   76-50334
ISBN 0-87855-137-9

Contents

Part III South Africa and the World

Part IV Looking Ahead

Contributors

Foreword

This is a valuable and timely book, offering a compendium of historical background, analysis, and provocative opinion on a preeminent issue in the international community today—the system of *apartheid* and its attendant policies of racial oppression, political repression, and dictatorial rule by the minority government of South Africa.

The editors, Ian Robertson and Phillip Whitten, have succeeded in persuading a group of distinguished authorities to contribute to the volume. Colin and Margaret Legum, for example, are characteristically perceptive in their review of South Africa in the contemporary world and their assessment of the future:

> Change in the Republic [of South Africa] will come primarily through effective black militancy posed against white supremacy, which will sharpen both the internal and external contradictions in the apartheid society, and . . . this will increasingly weaken the status quo. In terms of this thesis international pressures have played an important role—although not as important as the role of *apartheid* itself in radicalizing black attitudes. . . .The mood of white South Africa is complex: its public attitudes mostly exude confidence and resolute determination, but its private doubts show through in repeated warnings coming from its leaders about the dangers now confronting the Republic. To consider these elements in isolation can be misleading. . . .Changes in the attitudes of whites in fact have been much less significant than the growth of militant black consciousness over the last five years [a growth sharply heightened by the killing of Steven Biko and the widespread bannings and crackdown in the fall of 1977]; this radicalization of the black mood may, in the long run, be seen as the most important outcome of *apartheid*; it would be surprising if it were otherwise.

The Legums have hit upon the key to the future of South Africa—a future that will be determined largely by the people who are suffering the most inside that land. International pressures, to be sure, have a very significant bearing on the course of events in South Africa. The recognition of the importance of international action is a key part of the substantive revision of U.S. foreign policy toward South Africa since the Carter administration took office.

As for U.S. policy, the most difficult and controversial is: Just which kinds of pressures—multilateral and bilateral—are most effective in moving South Africa toward our goal of a peaceful transformation of that society into one of majority rule and racial harmony?

Donald B. Easum, one of the most sensitive American diplomats of our time and a man with extensive knowledge of Africa, speaks forthrightly in this book on the subject of developing and implementing our policy:

> The overarching problem will continue to be how to weight the several important U.S. interests that compete in uneasy interrelationship in the formulation of U.S. policies toward South Africa. There is no easy way to avoid the effect of *apartheid* on this interrelationship. There is general agreement in the U.S. and between the U.S. and black Africa, on the moral issues that *apartheid* poses. Differences of view exist, however, on the merits of U.S. pressures and on the effect that such pressures might produce on other U.S. interests. These will not be easy judgments. They will be seen throughout Africa as indicators of America's attachment to fundamental principles of human dignity and individual rights.

Our policy toward South Africa should remain flexible and under constant review, as it has been since early 1977. Whatever pressures we might adopt should be the result of careful analysis of the real needs of those who are suffering and struggling for freedom inside South Africa.

While admittedly it is hazardous to predict what will happen in South Africa, I must say that I do not accept the conclusion, held by some, that a bloodbath in that country is inevitable. What is inevitable, is majority rule, which I contend can be achieved peaceably. As I told an audience of white and black businessmen in Johannesburg in May 1977:

> I share with you a hope for you in South Africa. I get tired of hearing South Africans come to me saying that they are prepared to fight to the death, because I am not interested in anybody dying. I am interested in finding a way for South Africans to live together and with the rest of the world as brothers. And I think as brothers in a world community, the nation of South Africa has a tremendous amount to contribute.

That, I hope, is an objective shared by most of the world and one which the international community will address as international and bilateral relationships with South Africa evolve. This book certainly contributes to greater understanding of a momentous and historic issue that is a test of both the morality of world politics and the efficacy of international statecraft.

Andrew Young
United Nations, New York
January 1978

Introduction

The nature of the international order and the nature of the values on which this order was founded were profoundly changed in the aftermath of World War II. The Nazis had taken racist beliefs to their logical and gruesome conclusion, and had produced a deep-felt revulsion for racism throughout the world. Yet Hitler had been opposed, in the name of democracy and human freedom, by nations that owned large colonial empires or contained repressed ethnic minorities within their own borders. These contradictions could no longer be overlooked. There was a rapid erosion of white supremacist assumptions and of the belief in the right of one nation to rule over another; instead, the international community formally expressed itself in favor of national independence, the self-determination of peoples, and the protection of basic human rights. But one government set its face against this major historical trend of the second half of the twentieth century, and began with a new fervor to institutionalize racism and the absolute domination of a majority by the minority. The results of this policy—internal repression and tension, and international criticism and hostility—have grown steadily more intense for three decades. Today, with the attention of the world no longer distracted by events in Southeast Asia, South Africa is the focus of international concern.

South Africa was first occupied by a European power in 1652, when the Dutch East India Company founded a small refreshment station for its ships at the Cape of Good Hope. Although there was no initial intention to establish a colony, the settlement gradually spread, and the indigenous inhabitants of the area—the San ("Bushmen") and the Hottentots—were subdued by force of arms and decimated by smallpox. Slaves from Malaysia and elsewhere were introduced to the colony at an early date, and it has been suggested that the color consciousness of the present-day

Afrikaner has its origins in the mentality of the slave owner. To the Calvinist Dutch settlers the heathen slaves were inherently inferior, and slavery institutionalized this inferiority by formally identifying status with color. Neither the disdain for the nonwhite nor the intense puritanism of the settlers prevented miscegenation, however. Although the current official view is that the early settlers, deprived of the companionship of more than a handful of white women, remained stoically celibate for decades on end, the fact is that interracial sex and even marriage were common practice. This is the origin of South Africa's "coloured" people, who are, in effect, simply brown Afrikaners unable to pass for white. The Afrikaner's own mixed ancestry is never publicly mentioned in South Africa—it is the ultimate taboo—but it is an important element in the ruling group's own racial neurosis.

During the early eighteenth century Dutch *trekboers*—nomadic farmers—spread slowly into the interior of the country, until, some six hundred miles to the east, they confronted the westernmost advance of the Bantu-speaking tribes that were moving down the subcontinent. A series of bitter clashes, the so-called kaffir wars, continued for decades as these two nomadic peoples fought over land and cattle; and the Boers became steadily more disengaged from the mainstream of European culture. In his book *A History of South Africa*, de Kiewet gives a graphic description of the Boer's new life and its later implications for South Africa:

> In the vast, unmysterious, thirsty landscape of the interior the Boer race was formed. When the trekboers entered it with their flocks and tented waggons, they left the current of European life and lost the economic habits of the nations from which they had sprung. Though they never became true nomads, the mark of nomadism was upon them, and their dominant traits were those of a restless and narrow existence. They had the nomad's appetite for space and possessed the hardness and courage of men who watch their flocks and hunt their meat. . . .Their life gave them a tenacity of purpose, a power of silent endurance, and the keenest self-respect. But their isolation sank into their character, causing their imagination to lie fallow and their intellects to become inert. Their virtues had their obverse qualities as well. Their tenacity could degenerate into obstinacy, their powers of endurance into resistance to innovation, and their self-respect into suspicion of the foreigner and contempt for their inferiors. For want of a formal education and sufficient pastors, they read their Bibles intensively, drawing from the Old Testament, which spoke the authentic language of their lives, a justification of themselves, of their beliefs and their habits. . . .The remotest corner of Europe was better informed. . . .
>
> Their faith, like that of seventeenth century Puritanism, drew much of its inspiration from the Old Testament. Their religion, setting them apart from the unelected pagans around them, bred in them a special sense of destiny as a people.[1]

While the trekboers and the Bantu tribes skirmished on the frontiers, the British, recognizing the strategic importance of the cape for the sea route to East, occupied the colony by armed force in 1795. It was returned to the Netherlands shortly afterward by the Treaty of Amiens, and then taken over again by the British in 1806 as part of the peace settlement that ended the Napoleonic wars. The British governed the colony in accordance with principles laid down in London; in particular, they brought to the question of color an official philosophy that differed radically from that of the Dutch settlers and frontier trekboers.

In the early nineteenth century the British instituted a policy of equality of all races (except slaves) before the law, and the colonists were outraged. Then, in 1833, the British parliament emancipated slaves throughout the Empire, and the colonists found their former slaves their legal equals. This was the final indignity; contemporary documents show vividly how these Calvinist settlers interpreted the changed status of the nonwhite population as nothing less than an affront to the law of God. Their response, in 1836, was the pivotal event of South African history: the Great Trek. Over a quarter of the Dutch-speaking population of the colony abandoned its homes and farms and set forth into the unknown interior, trekking for years through constant hazards in search of its own kind of freedom, and in the process, subdueing the Bantu tribes whose lands they invaded.

After defeating the Zulu tribe in 1838, the Boers established a new republic in Natal, but their promised land was soon taken from them; the British annexed it in 1843. The trekkers moved further north, settling beyond the Orange and Vaal rivers, but in 1848 the British proclaimed their sovereignity there also. In the 1850s, however, the British lost interest in these outreaches of their territory and granted autonomy to the trekkers. The Boers created new independent states, the Orange Free State and the South African Republic (or Transvaal). By now a distinctive Afrikaner national consciousness was emerging, reinforced by the evolution of Afrikaans into a full-fledged language rather than merely a dialect of Dutch.

The new Boer republics, both with overtly white supremacist constitutions, were left undisturbed until gold was discovered in the Transvaal in 1886. By 1889 the Boer War had begun—ostensibly over the grievances of British fortune-seekers in the republics, but in fact over the gold. The Boer War, fought between Britain and the two tiny republics, turned out to be the largest military campaign the British had ever conducted; they met with such determined resistance that they had to put some 450,000 men in the field. Boer women and children were rounded up and placed in the first concentration camps of modern warfare, where some 20,000 of them died of disease. By the time of the final surrender of the Boers in 1902 a militant Afrikaner nationalism had arisen.

In 1910 the four territories of the Cape, Natal, the Orange Free State and the Transvaal were merged into a union. The Nationalist party was founded four years later as a mouthpiece of Afrikaner nationalism. Although the Afrikaners were a numerical majority of the electorate, enough of them, particularly in the Cape, voted with the English to prevent the Nationalists winning an absolute majority for decades, although the party governed as part of a coalition between 1924 and 1939. In 1948, however, the Nationalist party won its first full election victory and began to systematically remold South African society. Traditional forms of segregation were replaced by formal *apartheid* ("separateness") in every conceivable sphere of public and private life. The entire population was classified into four "racial" groups. Such political liberties as the nonwhites enjoyed were eradicated, and the civil rights of white critics were severely curtailed. The upper echelons of the military, police force, and civil service were filled with Afrikaner nationalists. The country was declared an independent republic and left the British Commonwealth. At successive elections the Nationalists strengthened their majority over an increasingly divided opposition, and it is generally believed in South Africa that if the party ever lost a general election, it would stage its own coup and remain in office.

South Africa today contains 4.3 million white people, about two-thirds of whom are Afrikaans-speaking; the English-speaking third dominates the country's economy but plays little role in its political life. The indigenous black population consists of some 18 million people belonging to several Bantu tribes and subtribes. There are 2.4 million coloureds, or half-castes, and an Asian minority of 800,000 people, most of them descendants of indentured laborers from the Indian subcontinent. The country's only real ally in the world is Rhodesia (Zimbabwe), the British colony to the north whose 274,000 whites, outnumbered twenty-two to one by their 6 million black compatriots, have declared unilateral independence.

The South African situation is a unique one, and parallels with the Rhodesian or other colonial situations can be superficial and misleading. In other former colonies, such as India or Nigeria, the whites were a small minority composed mainly of civil servants and others who viewed the subject land as a temporary abode, not as "home." But the whites in South Africa, and particularly the Afrikaners, regard South Africa as their permanent home, no less than the descendants of immigrants to the United States regard North America as their home. The Afrikaners are nothing less than a white African tribe, the creators of the original African nationalism, speaking a language incomprehensible beyond their borders, sharing a culture rooted in African soil, fanatic in their love of South Africa and their determination to make their way of life secure for themselves and their children. They are convinced that any sharing of power with the non-white majority would mean the end of all they struggled for three hundred years to achieve, and their ideology legitimates this stance as one imposed by divine dictates as well as economic self-interest.

Yet the Nationalist government has not been immune to world pressures or the forces for change. Dr. Hendrik Verwoerd, the Nationalist prime minister and abstruse theoretician who often befuddled parliament with his lofty justifications of government policy until he was assassinated in the House of Assembly in 1966, recognized that racial segregation and white domination had no moral basis. Instead, he proposed a modification: old style *apartheid* would have to go, to be replaced by "separate development." By this concept, Verwoerd envisioned nothing less than the territorial dismemberment of South Africa into a series of independent states: one for the whites, and ten for each of the major Bantu tribes, with the latter states centered on the traditional "native reserves" where few whites live. The logic of "separate development" is this: once a black person is granted citizenship in another state, he or she can have no claim to citizenship rights—such as the vote—within South Africa. By a piece of simple paperwork, a black South African is transformed into a citizen of another country, irrespective of whether that person has any ties to that other country or not. And no country, of course, grants the same rights to aliens as it does to its own people. In theory, then, the blacks can develop to their fullest potential in their own areas, and the whites in theirs; there are separate but equal freedoms for all.

That is the fiction of separate development. The facts are different. Millions of blacks, thoroughly detribalized, are permanently resident in the "white" areas, although their official status is that of migrant workers. In fact, two-thirds of the blacks live outside the reserves, and heavily outnumber the whites in the "white" areas. They want rights in the land where they live and work, not in distant territories that they may never have seen. The "bantustans," the supposed homelands of more than 80 percent of the population, comprise only 13 percent of South Africa's land area, and are almost entirely undeveloped—so much so that they cannot even support their present population at an adequate subsistence level. In effect, the "bantustans" are simply a staging ground for South Africa's labor and a dumping ground for her dispossessed. Neither does "separate development" provide any homeland for the coloured and Asian populations, who are offered nothing more than token power over limited community matters. Although some of the pettier forms of segregation have been relaxed in recent years, the physical separation of the races is still carried to absurd extremes. Racial inequalities are rampant; for example, the average white's income is twelve times that of the average black's income, and the government spends seventeen times more to educate a white child than a black one. In a thoroughly integrated economy where blacks comprise over 90 percent of the work force in industry and agriculture, the idea of territorial segregation can be nothing more than a grand illusion. Its only practical effects for the blacks resident in "white" South Africa are that millions of them have been uprooted from their homes as the boundaries between white and black areas are consolidated, and that all blacks over the age of sixteen are obliged to carry a pass on their persons at all times that indicates their status in the "white" areas. Unless the pass indicates that they are required for labor, they can be "endorsed out"—that is, deported—to the appropriate reserves.

These are the facts that cannot be disguised and which have ineluctably made South Africa a hotbed of racial tension and a pariah among the nations of the world. South Africa's obdurate stance has now divided the African subcontinent into two armed and hostile camps, from the borders of Angola and the South African-administered territory of Namibia on the Atlantic, through the border of Rhodesia and Zambia in the interior to the border of Mozambique and South Africa on the Indian Ocean.

The situation in South Africa has already spawned a rich descriptive literature, most of it partisan and polemical, and much of it deeply moving. It is not the purpose of this book to add to this tradition. Instead, we have tried to collect analytic writings, mostly by social scientists, in a form that will provide a useful general introduction to South Africa and its problems for the student and the interested lay person. Needless to say, it is impossible to adopt a "value free" position when writing about South Africa, and in fact all of the contributors are to a greater or lesser extent critical of the South African government and its policies. The general thrust of the articles, however, is toward factual analysis and interpretation.

The first part of the book is intended to provide a broad background to race and politics in South Africa. *Apartheid*, as Pierre van den Berghe points out in his classic article on the subject, operates at three distinct levels. Micro-segregation is the petty *apartheid* found in public and private facilities, such as washrooms and railway stations; its maintenance is not essential for the preservation of white supremacy and, as van den Berghe correctly predicted, this form of segregation is being progressively relaxed. Meso-segregation is the *apartheid* of enforced residential separation within multiracial urban areas. This form of segregation is essential for the preservation of the existing system, for it makes possible effective control of the urban black population—a fact amply demonstrated by the ease with which government forces contained the recent ghetto riots with virtually no loss of white life or damage to white property. Macro-segregation refers to the "bantustan" plan, and this is the most problematic of *apartheid's* guises. The "separate development" program contains serveral inherent contradictions, most notably the attempt at political segregation within an economically integrated society. If anything, van den Berghe cogently argues, the token rights granted in the distant "bantustans" to the urban blacks will merely increase their appetite for real rights in the urban areas.

In his controversial sociological analysis of the South African polity, Heribert Adam argues that the ideological posturing of the South African government often obscures the highly pragmatic basis, and indeed the flexibility, of the regime's strategy. Adam contends that the government's policies are by no means as irrational as they may at first appear: given the overriding objective of maintaining a racial oligarchy at any cost, these policies are rationally designed for maximum efficiency. Adam's analysis, unusually "hard-nosed" and implicitly somewhat pessimistic about the prospects for rapid change in South Africa, provides a useful corrective to the widespread assumption that white South African society must soon collapse under the weight of its own evil and the hostility that *apartheid* engenders.

The whites, always a minority within South Africa, have ruled the country for over three hundred years. To the outsider, the continued success of the oppressive regime seems almost an anomaly: why no revolution? John Daniel analyzes the history of radical resistance within South Africa, a history of uniform and dismal failure, and attempts to account for the lack of a successful uprising. He argues that a modern coup or revolution, if it is to be successful, must win the allegiance of a part of the armed forces. Unlike other societies in which successful revolutions have been fought, however, South Africa has an army whose members are drawn primarily from the ruling class, not the oppressed class. Moreover, the regime has been successful at the crucially important task of preventing access to modern weaponry on the part of the indigenous black population. Given the distribution of military power and the unshakeable determination of the regime to suppress any revolt at any cost, the prospects for a successful revolution seem less likely than demographic factors and the sheer provocation for rebellion would suggest.

The second part of the book discusses some critical institutions of *apartheid*. Randolph Vigne's article offers a useful survey of the various "bantustans" and their resources. His dispassionate account leaves no doubt that the "bantustans" have no prospect whatever of becoming politically or economically viable independent states; were it not for the grim implications of the "bantustan" program, the idea that these wretched, scattered parcels of land could achieve meaningful statehood would seem farcical.

Kenneth Carstens's article explores the role of religious organizations in South Africa, and particularly that of the Christian churches with their supposed dedication to human brotherhood. Carstens shows how the Dutch

Reformed Churches provide one of the bastions of the system by offering a systematic theological justification for *apartheid*; in so doing, they lend the oppressors the moral legitimation that they so desparately need. The "English" churches, on the other hand, are playing a more ambiguous and precarious role, reacting alternately in terms of their dislike of *apartheid* and their timidity toward the regime and their own white congregations.

Like other totalitarian governments, the South African regime systematically uses education as a tool for indoctrination, employing a segregated schools system and distinctive curricula to ensure that each child grows up equipped to fill the appropriate niche in a racial hierarchy. Ian Robertson's article shows how the ideology of Afrikaner nationalism and racial domination has been expressed in the educational system, in areas ranging from the differential funding of the schools to the indoctrinatory content of school text books.

David Mechanic's article on medical facilities in South Africa provides insights into the marked inequalities found in one institutional area, although it serves as a paradigm for many others. Mechanic found white South African medical facilities to be among the best in the world, while those for other population groups were woefully inadequate. He shows, too, how even the most well-intentioned white physicians unwittingly participated in the indignities inflicted on the nonwhite population: an object lesson in how white liberals may come to take for granted and to act on the racist assumptions of their society.

South Africa is exceptional among authoritarian and totalitarian regimes in that its rulers do not run the country purely by dictate and decree. One British institution that survived in South Africa is a parliamentary system founded on the Westminster model, and virtually every act of the government is based on laws passed with meticulous regard for parliamentary procedures, if not for the spirit of parliamentary democracy. In his article Albie Sachs shows how the law has become an instrument of repression; he details the steady accumulation of "race statutes" and the use of the prisons, bannings, whippings, and other legally sanctioned instruments to maintain the South African version of law and order.

The third part of the book focuses on South Africa's position in the contemporary world. South Africa is a country isolated from and reviled by the rest of the world, but one desparately anxious for detente with its black neighbors and for international respectability. Colin and Margaret Legum's article offers a concise overview of the military, political, and economic objectives of South African foreign policy, and of the extent to which the international community in turn can influence or even frustrate the country's internal policy.

Foreign investment in South Africa by Western countries, and particularly by the United States, has become a highly controversial issue in recent years. Reinier Lock surveys foreign investment in the country and looks pragmatically at the options available. One is a total withdrawal of investment from South Africa. This option, however, may prove unrealistic and is also open to the charge that it is supreme arrogance on the part of foreign liberals and radicals to wish to further impoverish black South Africans (who would bear the brunt of any recession) in their supposed best interests. A second alternative is to continue or even increase investment, either to improve black living standards or to create the climate of rising expectations among the blacks that has historically been a prerequisite for revolutionary change; but this option can too readily provide a rationalization for corporate greed. Lock suggests a third option, involving the selective use of both the withdrawal and the continued-investment strategies.

In his article, Randall Stokes looks at the external liberation movement, which hopes to bring about revolutionary change through guerrilla warfare rather than internal resistance. The Southern African liberation movements have already been successful in Angola and Mozambique, and clearly cannot be indefinitely resisted in Rhodesia. Taking into account the changing geopolitical context, Stokes shrewdly analyzes the liberation movement's chances of success against the sole remaining bastion of white supremacy on the African continent.

United States policy toward South Africa has often appeared to be vacillating and ambiguous. Periodic verbal criticisms, for example, have been combined with UN vetoes of all Security Council proposals that might have significant impact on South African policies. It is hardly surprising, therefore, that official United States condemnations of *apartheid* have been widely regarded as mere lip service and hypocrisy; the lack of any effective action by the State Department has translated into an implicit willingness to allow the status quo to continue undisturbed. Ambassador Donald Easum's article provides the first authoritative survey of United States policies toward South Africa in the past, and shows how these policies have been shaped by contradictions in the supposed American interests in the region.

The final part of the book looks ahead to South Africa's future, with three writers offering very different prognoses. Lawrence Gandar argues that an evolutionary solution is in the offing: the dynamics of the economy, the effects of external pressure, the burgeoning power of the urban blacks, and the whites' own increasing willingness to accept the inevitability of change are likely, he feels, to lead to a gradual transfer of power. Russell Warren Howe takes a diametrically opposed position and predicts a bloodbath. Believing that the regime will never compromise on basics, Howe sees black and white in South Africa set on a collision course from which there is no escape; revolution is an inevitability. The best that the whites can hope for in a postrevolutionary South Africa, he suggests, might be a white "stan" in a small part of the country. Edwin Munger takes a less fashionable and more controversial view, arguing that the South African government will make separate development a reality. The Afrikaner, he suggests, has no intrinsic need or wish to dominate others, and has done so in the past only to preserve the white tribe. In the short run, racial domination will continue; in the longer run, however, black South Africans will find political expression in a series of independent states, and the repressive apparatus within white South Africa will be dismantled. Eventually, there will be a United States of South Africa, with several fairly autonomous states existing in harmonious interdependence. If these are radically different predictions, they illustrate only the perilous uncertainty of South Africa's future.

Finally, we wish to express our thanks to John Daniel for his advice and help in the preparation of this book, and to Irving Louis Horowitz for the encouragement he has offered throughout the project.

Notes

1. C. W. de Kiewiet, *A History of South Africa, Social and Economic* (Oxford: Oxford University Press, 1957), pp. 17-22.

RACE AND POLITICS
IN SOUTH AFRICA

PART I BACKGROUND

Chapter 1

Racial Segregation in South Africa: Degrees And Kinds *

Pierre L. van den Berghe

No other state in world history has devoted as large a proportion of its energies and resources in imposing racial segregation as South Africa has done since 1948. While *apartheid* has been the object of an abundant literature, one of its important aspects has not received much attention, namely the degree of physical distance achieved by measures of segregation. We can distinguish three main degrees of segregation.

1. *Micro-segregation*—segregation in public and private facilities (such as waiting rooms, railway carriages, post office counters, washrooms, and so on, located in areas inhabited by members of several "racial" groups;

2. *Meso-segregation*—the physical separation resulting from the existence of racially homogeneous residential ghettos within multiracial urban areas;

3. *Macro-segregation*—the segregation of racial groups in discrete territorial units, such as the "native reserves" of South Africa, now re-styled as "Bantustans."

Originally published in *Cahiers d'Etudes Africaines*, vol. 6, no. 23, 1966.

The above distinction, however, is not only one of degree but also of kind. Each form of segregation fulfills different purposes from the viewpoint of the ruling albinocracy, and entails different consequences for South African society as a whole. Let us first examine the "gains" of the white group from the various forms of segregation, then analyze the internal contradictions inherent in macro-segregation, and finally turn to the differential economic effects of the three types of racial separation.

It is often said that the *apartheid* policies of the present Afrikaner Nationalist government constitute simply a more systematic and intensified version of traditional practices of racial discrimination and segregation. This statement is true in the sense that large-scale implementation of all three kinds of segregation extend at least as far back as the nineteenth century. In recent years, however, the Nationalist government has increasingly stressed macro-segregation. There are two apparent reasons why this should be the case. First, if one accepts the government's premises that interracial contact promotes conflict and that *apartheid* is the only salvation for the albinocracy, then it follows that maximization of physical distance between racial groups is desirable. Second, macro-segregation in the form of the "bantustan" policy can be presented, for purposes of international apologetics, as an attempt at equitable partition between separate but equal nations within a happy commonwealth. Indeed, a favorite argument of the apostles of *apartheid* is that their policy substitutes vertical nonhierarchical barriers between ethnic groups for a horizontal, discriminatory color bar.

Beyond these obvious considerations, this shift of emphasis in the implementation of *apartheid* from micro- to macro-segregation is motivated by more basic factors. To be sure, micro-segregation is still rigidly enforced, but not with the same order of priority. Micro-segregation with grossly unequal facilities is a constant symbol of the racial status hierarchy, and is a source of emotional gratification, economic advantages, and other practical conveniences for the white group. Substantial as the gains accruing from micro-segregation for the whites are, however, this aspect of *apartheid* is a "luxury," in the sense that it contributes little to the maintenance of white supremacy and that it further exacerbates the hostility of the nonwhite masses. (The Portuguese, for example, maintained their rule in Angola and Mozambique without any resort to legal micro-segregation, and thus claimed to be free of racial prejudice; similarly, the white-settler regime of Rhodesia has gone some way towards the elimination of micro-segregation without in any way jeopardizing its power monopoly.) The preservation of micro-segregation in South Africa serves mostly to indulge the albinocracy's phobia of racial pollution, but micro-segregation is definitely not a cornerstone of the sociopolitical order.

Meso-segregation, i.e., the maintenance of racial ghettos, arose in the nineteenth century as a way of making the nonwhite helotry as invisible as possible to the *Herrenvolk*, and of preserving the latter from the moral and physical contamination of congested, unhygienic slums. The presence of many domestic servants living on their employers' premises, however, made most "white" sections of town de facto interracial. In addition, there were a number of racially mixed residential areas in Cape Town, Durban, Johannesburg, and many smaller cities.

When the Nationalists came to power in 1948, they proceeded to make meso-segregation as impermeable as possible through the policy of "group areas." Hundreds of thousands of people were expropriated, expelled from their domiciles, and "relocated" according to their pigmentation. Even the number of nonwhite domestic servants allowed to live with their white employers was sharply reduced, a distinct departure from earlier practices. The enforcement of meso-segregation involves many hardships for nonwhites, threatens much of the Indian and coloured middle-class with economic ruin, and entails considerable profits for many thousands of whites. But, beyond these side effects, the complete ghettoization of South African cities is ostensibly being promoted as a cornerstone in the maintenance of the status quo.

The presence of millions of nonwhites in cities is deplored by the government, but reluctantly accepted as an economic necessity. Given the latter, the government endeavors to enforce a new style of rigid meso-segregation, in great part for reasons of internal security. With mounting unrest among Africans, military and police control becomes increasingly crucial. The older nonwhite shantytowns with their maze of narrow, tortuous alleys were often located close to white residential or business districts; they are now systematically being razed as a major military hazard. They are being replaced with "model townships" with unobstructed, rectilinear fields of fire, and wide streets for the passage of police vans and armored cars. The new ghettos are typically situated several miles from the white towns, with a buffer zone in between; they are sprinkled with strategically located police stations, and often enclosed by barbed wire.

Macro-segregation, because of its many practical and ideological implications, is perhaps the most interesting aspect of Nationalist racial policy, and hence deserves closer attention. Total territorial separation is the avowed ideal which *apartheid* seeks to achieve for all racial groups. Ideally, the government would like to cram the Africans into the impoverished, eroded, and entirely rural "native reserves" which constitute 13 per cent of the nation's territory. The rest of the country would then acquire a pristine white purity. While the government realizes that this aim is largely unrealizable, it is nevertheless implementing an elaborate scheme, the so-called "bantustan" policy, to keep as large a percentage of Africans as possible in these rural slums. Africans deemed to be "redundant" in the "white" areas are constantly being "endorsed out" of them and sent to their "Bantu homelands." The bantustans have several obvious security advantages: they are relatively isolated, dispersed, ethnically homogeneous, distant from the "white" cities, and devoid of any urban concentrations of more than a few thousand people; and communication within and between them is difficult.

In its basic conception, the "bantustan" policy of the South African government is not new. Interpretations of its "real" intention vary, but the limits of actual variability in implementation which the government is prepared to tolerate can be determined with a fair degree of precision. In "minimum" form, the bantustans are a revamping of the "native reserve" along the following main lines:

1. Geographical segregation of as many Africans as possible from non-Africans and of specific African ethnic groups from each other.

2. Pretoria-sponsored cultural revivalism, and the elaboration of pseudo-traditional authority structures.

3. An extension of the sphere of local autonomy under the authority of government-appointed chiefs, which, in effect, amounts to a shift from "direct" to "indirect" rule.[1]

Leo Kuper gives a vivid description of the "minimum" bantustan scheme as it is at present being implemented:

> Here the power of the White man is displayed in a comic opera of equality with the Black man, indeed of homage to his tribal essence. Here backward tribal reserves are in a state of Messianic transformation to satellite bucolic Ruritanias. . . .The policy is to retribalize Africans and to fragment them into separate tribal entities, self-policed, introspectively detached from each other and from the White man's world, and self-perpetuated by the insemination of tribal ardor.[2]

In this sense, the bantustan concept amounts to the transformation of the South African colonial empire from an internal one as analyzed by Leo Marquard,[3] to an external one: the "native reserves" are being restyled into semiautonomous puppet states or protectorates under a quasi-traditional aristocracy.

At the other end of the "tolerable" spectrum from the government's viewpoint is the "maximum" notion of bantustans as "separate black states." While this alternative is clearly distasteful to the government, since as early as 1961 it has been considered as a possible line of retreat in response to external and internal pressures. Former Prime Minister Verwoerd said in reaction to this possibility of separate black states: "This is not what we would have preferred to see. This is a form of fragmentation which we would rather not have had if it was within our control to avoid it."[4] Even under nominal political "sovereignty," the Nationalist government counts on the bantustans's ethnic division, small size, and utter economic dependence to perpetuate them in a colonial relationship to white South Africa. The political subservience to South Africa of the now-independent former British High Commission Territories of Swaziland, Botswana, and Lesotho has provided a reasonably good predictor of the likely behavior of the Transkei and other future independent bantustans, and has thus indirectly influenced Nationalist policies.

The basic question concerning the future of the bantustans and indeed of the country as a whole then becomes: will the government be able to contain the bantustan scheme within these fairly narrow limits? My argument is that it will not, in part because of international pressures, in part because of mounting conflicts in the "white" areas of South Africa, and lastly because of the dialectic unleashed by contradictions within the bantustan scheme itself. We shall focus here on this last point.

There are four major aspects to the contradictions evident in the bantustan policy; all of these are, to a large degree, unanticipated consequences of that policy, and threaten to make its implementation in the Transkei the opening of Pandora's box from the government's point of view.

The first aspect concerns the use of the magic word "independence." In 1951, Verwoerd was careful to emphasize:

> Now a Senator wants to know whether the series of self-governing Native areas would be sovereign. The answer is obvious. . . .It stands to reason that White South Africa must remain their guardian. . . .We cannot mean that we intend by that to cut large slices out of South Africa and turn them into independent States.[5]

Later, he ostensibly reversed his stand by stating eventual "independence" as a possibility. The lack of a time-table, or indeed of an even approximate definition of the term, made the statement vacuous, particularly in conjunction with Verwoerd's 1963 statement: "We want to make South Africa White. . . .Keeping it White can only mean one thing, namely White domination, not leadership, not guidance, but control, supremacy."[6] However, the magic word has been spoken, partly, no doubt, as a carrot to the collaborationist African chiefs, and perhaps also on the assumption that the statement would be taken at face value by some leaders of Western powers resulting in the nonintervention on which the future of *apartheid* hinges to a considerable degree.

It seems likely that the independence pronouncement, however vague, will encourage, or even create, rather than mollify, opposition. There are already signs that this is happening in two opposite ways. The strategy of many African chiefs who have decided to further their power and pursue their interests within the bantustan framework is to exert whatever pressure they can against the government in terms of the avowed goal of "independence." The most cautious form of "subversion from within" involves little danger to its advocates since it is couched in government rhetoric and ostensibly follows government logic. The sheer use of the term "independence" represents a retreat, if only a verbal one, on the part of the government, and it is in the nature of tightly oppressive regimes that concessions easily lead to an escalation of demands.

The rhetoric of independence has also opened up a new avenue of opposition to government policy. Unlikely as this may have seemed until 1961, the government is now under attack from the right, both from the *platteland* (rural) elements within its own party, and from the United party. The latter in particular claims to accept the indepence pronouncements at face value, and has taken the government to task for partitioning the Republic and creating hostile black states in its midst. Thus, de Villiers Graaff proclaimed:

> We would scrap the Bantustan plan. We shall retain South Africa as one integral unit with fifteen million people. We shall not fragment it into a group of States, some of which may become, and indeed are likely to become, hostile to White South Africa. We reject the idea of one man one vote, and we shall retain White leadership all over South Africa and not only in parts, as Dr. Verwoerd would have us do.[7]

Consequently, the government faces an interesting dilemma. On the one hand if it refuses to transfer sovereignty to the bantustans, the latter will be exposed more and more clearly as elaborate shams, and this may even precipitate a revolt of the puppet chiefs. On the other hand, should the government take definite steps towards granting political independence to more bantustans—a process begun with the independence of the Transkei in 1976—it must face the danger of losing the support of its reactionary Afrikaner electorate.

The second contradiction in the bantustan scheme is somewhat related to the first. It concerns the extension of universal adult franchise to Africans who live in the "native reserves" or whose theoretical "homeland" is supposed to be located therein. The government may have assumed that the cathartic effect of casting a ballot would reduce the hostility of Africans, and that this franchise would meet demands for "one man one vote." It is clear, however, that few Africans are satisfied with virtually meaningless voting rights which entitle some ethnic groups to elect a minority of members in a legislative assembly which is itself subject to Pretoria's veto and the jurisdiction of which is restricted to only *some* of the people living in a fraction of the Republic's territory. If anything, it seems probable that the exercise of an ineffective franchise heightens the level of discontent. What can be more frustrating than to be allowed to express one's hostility to *apartheid*, only to witness the establishment of a "self-government" led by government-appointed chiefs whose positions were in some cases overwhelmingly defeated at the polls?

In this respect, the Transkei scheme is fundamentally different from a Facist-type regime where ritualistic plebiscites, propaganda, mass rallies, and the like are used to create the illusion of consensus. In the Transkei, Africans have been allowed to express their strong opposition to *apartheid* at the polls, only to see their views disregarded and overridden. This use of the franchise seems to maximize discontent, in that it reflects the government's contempt for African opinion. Implicitly, the latter is regarded as so inconsequential as not even to be worthy of a concerted propaganda effort to "sell" *apartheid*.[8]

The third and perhaps most interesting contradiction in the bantustan scheme concerns the stand on the racial issue taken respectively by the collaborators and those in opposition. Ironically, the African opponents of *apartheid* in the "homelands" take what is ostensibly a "prowhite" position. They protested against the plan to make the Transkei an exclusively black state, and favor "multiracialism" with equal opportunities and rights for all, including whites. Conversely, the collaborating chiefs, under the leadership of Kaiser Matanzima, express their uneasy agreement with *apartheid* by raising the thinly veiled spectre of antiwhiteism.

Since *apartheid* is the product of white racism, it is not surprising that it calls forth black counterracism. The latter is, of course, repressed by the South African government when it takes a militant nationalist form as in the Pan-African Congress. However, black racism can also be couched in *apartheid* phraseology and take the form of extolling narrow ethnic nationalism, and giving vent to xenophobia. Indeed, there is no safer way for an African to express his hostility to whites than to make use of the official hate ideology. The government keeps warning Africans of outside "hyenas" and "jackals" who come to exploit or deceive them; it tells them what noble savages they are so long as they do not let themselves be spoiled by Western culture, and so on.

Thus *apartheid* and the bantustan concept can easily become latent platforms for a surreptitious and insidious variety of ethnic particularism and antiwhiteism. Such is Mbeki's interpretation of the Transkeian prime minister's motives: "A cold, haughty man who nurses an enmity towards Whites and wishes to escape their oppressive presence, Matanzima has chosen to try to do this by using *apartheid*."

The fourth contradiction inherent in the bantustans is the most basic of all, and indeed underlies the other three. Both the practicability of the bantustans and their acceptability to sufficient numbers of Africans hinge on a massive redistribution of wealth and power at the expense of the albinocracy.[10] More specifically, the economic viability of partition in South Africa depends on the manifold enlargement of the African (and indeed other nonwhite) areas, on the large-scale subsidization of subsistence agriculture by the money sector of the economy, and, consequently, on drastic land and income redistribution. Politically, if the partitioned areas are to retain any federal association, the basis of such association must clearly be an effective sharing of power between the constituent racial groups in the joint government rather than the bantustan blueprint of a white colonial state dominating a half-dozen or more labor reservoirs administered by puppet chiefs.

It is obvious, however, that these necessary conditions to any viable partition scheme are precisely those which the Nationalist government desperately seeks to avert through its bantustan scheme. The latter is apparently based on the assumption of the hope that Africans and the outside world are mistaking the "comic opera" of equality and the shadow of economic development for the real things. The bantustan scheme is thus in part an ineffective attempt to mollify internal and external opposition at minimal cost to the ruling caste, and in part a blueprint for the improvement of the state's repressive apparatus.

All four paradoxes or contradictions in bantustan policy we have briefly examined raise doubt as to the government's ability to control *apartheid's* latest litter of feral children.

In summary, *apartheid* aims to introduce between racial groups the greatest degree of physical separation consistent with economic imperatives in a highly industrialized society. Macro-segregation is deemed by the government to offer the greatest chance of continued white supremacy, but, where white industry, mining and agriculture require nonwhite labor, lesser degrees of segregation are acceptable.

The last aspect of our analysis concerns the differential economic consequences of micro- meso-, and macro-segregation. Many analysts of the South African dilemma have observed that *apartheid* involves a great economic cost and interferes with economic development. *Apartheid* certainly conflicts with principles of economic "rationality" and government policies often assign priority to political as opposed to economic aims. Directly and indirectly, the economic cost of *apartheid* is no less for being difficult to assess with any degree of precision. The three degrees of segregation, however, have different effects and entail different economic costs.

Micro-segregation is certainly the least costly of the three. Segregated nonwhite facilities are either vastly inferior to the white ones or altogether nonexistent. To avoid any suggestion of a "separate but equal" doctrine, a law was passed (the Reservation of Separate Amenities Act) providing for segregated and unequal facilities. True duplication of public conveniences is highly exceptional, and segregation often means nothing more than the exclusion of nonwhites from many places. This micro-segregation frequently involves a saving over what it would cost to provide adequate facilities for the entire population, and there is little or no economic incentive for the white group to abolish it.

With the introduction of the new style of meso-segregation, the government is deliberately paying an economic price for the maintenance of white supremacy. Much of that price, however, is not paid by the government, but by the Africans who have to finance many of the amenities in their streamlined ghettos, and bear the cost of transport to and from the "white" areas where they work. In addition, white employers of nonwhite labor suffer indirectly from the lower labor efficiency resulting from employee fatigue and time wasted in transit. Consequently, while the total economic cost of ghettoization is quite high, the direct price paid by the government and the bulk of the white electorate which votes for the Nationalists is relatively low.

Macro-segregation is potentially the most expensive for the government. The sums required to subsidize economic development in the bantustans in order to raise the standards of living above starvation would run into hundreds of millions of dollars. But, here again, the government only spends a small fraction of the necessary sum on the development of the "Bantu homelands."[11] What the bantustan policy does, in effect, achieve economically is to perpetuate the sharp distinction within the South African economy between a high-production money sector and a sub-subsistence one. The productive potential of the one-third of the African population which is kept in or even forced back into the reserves is thus vastly underutilized. In the same way as South Africa combines politically the properties of a quasidemocracy for the *Herrenvolk* and a colonial tyranny for the Africans, economically the country is at once a booming industrial nation and one of the most destitute of the "underdeveloped" countries.

From the above analysis, it seems that all three levels of segregation on which the policy of *apartheid* rests are doomed to economic and political failure for a combination of reasons. Micro-segregation serves little purpose in the preservation of the status quo, but also involves a minimum of cost to the government. Its major function is to provide a bigoted albinocracy with some psychological and material "fringe benefits" of oppression.

Meso-segregation is considerably costlier but on it rests the political control of the highly explosive urban areas. From the viewpoint of the maintenance of white supremacy, this meso-segregation is essential. Only through the compartmentalization of racial groups into streamlined ghettos can the dominant white minority hope to combat open insurgency. On the other hand, the implementation of meso-segregation with the entire repressive machinery of "reference books," "influx control," "job reservation," "population registration," and "group areas" is directly responsible for the overwhelming majority of acts of protest and revolt against *apartheid*. Thus the ghettoization of urban life brings with it the hypertrophy of the police and military apparatus. Not only is the militarization of an ever-growing proportion of the white population expensive, but its effectiveness is limited by at least two factors. First, the open and unrestrained use of military violence, given the climate of world opinion, threatens the government with outside intervention. Second, as the whites monopolize all key positions in government, industry, transport, communications, and so on, the simultaneous mobilization of the albinocracy on any sizable scale would bring about considerable disruption of civilian activities, not to mention the problem of the protection of dependents.

In the foregoing analysis, I have tried to show that the continued enforcement of meso- and macro-segregation is essential to the preservation of white supremacy. However, *apartheid* also generates conflicts and contradictions the control of which involves an ever-rising cost in economic, human, and military resources. Micro- and meso-segregation in urban areas create an undercurrent of revolt precariously held in check by a growing police and army apparatus, and the bantustan scheme unwittingly threatens to destroy the entire edifice of white supremacy.

Notes

1. For an analysis of the role of African chiefs in the Transkei see W. E. Hammond-Tooke, "Chieftainship in Transkein Political Development," *Journal of Modern African Studies* 2 (December 1964): 513-29.

2. Leo Kuper, *An African Bourgeoisie* (New Haven: Yale University Press 1965), pp. 22-23.

3. Leo Marquard, *South Africa's Colonial Policy* (Johannesburg, 1957).

4. Quoted in Brian Bunting, *The Rise of The South African Reich*, (Harmondsworth and Baltimore: Penguin, 1964), p. 310.

5. Quoted in Pierre L. van den Berghe, *South Africa: A Study in Conflict*, (Middletown, Conn.: Wesleyan University Press, 1965), p. 118.

6. Ibid.

7. *African Digest* 12 (December 1964): 81.

8. This is but one of the several ways in which South Africa differs from a Facist-type regime. See van den Berghe, *South Africa*, for a more extensive treatment of this point. Bunting on the other hand stresses, and indeed overstresses, the similarities of South Africa with Nazi Germany. See Bunting, *Rise of the South African Reich*. The southern United States constitutes a closer parallel to South Africa than does Nazi Germany, Facist Italy, or Franco's Spain.

9. Govan A. M. Mbeki, *South Africa: The Peasants' Revolt* (Harmondsworth and Baltimore: Penguin 1964), p. 137.

10. Although the vast majority of African leaders have rejected the partition of South Africa on any terms, there have been a few dissenting voices. For example, Jordan Ngubane has advocated an ethnic confederation accompanied by drastic land reform. Cf. his book *An African Explains Apartheid* (New York: Praeger, 1963), pp. 220-32.

11. Only a small fraction of the conservative 1956 estimate of 104 million pounds recommended by the Tomlinson Commission for a ten-year period was expended.

Chapter 2

The Political Sociology of South Africa: A Pragmatic Race Oligarchy*

Heribert Adam

Democratic Police State

While the content of racial beliefs is always irrational, propagated as a justification for existing privileges or, as in anti-Semitism, adopted as a fictitious explanation for economic frustrations, this irrationality does not necessarily characterize the implementation of racial discrimination, which can be "rational" and efficient with respect to its intended purposes. It is precisely this means-end rationality that seems the decisive new feature of South Africa's version of racialism. This pragmatism treats racial and related historical experiences only with reference to their practical lessons. It overrides the ideological implications of racial beliefs and is oriented solely toward the purpose of the system: the smooth, frictionless, and tolerable domination over cheap labor and political dependents as a prerequisite for privileges of the minority.

Originally published as "Consequences of a Pragmatic Race Oligarchy," chap. 4 in Heribert Adam, *Modernizing Racial Domination: The Dynamics of South African Politics* (Berkeley: University of California Press, 1972), pp. 53-118. Slightly abridged.

13

This domination, which is rationalized by slogans such as "securance of white survival" or "preservation of Christian-national identity," however, is secured ultimately by coercion. Decade-long efforts to achieve some non-white political rights by peaceful means outside the *apartheid* framework have been rejected with increasingly sterner measures: these also have been directed against radical white opponents of the system. In terms of the questionable distinction between "criminal" and "political" offenses, approximately thirteen hundred persons had been imprisoned for political offenses under the various security laws by the end of the sixties.[1] Almost one thousand persons (126 whites, 853 nonwhites) have been banned since the "Suppression of Communism Act" became law in 1950.[2] Of these banning orders, 355 (50 whites, 305 nonwhites) were in force at the end of 1969. While several hundred orders were apparently withdrawn or not renewed after expiry, a number of persons have been banned for a second and even third period. Hundreds have had their passports withdrawn or refused. Many political prosecutees have left the country on exit-permits. This new form of silencing political opponents—applications for exit-permits are usually granted—decreases the domestic political pressure and can be viewed as another new device of pragmatic domination, compared with traditional totalitarian practices elsewhere. The calculated risk which is incurred by allowing opponents to go into exile has so far proved relatively harmless, since the refugees soon lose the vital contact with the local scene and confine themselves to the already existing verbal attacks from outside.

There are various other sophisticated laws, apart from those entailing imprisonment and house arrest, that achieve efficient control of political opponents. The "Suppression of Communism Act" provides for listing of members or supporters of banned organizations. It is an offense for listed persons to change their places of residence or employment without notifying the police, or for their utterances or writings to be disseminated or reproduced in any form. Approximately four hundred persons are listed, and may not be quoted in South Africa, in some instances, even though they are now living abroad. Law professor Ellison Kahn (University of the Witwatersrand) estimated that there are thirteen thousand prohibited publications, including those banned by the Censorship Board before the Publications Control Board was created in 1963.[3]

One of the most striking features of South African cultural life is the relative intellectual isolation and ignorance about the changing world of ideas, which whites in particular hardly seem to notice. While the Boers in the eighteenth and nineteenth centuries were cut off from the ideas of the French enlightenment by geographical isolation, the ninety-seven definitions of what is "undesirable" in the Publications and Entertainments Act achieves largely the same result, in an era of satellite communication, and this despite the advantage of the universality of the English language in facilitating access to the ideas of the Western world. It is not surprising then that South African whites display the greatest ignorance about the people with whom they are in closest contact. The enrichment of creativity and new perspectives through the experience of cultural diversity exists in theory only. The works of African writers who have most to say, such as Mphahlele, Nkosi, and Modisane among others are banned and even their names are unknown in South Africa. Deviant whites are still allowed to deal with African problems and suffering, but even this tolerance might be more in the interest of white domination than black liberation, as Nadine Gordimer has speculated self-critically:

> When it comes to literature, and in particular the literature of ideas, there has been precious little tolerance to disguise the repression. Tolerance has oper-ated in one small area only, and provides a curious half-light on the psychology of white supremacy. Literature by black South Africans has been successfully wiped out by censorship and the banning of individuals, at home and in exile. But white writers have been permitted to deal, within strict limits, with the disabilities, suffering, hopes, dreams, even resentments of black people. Are such writings perhaps tolerated because they have upon them the gloss of proxy—in a strange way, although they may indict white supremacy, they can be claimed by it because they speak for the black man, as white supremacy decides for him how he shall live? . . .[4]

Under these circumstances the still-legal, white *apartheid* opposi-tion—the English-speaking press, Progressive party, National Union of South African Students (NUSAS), Black Sash, Institute of Race Relations, and some church circles—serves the function of keeping alternatives in the public opinion alive or, at least, of branding the injustices in the manner of a democracy-conscious enlightenment. Without doubt, such critiques have, on occasion, embarrassed the government, sobered what might be more extreme race laws or ameliorated their implementation. With non-white opposition organizations banned, however, it remains essentially in-effective. Apart from sections of the English-speaking press, which sur-prises the observer accustomed to totalitarian techniques elsewhere by its outspoken criticism, potential opponents are in general so intimidated that only a small core of dedicated people keep the antigovernment organiza-tions alive. The English-speaking press enjoys its restricted freedom, partly because of its ineffectiveness, but also because it receives the backing of business interests.

Some members of the clergy, including the Afrikaans-speaking churches, have distinguished themselves as defendants of racial equality and suffered personal consequences for their stand. The members of the

South African Council of Churches have regularly condemned *apartheid*, but this critique was mostly confined to the un-Christian consequences of the race policy, assuming that there is a just *apartheid*. It was not until September 1968 that this church body denounced racial separation on principle. Whatever the wording of public statements may be, their influence on the churchgoer is minimal and the discrepancy between theory and practice continues. As representatives of an institution based on the voluntary membership of prejudiced supporters, even a progressive clergyman cannot afford to dissociate himself too radically from his basis. The English-speaking churches in particular need the personnel of foreign missionaries whose visas are dependent on the benevolence of the government, and a substantial number of foreign priests have had to leave the country for political reasons.[5]

Where the domestic institutions dominate, as for instance in the Catholic Church, the vested interest in their continued existence and proper functioning leads to a resigned accommodation to the prescribed conditions. When the then archbishop of Canterbury, Dr. Michael Ramsey, announced his visit to South Africa, a spokesman for the church explained: "The Anglican Church in South Africa is in a difficult position. It is against Apartheid, but cannot afford to be too outspoken, as the deportation of Bishop Amrose Reeves showed. If all your Bishops are deported you cannot carry on, can you?"[6] Faced with the choice of institutional continuation or institutional suicide for an uncompromising moral stand, the churches in South Africa have so far preferred the former, similar to the attitude of Pius XII toward Nazi Germany on the question of the extermination of Jews. Increasing verbal militancy, especially on the part of individual clergymen, has been paralleled by practical resignation and declining moral influence over a largely indifferent parish, which reduce the manifestos to well-meaning rhetoric.

It is within this stifling climate of repression that white student opposition has gained particular significance as an articulator of the forgotten. *Die Transvaler* views the National Union of Students (NUSAS) as a "a fifth column of enemies of the Republic and an obstruction in the smooth running of healthy race relations in the country."[7] The unpredictable student activity at the white English-speaking universities has developed into a propaganda annoyance for the government. The active members of NUSAS, though a small minority, have succeeded through their imaginative actions in keeping the mood of protest alive. The invitation of Robert Kennedy to South Africa has, thus far, been the most spectacular action, apart from a sit-in at Cape Town University in 1968 against the university's yielding to government demands in academic appointments. Issues which have elsewhere created only internal interest within the university have tended

to grow here almost immediately into questions of general political principles. Taking place within the privileged framework, the actions of the
white opponents tend to be considered more subversive. On the other
hand, the symbolic protest of students who face various personal risks has
the same clouding functions as any protest under totalitarian conditions,
even though one should not dismiss too easily these isles of liberty. The
total boycott of the South African universities as propagated by *apartheid*
opponents in England is also welcomed by the government in Pretoria,
while all admissions of foreign students are carefully screened.

However, it is hardly meaningful to compare the internal South African
resistance against *apartheid* with political protest movements in Western
countries. The specific racial problem has caused political contradictions
which lend significance to movements which would elsewhere be classified
merely as frictions within a broad right-of-the-center spectrum. In some
aspects, particularly with regard to economic planning, the ruling Nationalist party with its state capitalism might well be regarded as being to
the left of the opposition United party. Some of its supporters and the
voters for the small Progressive party represent a liberal bourgeoisie, which
views racial separation as basically detrimental to the economy and unwise
with regard to the urban Africans. Similar to the church spokesmen, they
condemn the inevitable injustices of racial separation without seriously
aiming at real equality or equal opportunities for all groups. The Progressive party advocates a qualified franchise for "educated" Africans, thus
substituting for an obstructive racial system a less-obnoxious class system.

The Nationalists do indeed score a point when they ridicule Progressive
nonracialism as inconsistent and false in comparison with the homeland-
franchise of separate development: "Dr. Jan Steytler [then Progressive
party leader]. . .cannot seem to see how ludicrously his ardently accepted
proposition that 'no person may be denied full political or economic opportunities on grounds of race or colour' contradicts the well-known Progressive policy of a 'qualified' franchise.[8]

Compared with the federation program of the rapidly disintegrating
United party, the theoretical "separate development" of the Nationalists
can be considered as radical and democratic. The United party proposes
separate voters' roles in a federal constitution of a centrally controlled
state. These separate roles are supposed to provide representation for (1)
coloureds, by six members of Parliament and two senators (who may be
white or coloured), (2) for Africans by eight M.P.'s and six senators who
will be whites, and (3) for Indians, by two M.P.'s and one senator who will
be white. "I know" exclaimed the leader of the opposition, de Villiers
Graaf, "I shall be told by the idealists that this means that there will not be
equality between the race groups. . . .Of course there won't be. Why

should there be? The real interests of South Africa as a whole, as well as of the races constituting South Africa, can best be served and advanced by the leadership of the White group. Why should we deny that leadership to the people of South Africa?"[9]

The English language press (with the exception of the *Rand Daily Mail*) applies a similar perspective, which criticizes the government vehemently but agrees with the principle of racial separation. The authoritarian method of implementing this policy with its inhumanities and injustices, not the policy itself, is attacked. Occasionally, English journalists even show signs of deference, thanking the government for a gesture of benevolence toward political opponents as if it were a relieving gift, instead of a right to which they are entitled. An illustrative, satirical comment on this topic has been provided by columnist Hogarth Hoogh, of the *Sunday Times*, on the occasion of Sobukwe's release from Robben Island.

> My very warm congratulations to the Minister of Justice, Mr. Pelser, on his decision to release Robert Sobukwe. I will not dwell on the fact that it should have been done long ago. Let us count our blessings and be thankful that this indefensible incarceration is now coming to an end. The Government has feared, of course, that Sobukwe would become a danger to the State if he were released. This is always a possibility, but I doubt whether we really have much to fear (a) because Sobukwe is unlikely to try anything and (b) he won't get very far if he does. The important thing is that a man's liberty is no longer curtailed by arbitrary decree. I always felt a little ashamed when I thought of the way Sobukwe was restricted. Many of us will now be able to hold our heads a little higher as we walk down the street. We thank the Minister.[10]

However, the favorite subject of the English-language press in South Africa is the lack of realism on the part of the Nationalists. Again and again, they are accused of ideological obsessions which would prevent a tolerant treatment of the nonwhites. Neglect of the African's feeling of dignity, it is said, reflects a dangerously unrealistic assessment of economic interdependence. The editor of the largest Sunday paper in the country writes in a debate with his Afrikaner counterpart Dirk Richard: "I quite agree that we would all prefer not to have 'integration'. But that is rather like an Eskimo saying he would prefer not to have ice in Winter. . . .To pretend that the non-Whites are not there, or to persist in futile efforts to remove them is dangerously unrealistic."[11]

Even the irreplaceable Institute of Race Relations whose documentation, research, and objective information is one of the most important sources of internal enlightenment, presents itself as opposing "injustice and unfair discrimination,"[12] which obviously implies the existence of a "fair" discrimination. Its language frequently resembles official announcements, often more or less identifying with a South African nationalism against the liberation movements in other African countries. The institute's *Fortieth Annual Report 1968/1969*, for example, states, without qualifying the terms used: "Terrorism will continue to be a potential threat. Despite internal problems, other African territories must continue to arraign South Africa and will continue to agitate against South Africa's membership of international organizations." One can anticipate the time when "the emergence of a sense of 'Black Power' in undemonstrative assertions of purpose," which the same report mentions, will dismiss the institute's well-intentioned striving for a nonracial society as the irrelevant and futile efforts of guilt-ridden dogooders.

Since the Rivonia arrests, active opponents inside the country have learned to assess realistically the power of the state machinery. The system of police informers in all potential opposition groups has been improved to such an extent that this surveillance alone guarantees an effective check on all opponents inside and outside the country. Wide powers, without interference of the courts, together with effective methods of interrogation, give the political police virtually unlimited authority. Solitary confinement and permanent interrogations replace direct physical torture.

Police brutality is present in South Africa as it is in various other countries; but on the whole it has become the exception rather than the rule since psychological torture makes physical assaults unnecessary. Officially, police brutality is not encouraged; confrontations such as the Sharpeville massacre and the urban riots of the mid-seventies have become extremely embarrassing for the government, since they demonstrate that the system does not, in fact, function as smoothly as propagandized. Apart from individual sadism and the institutionalized violence of repressive laws, however, the direct brutality of traditional master-servant relations remains an ever-present threat, in spite of official admonitions to avoid embarrassing incidents. Sharpevilles on a smaller scale still occur as a matter of routine, and are hardly noticed as exceptions, since they have become part of the accepted body of sanctions against deviations from role expectations.

The report of a clash on a Transvaal farm characterizes the typical mentality of the police when confronted with a threatening situation involving Africans who are ready to challenge police interference.

> According to Brig. E. de W. Brandt, Divisional Commissioner of Police for the Western Transvaal, a strong force of police (35 White and African men) was sent to the farm of Mr. Faan Bekker after a complaint had been received. The police parked their vehicles some distance from where the group of about 150 Africans were screaming and holding war dances. The Africans all work on near-by mines. Brigadier Brandt said the mob taunted the police

and refused to disperse despite repeated warnings. When the mob started throwing stones, the police opened fire. According to Brigadier Brandt, the crowd scattered in all directions after the first burst of fire. Police arrested 22 during mopping-up operations and found four wounded Africans.[13]

More indicative than the actions of the police is the reaction of the white public toward such reports. The Afrikaner press, if it reports such incidents at all, does so in the same manner as road accidents—regrettable, but hardly altogether avoidable. The English opposition press similarly reveals the basic consensus about white authority enforcement, only modified through a more humane implementation. In this vein, *The Star* comments:

> There ought to be a great deal of understanding for the police when duty requires them to face a mob that has got out of hand. Their position is often dangerous. In the last resort there may be no alternative to firearms, but are there not other steps that could be taken before this drastic order is given? For instance, tear gas.[14]

On the other hand, the guilt feeling of whites, when confronted with obvious injustice, is an important factor of the South African political scene. The *baasskap* (white domination) attitude, even in its bureaucratized form, disturbs the conscience-easing tranquility of many whites whose professional ethics are closely linked to universal values of equality and justice. The more South Africa deviates from world trends and the *total* subordination of her colonized population becomes a necessary fact of *apartheid* life, the more pragmatic domination has to insist on its proper legitimation in terms of otherwise acceptable values. The guilty white frequently articulates this gap, however, without being aware that his own group policies lie at the root of his uneasiness. He hopes to reconcile the unreconcilable; his moral indignation remains confined to the realm of self-assuring protest without impact; if there are consequences of his protest over secondary injustices it lies in a further streamlining of the system of primary differentiation.

The South African system of internal colonialism has largely managed to convey the impression that the colonized are no longer entirely the victims of their masters. Courageous verdicts from some members of an independent judiciary have contributed to an awareness of injustice as much as the public discussion about it. It is still possible for example, for twenty-one Africans, held in prison for seventeen months and charged with Poqo membership, to be finally acquitted after the judge found that the key witness of the secret police had lied.[15] The insistence of white domination on properly legalized repression to a certain extent clouds the content, and the power of the state seems impartial, merely abused by individual transgressions. The South African sociologist, Fatima Meer, emphasizes the political significance of this legalistic attitude. She argues that South Africa preserves its

> structure through a highly sophisticated administrative technique which carefully mixes personal benevolence with the impersonal and hence impartial mystique of the law, which transcends mere human considerations. The non-White victim is beginning to believe that he has the sympathy and support of minor and senior officials, including the Prime Minister, and that both Blacks and Whites are equally victims of South African customs and the laws of Apartheid. This myth has the probable effect of improving race relations while retaining the deprived status of the non-White.[16]

The arbitrary powers of government officials are also counterbalanced to a certain extent by the relative "integrity" of Afrikaner bureaucracy. Compared with the widespread corruption in Latin America and many other states, the Afrikaner civil servant adheres to a Calvinist-inspired work ethos that is more oriented toward the benefits of his group than toward individual advantages. Laws are created and bent to fit this collective goal of group protection and not to further the advancement of officials in power or lobbyists connected with them. Although the typical rank-and-file public servant is known to represent one of the staunchest supporters of the National party, he has hitherto been debarred from formally belonging to political parties because of his image of objectivity. When the government counters criticism with the assurance that the sweeping powers of its executives will not be misused, it can, for the most part, rely on this ingroup integrity which has proved to be a considerable source of strength and efficiency in the implementation of extralegal control.

The freedom of helpless protest the few dissident whites enjoy also contributes to the overall strength of the system rather than to its downfall. If the much misused formula of "repressive tolerance" has any meaning, it applies in South Africa. For example, with a kind of masochistic satisfaction, cabinent ministers undergo the experience of being heckled by white nonbelievers, thus demonstrating their democratic tolerance toward a powerless opposition.

The press reported a meeting between two thousand Witwatersrand University students and a cheerful minister of mines: "The last question put to Dr. de Wet concerned the deaths of political detainess. In reply he said there was a procedure by which magistrates could visit political detainees, adding the question was an attack on the integrity of the Bench, not the Government. At the conclusion of the meeting nearly half the students stood up and, after lifting their hands in the Nazi salute, chanted Sieg Heil, Sieg Heil for a good 30 seconds."[17] While such expressions of dissent would hardly be tolerated in totalitarian regimes of the fascist or Stalinist version, the South African rulers can afford such marginal deviation among the members of their restricted constituency.

What really matters is the successful check on the nonwhite opposition. As long as this potential threat can be arrested, and the organization of the fragmented and atomized subordinates can be prevented, no real danger for white rule exists. With all the nonwhite leaders of the *apartheid* opposition either in jail, in exile, or under house arrest, and with their organizations banned, the active mass resistance within South Africa is paralyzed. It is wishful thinking to state from a position of safety abroad: "But the tendency for new men to take the place of those imprisoned or on trial shows no sign of halting or of being intimidated by countermeasures."[18]

Nevertheless, it is not only the development of the country into a democratic police state that secures the white supremacy. Given the numerical ratio, increased terror by the white minority would have enhanced the likelihood or a revolutionary upheaval. The key to an explanation of the present situation lies in two other factors: (1) the partial successes of the program of "separate development," and (2) the consequences of an unexpected economic boom, neutralizing dissatisfaction by channeling it into other goals.

Apartheid as Utopia and Reality

Promise of Independence Instead of "Petty Apartheid"

Any analysis which focuses only on the repressive aspects of the South African race system overlooks the new elements of the pragmatic oligarchy. These are most clearly embodied in the utopian aspects of *apartheid*, from which the traditional race separation can be distinguished. The traditional *apartheid* represents no invention of the National party, but has always been part of the South African way of life, whether in English-speaking Durban or in Afrikaans-speaking Pretoria. These special relationships of contact, or rather distance, between the race groups, were simply legalized by the laws of petty *apartheid*, and only in a few instances newly introduced. Pierre van den Berghe has called the sphere micro-segregation as distinguished from meso- and macro-segregation.[19] Meso-segregation aims at the geographical separation of residential zones in the urban areas, while macro-segregation is directed toward the future separate coexistence of ethnically homogenous nations. It is this third aspect of *apartheid*, occasionally referred to as "ideal" or "theoretical" *apartheid*, that dominates the contemporary discussion compared with the two other forms of separation. This partly reflects the fact that micro- and meso-segregaton have largely been realized. There is hardly any sphere which has not yet been separated. In addition, the emphasis on utopian *apartheid* can be understood as an attempt to overcome the repressive features of this traditional pattern, and in face of this endeavor, the significance of petty *apartheid* is steadily decreasing. It is with the dominance of macro-segregation or utopian *apartheid* as compared with administrative-repressive *apartheid* in mind that the new forms of racial oligarchy can best be analyzed.

Afrikaner domestic neocolonialism, at least the Verwoerd and Vorster version, is much more enlightened than the traditional colonial methods of an Ian Smith in Rhodesia or those of the late Portuguese administration in Mozambique and Angola, both of which have managed without formal racial separation. Under the pressure of world opinion and a growing ur-banized African proletariat, as well as a small nonwhite professional elite with a fifty-year-long struggle for emancipation behind it, Verwoerd realiz-ed that he had to create a political outlet for African nationalism. The ban-tustan policy is supposed to fulfill this function. It deflects political aspira-tions to areas where they are no danger to white rule. It meets the worldwide demand for African political rights in a fading colonial period by granting them the vote in remote areas—but not in their living and working places where they are merely given the status of rightless "guest workers."

Furthermore, the bantustan policy conceals continued white control over development under the guise of convincing examples of African pseudo-independence. This device has already proved useful in the case of the other independent neighboring states of Lesotho, Botswana, and Swaziland. The status of "satellite" applies to the independent neighbors of South Africa at least as much as in some Latin and Middle American coun-tries, where the economic dependence on the United States had led to a situation "in which sovereignty of a country becomes a mere fiction in many spheres."[20] The planned bantustans will constitute a new model in this respect. Numerous studies point convincingly to the illusory aspect of the program, and the increasing gap between promise and reality is regret-ted even among Afrikaner intellectuals.

After a thorough survey of the Transkei, American political scientists Gwendolen Carter, Thomas Karis, and Newell Stultz reach this conclu-sion:

> The almost total dependence on the South African economy for even the livelihood of those in the territory, the lack of attractiveness of rural life to Africans brought up in urban areas, and the relatively small numbers affected in relation to the total African population of South Africa would all seem to make independence for the Transkei relatively unimportant in the total con-text. Even if the South African government should decide to pour massive

funds into the Transkei and other African areas for which it plans comparable development, it can hardly be expected that either the Africans themselves or the outside world would feel that what was virtually a unilateral settlement by Whites for a small, impoverished area would compare with the progressive extension of political, social, and economic rights for Africans within the present boundaries of South Africa.[21]

This prediction has been borne out by the refusal of the international community to recognize the independent status of the Transkei. Nevertheless, the program of separate development has been partially successful, not through a real redistribution of power, but through psychological impact. This is true mainly for two aspects: (1) the compensation for absence of real political rights by so-called local self-governing bodies and (2) the increase of nonwhite fragmentation through the separation of the population groups.

Less important political decisions and bureaucratic functions are delegated to various nonwhite local and regional self-governing bodies, whose members work under white supervision. Apart from the propaganda effect, these institutions prove useful for the central authority in at least three respects: (1) upwardly mobile and politically ambitious individuals are absorbed into this administration, (2) immediate discontent of nonwhites is directed toward members of their own groups, since they represent the overall system; and (3) the real authorities are freed from burdensome and tedious spade work and thus can confine themselves to "advisory" functions without losing factual control. As Barrington Moore writes: "totalitarianism represents, in part, an attempt to allocate functions without granting control over the resources that the function requires, in order to prevent the growth of independent bases of power in the hands of subordinates."[22]

Under these circumstances the pragmatic Afrikaner no longer insists on *baasskap* but practices an enlightened coexistence. For the first time in their history, they shake hands and organize civil receptions for foreign African dignitaries; as Nationalists of similar status they are allowed entry into the best white hotels while in daily life, black and white are often still not even allowed in the same elevator. In contrast to Portuguese and Rhodesian politicians, the enlightened sector of Afrikaners have long realized that the era of traditional colonialism is definitely over. The editors of two Afrikaner papers, P. Cillie and S. Pienaar, have expressed this attitude frankly: "Old-time colonialist *baasskap* has not only become impractical in the modern world; nor does it only make our coexistence with other people impossible; we can no longer live with ourselves under such an order. . .we cannot and may not become the last fortress of a wrong order in the fighting against which the Afrikaner people were formed in a larger degree."[23]

From the awareness of this necessity the practice of racially defined discrimination arose; it was not however, justified with the classical ideology. According to a frequently used distinction, the South African system is characterized by "racialism," but no longer by "racism." The practice of pointing to the biological inferiority of the blacks and the natural superiority of the whites—a central feature of Social Darwinist race theories—is officially regarded as outdated, though latently still assumed; the underprivileged are no longer held to be inferior but solely different. Furthermore, from this perspective, the underprivileged are depicted as desiring to be different. The tendency toward greater rationality in the implementation of domination has been preceded in the ideology by a focus on social and cultural traditions instead of on dubious biological assertions. The inherited inferiority was a matter of mere belief, fictitious and constantly refuted by experience to the contrary; but the reference to cultural pluralism has a real basis indeed, especially since it is promoted by the forced separation of an ethnocentric policy. This policy no longer requires traditional ideological rationalization: its justification is demonstrated by its very existence.

Apartheid reinforces the existing group differences. It need not create them altogether but can build on the traditional syncretic structure and thus prevent nonwhite unity. Nothing seems further from reality than to assume a conscious homogeneity of nonwhite interests as opposed to their rulers. In Marx's categories, they constitute most certainly a class "in itself" but they are further away than the European proletariat ever has been from a consciousness with which they form a class "for itself." So far as subjective intensity is concerned, the conflicts among the nonwhite groups at many levels exceed the frictions between white and nonwhite. Fostered by this situation, the government was able to propagandize a policy that effectively blocked the politicizing attempts for nonwhite solidarity. Anthropologist Ellen Hellmann states that tribalism was until recently a waning force in South Africa. "Under the spur of the present Government's policies and in the absence of any alternative, Bantu tribalism is growing in strength in this country. The signs of this abound."[24] It is, however, not the disunity among the subordinate groups that accounts for the present stalemate, but rather the strength of the ruling group.

The ethnocentric nationalism provided by *apartheid* is thus distinct from cultural imperialism, particularly of the French version, which aimed at the extinction of any memory and pride of the colonized toward their own history and dignity in favor of complete adoption of colonial culture. In a way, the *apartheid* ideology has anticipated what Frantz Fanon describes as the central feature of the "Wretched of the Earth," and what concepts such as "Negritude" and similar ideologies of black nationalism attempt to revive. Theoretically, *apartheid* promises the abolition of cultural and finally material discrimination. The defensive Afrikaner nationalism does not glorify its own superiority toward other nations as was the rule among the aggressive European nations of the nineteenth century. Whether the Afrikaner past with its former progressive nationalism is projected onto the other groups, or whether *apartheid* is merely a witting device of *divide et impera,* is hardly significant compared with the fact that obviously a widespread ethnic narcissism in all groups responds to such offers. That for which minorities in other parts of the world struggle—the right to keep their cultural identity—is granted readily in South Africa. While in other countries the quest for autonomy on the part of minorities has a progressive function in furthering their partial liberation from the majority's domination, the same process under South African conditions means that the existing domination thereby secures its continuity and refuses political autonomy to the majority.

Control through Self-Government

In this endeavor, the South African whites are, however, confronted with a dilemma that makes the effective use of indirect rule, as successfully practiced by colonial predecessors, difficult if not impossible. Indirect government through the chiefs and headmen presupposes respectful acceptance by their subjects: it was successful because of the unchallenged loyalty of the illiterates in the wisdom of their leaders. However, today the traditional rulers often represent the backward part of the population and often are illiterate themselves, and thus for a growing number of tribal people their legitimacy derives solely from their white mandators, by whom they are paid and controlled. This does not necessarily decrease their actual power. Although the prestige of the collaborating bureaucrats within their group might be questionable, even their most outspoken enemy is forced to yield to the channels which they provide if he expects any chance of obtaining any gratification from the system. The increased bureaucratization and regimentation of life of the nonwhite population has thus strengthened the power of these secondary rulers, despite their waning tradional legitimacy. Whereas under the former "sure" colonial conditions, the white bosses were satisfied if the chiefs kept their followers "in their place" and provided the imposed services and taxes, they now have to insist that the politicized subjugates are in fact ruled, administered, and controlled.

This task, however, seems to be beyond the capacity of the traditional chiefs under *apartheid* conditions. In their public statements, especially in their speeches to their own group members, many avoid identifying themselves too much with the government's race policy. If they intend to be not merely policemen who implement the duties delegated to them by a foreign dictate, then they must demonstrate their independence and usefulness in order to counteract the charge of being collaborators and traitors. This is especially so for the coloured and Indian representatives who lack traditional legitimacy and are thus faced with an even greater ambivalence. The following speech delivered by the chairman of the South African Indian Council at its constitution is characteristic of the way the council members reconcile their dependent role with the fact that they hold their position due to their readiness to cooperate and not on the basis of an electoral mandate. In a similar way the African speakers defend their cause by emphasizing that they, for the first time, are allowed political influence:

> Under the Chairmanship of Mr. Maree [the minister of Indian Affairs], during the last four years, members enjoyed complete freedom of speech, a privilege that will be maintained in all our future deliberations. In this regard, I wish to recall the words of Mr. Maree, when he said that he did not want stooges, neither did he want members to regard themselves as a rubber stamp for the actions of the government.[25]

While one is easily inclined to dismiss such statements as rhetorical declamation, they, nevertheless, reflect an important aspect of rational oligarchy. System theorists have stressed the negative correlation between the information a government has about a specific situation and its use of force. Under South African circumstances, the government is indeed interested in the disagreement and not the conditionless agreement of the controlled voice of its dependents. In the absence of other representative channels for complaints and demands, "constructive criticism" in the framework of the prescribed responsibility serves to illuminate early dangerous areas within the system. The recognition of dissatisfaction among the ruled becomes in itself an important instrument of enlightened neocolonial domination. Potential conflicts are no longer merely suppressed, with the risk of their becoming explosive as in former authoritarian regimes, but are disarmed and mastered by controlling dissatisfaction within the framework of the system.

> Mr. Maree invited members to express their disagreement whenever they were so inclined, or to differ with actions and decisions. However, if the Council found it necessary to express any disagreements, he appealed that they do so in a sensible, constructive and reasonable manner as might well be expected of a responsible Council.[26]

On the other hand, the granting of codetermination and political rights, though minimal, does contain the nucleus of future conflicts that inevitably will change the carefully established system in its old form. The dialectic of oppression and necessary concessions to the oppressed leads to an increase in opposition demands which in their turn either sharpen the conflicts or have to be countered by steadily greater concessions, for which, however, shifting limits exist in the system of totalitarian domination. Suppression is either absolute and total or it develops an inner dynamic toward its own abolition. In this sense, the promise of independence for the bantustans and similar self-governing bodies for the other groups indicates not only strength but also the retreat of formerly undisputed domination.

A closer look at nonwhite elections, at the program of nonwhite parties, and at the behavior of their representatives under *apartheid* conditions can illustrate this dialectic inherent in the concession of self-administration.

An ill-founded assumption widely held within white government circles is that the so-called pro-*apartheid* groups do indeed support the white policy. However, in the first coloured election in September 1969, all three progovernment parties defended only "the positive aspects of separate development" (expanded educational institutions for example) and were strongly opposed to petty *apartheid* and some of the ways the Group Areas Act is being implemented. The rival Labour party which won a clear majority of elected seats in the Council rejects any form of *apartheid* whatsoever, and is in principle and spirit a multiracial party.

It is possible to classify the political activity of nonwhites in South Africa into three main groups, according to program and tactics:

1. Groups that reject the discriminatory aspects of *apartheid*, but work legally within the prescribed limits to improve their racially defined situation. In all important questions they collaborate with the central government (Federal Party of the Coloureds, Transkei National Independence party under Kaiser Matanzima before independence).

2. Groups that use permissible political activity to combat *apartheid* as a principle, and secondly to oppose ethnocentrism within their own group members (Labour Party of the Coloureds, Democratic party in the Transkei under Knowledge Guzana before independence).

3. Groups that consider any legal political activity in the prescribed *apartheid* framework meaningless, and, therefore, recommend passivity and the boycott of elections.

It is impossible to draw definite conclusions about the strength of the three groups simply from election results. The voting system of single constituencies and also the form of participation leave scope for contradicting explanations. For example, between 75 and 80 percent of the Transkeian voters (men and women over twenty-one) are illiterate: at the polling station they communicated their vote verbally to the officials who marked the required "X" for them. In the coloured elections, the total percentage poll was 48.7 percent, the highest participation in the rural constituencies and the lowest in the urban areas of the Cape, only 16.4 percent in one Cape Town seat.

In the coloured elections the Labour party (group 2) won a majority of seats but not the majority of votes. In the second election in the Transkei the Democratic party (group 2) won sixteen of forty-five elected seats, a loss of thirteen compared with the previous election, and there was no coercion.

However, to ensure that the institutions of separation are not used against government's intention, one-third of the members of the Coloured Representative Council are appointed by the government; for the most part, candidates have been appointed who were in fact defeated in the elections. The appointed chairman of the Executive of the Council Tom Swartz, for example, ran third in his constituency in the election. The blatant action of the government, which did not even attempt to conceal its motives by appointing seemingly "neutral" candidates, was aimed at silencing its right-wing critics. Among the subordinates it dispelled any illusion that the elections could in practice be anything more than symbolic demonstrations.

Nevertheless, there is a discernible trend among the politically conscious nonwhite elite in South Africa to move away from protest through passivity and boycott, and to use the limited possibilities for practical political action. In the face of total subordination, political behavior becomes redefined as a technique of maximum survival. No longer can victory be expected or even sought. The choice they have to make is between political suicide or accomodation. Realizing this alternative, many opted for pragmatic survival. "One has to be practical in one's approach. Here in South Africa we are faced with a situation that is not our making. We have learnt from previous experience that total opposition does not help us in any way. So what do we do? I know that we on the Council are often called Government men. This is absolute nonsense. We serve on the Council only because we feel that we might be in a position to obtain opportunities for our people that were denied in the past."[27] If this view is correct in expecting opportunities to improve the fate of the governed, than it must coincide with the rulers' readiness to make concessions.

The interest of the rulers in the smooth functioning of the subordinates' self-administration is based mainly on political and propagandistic considerations. But, in addition, the expansion of *apartheid* administration using only white manpower would be economically impractical. One out of every nine white South Africans is already employed in government service (central, provincial, local agencies, and railways). This high ratio of state employment as compared with other Western countries such as Britain or the United States results partly from the increased bureaucratization required for the implementation of *apartheid* laws, but above all from the exclusion of nonwhites from state administration in the past. Given the white manpower shortage, the "self-policing" of the colonized on the payroll and under the control of the colonizer becomes a desirable if not necessary goal.

Table 1 illustrates the well-known fact that public service employs a higher percentage of white workers than does the private manufacturing industry.[28]

TABLE 1

	Whites	*Coloureds*	*Indians*	*Africans*
Public Service	40.2	10.0	2.2	47.6
Provincial Administration	50.1	6.8	1.2	41.9
Private Manufacturing	25.3	16.2	5.9	52.6

If this employment pattern is to change, the middle and upper stratum of nonwhite administration will have to be staffed by the nonwhites themselves. This would mean creating entire civil services including a formal top of the hierarchy for each racial group. After stating that only one in every thirty Bantu is employed in government service, *Current Affairs*, the outspoken daily political commentary of the South African Broadcasting Corporation, elaborates: "This means that the White population is carrying a grossly disproportionate burden in the management of the country and people as a whole. There is only one effective solution here: it is to enable and encourage more Bantu—and Coloureds and Indians—to participate in the running of their own affairs. Only when the various groups have civil services of their own will the imbalance be corrected—and this is a major objective of the policy of separate development."[29]

"Running their own affairs," however, is an issue where white and nonwhite interests will inevitably conflict over the extent and meaning of autonomy and participation in power. The limitations presently set on self-control will affect political consciousness among the men in a new ethnic political context. The more clearly the nonwhite administrators become aware of their pseudo-control, the more their resentment increases. To be sure, there are for the first time channels within the system through which ·complaints may be launched and limited changes obtained, but these possibilities prove insufficient, if for no other reason than the continued economic dependence. Although criticism has now become legal, this does not necessarily render it less dangerous; for the former clearcut fronts between the system's enemies and its supporters have now been obscured.

Subversion within the scope of permitted political activity could become difficult to control. As long as such activity uses the logic and the jargon of the government, it remains relatively safe for its advocates. Informed observers point to some of the chiefs in the Transkei who have cleverly used *apartheid* to fight the *apartheid* inventors with their own arms.[30] Although such chiefs share governmental interests in the maintenance of the traditional tribal structure, the latent potential of conflict between these uneasy allies could develop into a major political factor. Similarly, the pressure emanating from the voters, merely administered on behalf of the real power, increases. Granting the franchise for all Xhosas of the Transkei inevitably raises the question for the voter as to what his vote really means and decides. Politicized for the first time by fictitious alternatives, they will probably feel more frustrated in the long run than before, by having formal political rights and yet remaining basically rightless subjects.

In the short run, however, the extreme racial structure in South Africa might well support the temporary "satraps"; that there are fellow non-whites with certain minor privileges has a powerful appeal for those who are used to nothing but subjugation. The historical degradation of the South African nonwhites is so absolute and uniform that any role of authority feeds the desire to identify and participate, if only symbolically, in the control of their own lives.

Having launched the program of self-government for ethnic minorities, and having now granted independence to the Transkei, its initiators cannot now reverse the process even if it should backfire on them. A return to the former *baasskap* policy is no longer possible. Were the government to withhold from other bantustans the realization of these heightened expectations, greater dissatisfaction and subsequently more direct oppression would be the inevitable consequence. The rulers too are subject to the dialectical forces inherent in the conditions of modified rule. The more the bantustan populations, for whatever reason, applaud the *apartheid* cooperation of their tribal leaders, the greater the pressure on the government to discharge the promise of independence. What seems advantageous for propagandistic reasons and of limited significance in view of the continued economic dependence of the territory does, however, include a military risk. In contrast to the geographically isolated former British territories, the maritime Transkei can import armaments by sea. It would seem, therefore, that the white state cannot afford to relinquish its indirect control of the territory, which could in the long run become politically explosive.

Stabilization Through New Role Relations

The utopian *apartheid* program has resulted in developments often un-noticed outside the country. Compared with the *baasskap* era, race rela-tions appear to have assumed the form of a relatively smoothly function-ing, correct business relationship despite increased institutionalized separa-tion. Nonwhite customers assert they are now served more politely in the shops due to their growing purchasing power. The civil servant has official-ly been told to avoid blatant discriminatory treatment, and direct confron-tation in an arrest or a police raid is largely carried out by black constables. It would appear that the African in Pretoria, at present, has a greater chance of being correctly treated by the police than the black in Chicago. These superficial changes in race relations do not indicate a greater tolerance of the South African system, but rather the complete absence of alternatives for the ruled. The control of the state machinery is so absolute, and the certainty of this total dependence is so universal, that no individual dares to claim what ought to be his rights. The state official, therefore, can afford to demonstrate a generous benevolence.

On the other hand, the rulers are for the first time making conscious ef-forts to dampen potentially explosive situations. The commander of the Johannesburg police declared that policemen treating Africans not as human beings would be regarded as "saboteurs."[31] Piet Koornhof, then deputy minister of Bantu Administration and Education, emphasized that government officials who had to deal with Africans were taught early in their careers that the African was "a human being just like the Whites" and that he merited his own place in the sun.[32] The Bantu Affairs commis-sioners were proud of the fact that the African rightly looked on them as "fathers." "We do not believe in fraternization—but we do believe in honesty and sincerity. We do want to create false illusions and we want the Bantu to know exactly where he stands and what our intentions are with him." To a large extent this intimidating bluntness would seem responsible for the overtly smooth race relations. The Afrikaner does not allow any doubts that he would use his powers. This clear role definition allows him to behave according to collective dictates and to avoid as far as possible, individual deviations. Other emotions which always characterized and "humanized" even the most brutal master-servant relationship are ideally excluded in this definition. Master and servant ought to be reduced com-pletely to their prescribed role. The surprise effect of individual reactions precludes calculation and, therefore, has to be avoided.

The former racialists have realized pragmatically that the future of white South Africa depends on the extent to which it can gain the acquiescence of the African masses. When the army goes into maneuver to exercise guerrilla warfare it is accompanied by ethnologists and other experts to make sure the native population is not offended by white ignorance of local customs, and that they understand their intended part of the armed struggle. An editorial of the *Die Burger* states: "Today we realize better than before that the stirring up of race tensions is preparatory to revolutionary war, which cannot be carried out without the enemy winning friends within our internal life. And to counteract these race tensions is not just a military task in the narrow sense. It calls for effort at all levels under the leadership of our chosen political High Command. It is time for all South Africans to see the connection between the Government's political plans for the non-White people of the country and our military security."[33]

Even though the practice of such insights in daily routine is often still more an exception than the rule, and though paternalistic master-servant relationships dominate in the working sphere, an African is no longer only an object of personal white arbitrariness. Awareness among nonwhites of at least their formal rights when confronted with individual discrimination has contributed in some measure to the belief in the justice of *apartheid* order. Frequently the subordinate prefers this openly announced and admitted dictate to the facade of equality presented by many of the English-speaking whites. All empirical surveys revealing the attitudes of Africans toward the openly racialist Afrikaners and the less outspoken English-speaking whites showed greater suspicion and aversion toward the latter.[34] The guiding theme of many responses is that the Afrikaner could be taken seriously, in contrast to the Englishman who was too hypocritical to admit his prejudice. This reaction suggests that the group discrimination by the confessed racialist is experienced as less offensive than the mere rhetorical advocacy of equality. The awareness of belonging to a group of people who are equally oppressed provides collective psychological protection; while in the case of individual discrimination, disappointed expectations are frequently explained as personal failure.

White Resistance against Race Utopia

A decisive obstacle for the implementation of theoretical *apartheid* is that it is accorded only rhetorical rather than factual support among the white electorate. The majority are openly unwilling to support a government that would take such a program seriously. The gap between the *apartheid* ideologists in the government or press and the reactions of the majority of white citizens is openly admitted and regretted in many editorials. In a preindependence commentary on the Transkei elections, *Die Beeld* wrote:

The Transkei must—and not some day in dreamland but acceptably soon—develop in such a way that it will become a vital Southern African state, capable not only of maintaining its own people but also of attracting its best sons and daughters back from across its borders, where they are liable to become permanently estraged from it. It is doubtful if the South African general public, too, has any conception of what such a task embraces, and it is, therefore, doubtful if the South African public is in a position to view the result in its proper perspective.[35]

Here only abstract economic and political sacrifices are demanded, but the real attitude of the white South African becomes evident in matters that affect his immediate comfort. Nearly all white households employ African servants; the early morning coffee or tea served at the bed of the *baas* belongs as much to the sacred colonial relic as the freedom of women from tedious housework and supervision of children. The purists in other spheres have no objection to their children being bathed, dressed, and sometimes tutored in their school work by African servants. Some women, reports a paper with disgust, even ask their servants to curl their hair and permitted African men to make beds and handle nightwear.[36] When, during the resistance campaigns, the number of Africans being housed in white backyards reached a supposedly dangerous limit, a law was passed that allowed only one servant per household to stay overnight. All futher attempts "to keep the cities white" at night encountered fierce rejection by housewives and other affected parties.

> Householders can allow only one servant to sleep in without a permit. But experience shows that the local authorities are not sparing in the issue of permits, for after all, fewer Bantu in White back yards imply a greater demand for accommodation in municipal locations and the White ratepayer is not prepared to supply it.[37]

The following selection from editorials of Afrikaans papers during a single week in November 1968 gives a further insight into the reality of separate development from the perspective of its most active interpreters. It documents at the same time the thinking of leading government circles.

> People who call aloud for a solution of the race question continue to keep a small army of non-Whites in their homes or on their farms. They even shut their eyes to the fact that Bantu stay overnight on their property. It simply does not enter their heads to investigate who is sleeping on their property. Early in the morning, it is not only Lyttleton that looks like a "black antheap." Let every Johannesburger, for example, take the trouble to stroll through the streets of his suburb between five and six in the morning. He will then see how potential thieves, thugs, robbers and so forth are exuded in their dozens from the backyards.[38]

In contrast to such statements it looks like a magic incantation when the same paper writes six days later:

> The Nationalist Afrikaners are like other people, selfish, as Mr. Gerdener says; unthinking, as Professor Rhoodie avers. But one thing is certain about them: they are prepared to make separate development a vital, practical reality in South Africa and when the sacrifices for doing so are required of them, they will be ready for them.[39]

The contrary view seems more realistic despite the fact that it generously overlooks the government's inability to do much against the interests of its electorate:

> It is very clear that there can hardly be any question of voluntary cooperation. The Government will simply have to see that its laws are carried out, for to an increasing extent, Nationalist governments will be required to give an account of the way in which their "white cities" policy is being implemented—even though the big critics will also be the big offenders. The excuse that the public will not cooperate will in course of time become an indictment.[40]

Ominously realistic, another Afrikaans paper close to the government warns:

> Should things one day collapse here in the Republic the Whites will only have themselves to blame. There have been enough warnings to make everyone appreciate the race problem properly, but too many Whites choose not to take notice.[41]

An Afrikaner psychology professor seemed to represent the mood of many similar statements of his peers when he ends an article on the topic, "The Afrikaner Intellectual and Apartheid" with the conclusion:

> The acceptance of ethnical equality means that those of us who believe in the positive aspects of Apartheid can be satisfied with nothing less than the implementation of policies aimed at the eventual complete independence and viable nationhood of those peoples with whom we do not wish to integrate and who are at present under our control. If we fail to achieve this, I see a dark future for my people, whose need for apartness may lead them in the event of a catastrophe to a wandering existence such as befell the Jews, who also saw themselves as a chosen people.[42]

This extensive documentation of the self-understanding of Afrikaner intellectuals seems to indicate a schizophrenia that, on the one hand, realistically assesses its own situation and sees the hopelessness of continued rule in its traditional form, but, on the other hand, adheres to fictions that prevent a realistic policy. Karl Mannheim has described such a consciousness as the "utopian mentality" which tends to burst the bonds of the existing order. "A state of mind," Mannheim defines, "is utopian when it is incongruous with the state of reality within which it occurs. This incongruence is always evident in the fact that such a state of mind in experience, in thought, and in practice is oriented towards objects which do not exist in the actual situation."[43] For this state of mind, *apartheid* functions as a magic formula with which the status quo is conjured and transformed into a past utopia at the same time. The more the fiction becomes obvious, the more its reality has to be averred. In an editorial on the practicability of *apartheid*, the author states: "If there is one thing we must guard against it is the spreading of doubts."[44]

Political Intentions and Demographic Trends

The belief in the possibility of implementing *apartheid* goals with regard to the geographical separation of the racial groups, and the return of Africans into developed "homelands," is refuted above all by simple demographic and economic data. The success of the policy is no longer measured against the initially proclaimed goals, but against the speculation of what would have happened without influx control. Some more realistic politicians of the opposition suggest that the African townships in the urban areas be declared part the "homelands." Other officials of the white bureaucracy think that urban Africans could best be induced to settle in the bantustans by increasing their insecurity in towns and restricting their recreational and educational facilities.

Press reports that the Department of Bantu Administration had circulated an order to local authorities that nonwhite doctors and other professional men should not be granted consulting rooms and offices in urban African townships because such communities were in white areas, were later denied by the minister, M. C. Botha. He declared that established African doctors would be allowed to continue practicing in the townships, but would however, "be encouraged to offer their services in the homelands." New African doctors who applied for facilities in the townships in the white areas for the first time would, therefore, "not be granted these facilities lightly."[45]

The very existence of Africans in the townships has become increasingly dependent on labor needs and centralized government decisions. If the government should implement the "Bantu Administration Boards Bill" then the last guarantees and securities of Section 10 of "Bantu (Urban Areas) Consolidation Act, 1945" will have been abolished. This means that even those Africans who were born in the cities or have continuously worked there for ten or fifteen years will have no guaranteed right to live there any longer. In 1969 the minister for Bantu Administration stated: "As far as I am concerned, the ideal condition would be if we could succeed in due course in having all Bantu in the White areas on a basis of migratory labour only."[46] This legislation alone makes clear that the *apartheid* ideal can only be achieved by coercion and force, against the will of the people concerned. Assuming for a moment that the bantustans were indeed to be developed or the government were to succeed in reducing the number of Africans in the cities, it would never be considered a "success" in the view of the Africans.

Dozens of competent observers have pointed to the demographic and economic factors that make the utopian *apartheid* program illusionary. Some of the facts, familiar to the most superficial analyst of the South African political scene, are: the influx of Africans into the urban areas is continuing, despite increased control and rigorous enforcement of existing restrictions. Although according to official statistics the African population of the "homelands" increased from 37.5 percent in 1960 to 46.5 percent in 1970 (from 4.1 million to 7.0 million), nearly 8 million Africans now live in white areas, compared with 6.8 million in 1960. While the proportion of Africans in white areas has fallen from 62.5 percent in 1960 to 53.5 percent in 1970, the black/white ratio has not changed.[47] All these figures, however, are arbitrary, based, for example, on the registration of migrant workers in the "homelands," although most of their time is actually spent living and working in the white cities on which they are so totally dependent. On the basis of the conservative estimate of the Tomlinsson Commission that in the year 2000, 10 million Africans could live in the industrialized reserves, including 2 million migrant workers, the majority of the then living Africans will still have to live outside their prescribed "homelands." C. J. Jooste, director of the government-aligned South African Bureau of Racial Affairs (SABRA), estimates the expected African population in the year 2000 at 30,591,000 of whom 22,838,000 (at present less than 5,000,000) will be in the urban areas.[48] The development of the reserves, however, has hardly progressed during the sixties. Consolidation of the over 200 separate territories remains a catchword in spite of limited state purchase of land for this purpose.

The military budget alone is six times the amount of expenses incurred for the reserves: only about 6 percent of all investments for public projects are flowing into the bantustans. Within the Transkei, the most progressed bantustan, only 42,401 Africans were in paid employment in 1969. The Bantu Investment Corporation through which all investments are channeled has, during its existence since 1959, only succeeded in establishing some small enterprises which employ no more than 2,000 people. In the

Transkei, where 285 of the 600-odd trading stations have been taken over by the Xhosa Development Corporation, a mere thirty-five have been sold to African owners.[49] The reserves, altogether 13 percent of the South African total territory and approximately 25 percent of the country's fertile soil, are already hopelessly overcrowded, with 110 persons per square mile compared with 34 in the other parts. Although in many respects capable of developing, the rural bantustans are dependent on additional food imports due to soil erosion, unprofitable farming methods resulting from lack of capital for mechanization, and disproportional livestock. The white agricultural officers and other civil servants work with undoubted dedication to produce a higher maize yield or better bull breeds in the reserves. They blame failure on the resilience of tribal attitudes and the human potential of their black clients, but fail to take into account the political aspects of their role and African reactions toward it. Official predictions that with the development of the reserves the influx of Africans in the urban areas will be reversed by 1978 are pure illusion in the face of the above data. In the country as a whole, as well as in the urban centers, the percentage of whites decreases in spite of a net gain of approximately 35,000 immigrants annually. However, it can be expected that the incentives to white immigrants will be increased substantially.

Increased mechanization and the general trend toward more qualified work in highly industrialized societies could diminish the demand for unskilled African labor. As yet, however, the abundance of cheap labor has prevented increased mechanization, even though the migratory labor system keeps the individual productivity extremely low. Furthermore, any intensive mechanization and automation would presuppose a mass market with high purchasing power, which as yet does not exist in Africa.

The program of developing border industries on white land close to African reserves, with which the government hopes to counteract the influx to the cities, has to be considered as essentially political self-delusion, regardlesss of the increasing success of this decentralization scheme as such. In its initial stages the border industries program appealed almost en tirely to labor-intensive industries such as textiles. Border industries have been established in close proximity to an already existing urban infrastructure, favorable for future development. Since 1969, however, more and more companies operating in capital-intensive industries have announced plans to expand to, if not actually move to, border areas. There are several reasons for this new trend:

1. The government has encouraged this development by compensating investors for the loss of advantages in the urban areas. These compensations include tax concessions and other financial assistance as well as the provision of basic services and technical aid.

2. While new growth points in remote areas were actively encouraged, expansion of the Witwatersrand has been drastically restricted. But so much hinges on the mobilization of African labor resources that industrialists had to follow the political restrictions.

3. New state-sponsored developments in rural areas have also created new growth centers closer to African reserves.

However, even an increased border industry development does not solve the issues of white-African contact and competition in urban areas; it even multiplies or at most decentralizes them. Although the individual African worker enjoys greater freedom from restrictions with regard to his family life and the right to own land, he still encounters the disadvantage of lower wages and the low ceiling of job reservation. With regard to wider questions of economic growth, the Stellenbosch sociologist, S. P. Cilliers, suggests that border industrial development, although "admirably suited to the policies and needs of South Africa" will be insufficient to provide a continued high growth rate for the economy of the country as a whole. "Development in and around the existing industrial complexes will, at the same time, have to be maintained at a steady rate, and although it may be expected that the intake, especially of Bantu labour, into this growth will be slowed down and supplemented by immigration and by the use especially of indigenous Coloured and Asiatic labour, no great exodus of Bantu from these areas can at this stage be foreseen."[50]

Discussion about theoretical *apartheid* among the whites has become more or less an abstract matter of definitions and classifications, untouched by the suffering of those concerned, so long as white dominance is not jeopardized. The pompous debates over the proper use of the labor commodity become cynical rationalization of a reality in which the nonwhites, the white electorate, and the audience abroad are fed utopias that, because of only minimal political concessions, prove to be guarantees of continued white rule. It seems possible only post facto to indicate how this device for the perpetuation of white rule has on the contrary fostered its decline.

Implications of Economic Integration

South African society, with its repressive oligarchy and its deep group antagonisms, is above all cemented by a common economy. Although the various racial groups realize differential rewards from this economy, they are, nevertheless, dependent on each other. Leo Kuper has frequently emphasized this mutual interdependence as a factor in thus far preventing the breakdown of the racial order, but argues that it does not necessarily exclude a sudden explosion.[51] At present, however, the integrative forces of a rising economic growth rate dominate. Both antagonists are interested in its continuance.

As in no other capitalist society, the producers here are reduced solely to their role in production—elements in an exchange process, cheap raw material in the calculation of costs. A Nationalist member of parliament summarized this situation with the statement that the Bantu "only came here to supply labour. They are only supplying a commodity, the commodity of labour. . . .As soon as the opposition understands this principle that it is labour we are importing and not labourers as individuals, the question of numbers will not worry them either."[52]

This view, however, avoids the omissions of its European predecessors. Forewarned by the events that characterized European industrialization, and alert to the potentially explosive racial situation, the South African hegemony introduced, at an early stage, a social policy designed to prevent extreme and dangerous poverty. The typical African industrial worker has been moved from self-built shacks into tolerable housing schemes. Compared with the fifties or the conditions of his tribal fellow brothers elsewhere, he now has easier access to medical care; his children can attend better equipped schools; and he himself can enjoy more of the comforts of a westernized consumption culture, according to his financial limitations. All sections of the African population have increasingly become part of the money economy. The number of wage earners (economically active persons) has increased from 5,692,000 in 1960 to 6,744,000 in 1968, and 68 percent of these were Africans. Wages increased at a considerably faster rate than did the cost of living index. In spite of recent wage increases for all groups, the gap between white and black wages has widened, as it has, for example, in mining from 17.6:1 in 1968 to 19.19:1 in 1970. Economists point to the increased food consumption as perhaps the most striking quantitative illustration of the gain achieved in real living standards—but also of the tremendous income disparities which exist.[53] While urban whites spend only 19 percent on food consumption, the underprivileged majority has still to devote around 40 percent on food.

Even though half of Soweto's 500,000 Africans still live below the poverty line,[54] the relative improvement of their economic situation takes the sting out of their deprivation. (See Table 2) After the widespread slums of the fifties were cleared, for strategic reasons among others, their dwellers, though reluctantly at first, settled down in the prepared standard homes; the experience of a more hygenic civilization here has soon made the white patterns of consumption a dominating desire. In 1968, 31 percent of the urban Africans had electricity in their homes and 66 percent

TABLE 2
Employment and Wages in the Major Sectors of Industry

	1958		1968	
	Nonwhite	White	Nonwhite	White
Mining and Quarrying:				
Employment	499,000	65,000	550,000	61,000
Proportion of total	88.5%	11.5%	90.1%	9.9%
Compound average rate of increase			1.1%p.a.	-0.65%p.a.
Average wages per year	R145.6	R2,079	R372.5	R3,389
Compound average rate of increase			9.8%p.a.	5.0%p.a.
Manufacturing:				
Employment	462,000	163,000	772,000	259,000
Proportion of total	74.0%	26.0%	74.9%	25.1%
Compound average rate of increase			5.2%p.a.	4.7%p.a.
Average wages per year	R371.9	R1,816.4	R627.0	R2,998.6
Compound average rate of increase			5.3%p.a.	5.1%p.a.
Construction:				
Employment	93,000	28,000	212,000	50,000
Proportion of total	76.9%	23.1%	80.9%	19.1%
Compound average rate of increase			8.4%p.a.	5.9%p.a.
Average wages per year	R332.8	R1,485.3	R680.3	R3,158.7
Compound average rate of increase			7.4%p.a.	7.8%p.a.

Source: Merton Dagut, "The South African Economy through the Sixties," *Optima* 9, no. 3 (September 1969): 119.

had water. Over a period of two years (1966-68) radio ownership among the urban Africans increased from 26 percent to 48 percent.[55] The number of private cars owned by Africans doubled within five years and stood at 7.8 percent of all registered private cars in South Africa in 1968 (whites 85.4 percent). Firms that aim at African buying power in the townships advertise increasingly with African models and African themes. (See Table 3)

Although the white builder earns more in two hours than his "boy," who does most of the actual work, during the whole day, this inequity has been clouded by gradually rising wages. Due to the continuing boom, the average African worker receives more than he could otherwise realistically expect. Such experiences and hopes encourage him to scratch along. In

TABLE 3
Estimated Per Capita Income by Racial Group

	1962	1967
Whites	R782	R1141
Coloureds	120	165
Indians	139	233
Africans	62	82
All races*	207	298

Source: W. Langschmidt, Managing Director of Market Research Africa, derived from National Readership Survey 1967/68 as reported in *STATS*, February 1968, p. 906.

*The differential wages between the race groups are most evident in cases in which the persons have equal qualifications. Thus for instance, male teachers with Standard 12 start with the following annual salaries: Africans-R660, Coloureds and Indians-R1320, whites-R1920. (*The Star*, 10 October 1969). The provincial government of Natal declined in 1967 to adjust the 50 percent income of the nonwhite doctors to the level of their white colleagues at the same hospital in Durban. The reason given was that the nonwhites in South Africa traditionally have a lower living standard and, therefore, need no pay raise. The average African servant earned R17.40 ($24.50) monthly in 1968 plus housing and food for a working day which often exceeds twelve hours.

material terms the South African black proletariat is without doubt far better off than most of the workers in the neighboring industrially underveloped African states, for whom migratory work in the African mines is often the only opportunity for case income.

With regard to educational opportunities, the five nonwhite universities have on the whole been successful in terms of the *apartheid* programs, despite the limitations placed on them as separate institutions under paternalistic Afrikaner guidance. (See Table 4) Their facilities are frequently better and the teacher-student ratio much lower than in the white universities, now as well as previously when they were "open." This limited advancement in nonwhite higher education has been allowed partly for propaganda reasons and to meet economic needs.

An equally important consideration, however, was that this expansive provision of separate institutions proved to be the most expedient way for the government to retain control of facilities for nonwhite education. At the same time it opened new avenues for an ambitious nonwhite middle class for whom other channels of upward mobility were blocked.

There are contrary opinions in the studies on South Africa regarding how revolutionary consciousness may be influenced by a rising standard of living. Leo Kuper, obviously with the bourgeois revolutions in mind, comments: "The greater the advance, the greater the impatience with arbitrary

TABLE 4
Comparative Enrollment in South African Universities

	1958				1970			
	White	Coloured	Asian	African	White	Coloured	Asian	African
Orange Free State	1,709				4,222			
Potchefstroom	1,474				4,212			
Pretoria	6,324				12,500			
Stellenbosch	3,694				7,827			
Port Elizabeth*	—				1,144			
Cape Town	4,408	388	127	37	7,528	291	148	2
Natal	2,530	31	373	188	5,706	43	331	163
Witwatersrand	4,756	22	158	73	9,041	29	293	5
Rhodes	1,098				1,803		40	
South Africa**	6,144	204	601	1,179	17,899	584	1,006	2,397
Rand Afrikaans*					1,322			
Fort Hare		59	59	320				610
The North								810
Zululand								591
Durban-Westville							1,654	
Western Cape						936		
	32,137	704	1,318	1,797	73,204	1,883	3,472	4,578

*A new university founded in 1967.

**Bilingual correspondence university.

Source: M. Horrell, *A Survey of Race Relations in South Africa, 1959-1960,* p. 227: Ibid., 1970, p. 243. The percentage of pupils in secondary schools per group is: Whites-38.1; Coloureds-11.1; Indians-23.9; Africans-4.2.

restraint."[56] Other authors surmise on the contrary, "If a revolution is to have a chance to succeed in South Africa, the economic situation will have to grow worse instead of better."[57] Both opinions are able to point to strong arguments and historical experiences in other circumstances. Nevertheless, both seem insufficient in this generalized form for the South African circumstances since they fail to take specific aspirations into account. Only where concrete expectations are disappointed and where a general politicization emphasizes the gap between claim and reality, can revolutionary action be expected. Dire poverty alone has hardly ever led to political initiatives. In South Africa, an expanding economy has made it possible so far to meet the rising material expectations and not to heighten the discrepancy between ideology and reality.

While relatively unthreatened by an economically motivated rebellion, however, most observers suggest that the status quo is particularly vulnerable to the political aspects of race relations. Frequent arrests and charges with respect to the pass laws or other noncriminal offenses, it is argued, create an explosive potential of hate and threaten the dissolution of a social order based on compliance with laws. However, the restrictions imposed on the mobility and freedom of the urban worker have as yet had no visible political effects since the final prohibition of African political organizations in 1961. The necessity for migratory workers to live alone and leave their families behind in the reserves has had more severe consequences for the rural families than for the urban dweller who soon finds substitutes. One effect of such repressions is that the crime rate in the urban locations has risen dramatically to a level that is possibly the highest in the world. The frustration generated by this imposed coercion is increasingly released through aggression against other ingroup members, since they are the most vulnerable persons. In only one out of every ten cases of known assault and robbery committed by a nonwhite is the victim white. (See Table 5) Reports describing the hazards of life in the townships are typical in South African papers:

> The Russian Gang—the dreaded township mobsters—was active in Naledi Township, Soweto, at the weekend. Armed with iron bars, kieries and sjambocks and chanting Sotho tribal songs, they roamed the streets, molesting and terrorizing residents. And not far from the sports field in Naledi, they pounced upon a man who was walking past them in the street. The man, not known in the vicinity and thus unidentified, was beaten to death. Terrified residents, including children, simply stood in their yards watching as the mobsters killed their victim. They dared not intervene.[58]

The statement by an unknown African in Johannesburg has become famous: "A lot of people die in Soweto and not all of them were sick."

TABLE 5
Convictions for Violence by Racial Groups

Crime	Race of victim	Convicted Persons			
		Whites	Coloureds	Asians	Africans
Murder	White	20	15	3	59
	Nonwhite	10	151	14	1,381
Rape and attempted rape	White	57	93	4	29
	Nonwhite	24	362	19	2,290
Culpable homicide	White	21	8	—	15
	Nonwhite	23	264	3	1,533
Totals 1966-67		155	893	43	5,307
Totals 1965-66		134	748	33	4,516

Source: M. Horrell, *Survey of Race Relations in South Africa, 1969.* 50.

Observers estimate there are a thousand and more murder cases annually in Soweto alone. In a letter to a newspaper an African housewife describes "Zola and Emdeni, where the knife is used in the worst form of assault and children seem to be used to seeing corpses lying around as if that was just one of the day's happenings."[59] Such immediate fears of survival affect political consciousness and revolutionary potential. Among the various anxieties of an urban African, the fear of being robbed after being paid on a Friday evening perhaps ranks first. The growing number of criminals in the townships—plus the young *tsotsis* who have developed a specific sub-culture of violence to compensate for the omissions and frustrations of the system, comprise a considerable reservoir of brutality. While the displacement of hostility away from political goals and the whites functions for the time being to support the status quo, it, nevertheless, represents a continuing menace. The perpetuation of frustration and hostility always leaves open the possibility of its being mobilized and directed toward political ends. For an African, being political is becoming increasingly synonymous with being antiwhite, making a transition from unpolitical criminal behavior to politicization. On the other hand, under these circumstances, the government encounters no difficulties in recruiting African policemen. As remarked by Alan Paton, as long as the police force continues to be able to recruit African policemen, a strata that would be the first object of hate from the general population, there can be no hope of revolution.

Similarly motivated, though more masochistically exhibited substitute reactions are the Sunday rituals of the growing Zionist sects. Recent estimates suggest there are five thousand independent church sects scattered throughout the thirty-four African countries, more than half of them in South Africa. While in 1946 approximately 10 percent of the African population in South Africa belonged to these organizations, their numbers had increased to 21.2 percent by 1960. The original close association between the sectarian ideology and the anticolonial, political resistance movement cannot explain their growth, which continued after the achievement of independence and even survived prosecutions of the new governments, as in the case of the Lumpa-sect in Zambia. Sundkler states in the second edition of his book *Bantu Prophets* that the politically conscious and activists in South Africa, insofar as they belong to Christian denominations at all, are not among the nativist separatists.[60] An explanation of the sectarian appeal must take into account the cultural discrepancy between the traditional African way of life and the norms preached by the Christian churches as well as the simple continuation of material frustrations for the mass of the population. In South Africa particularly, rational behavior cannot be expected where irrational conditions officially dominate and the frustrations reach a particularly depressing level.

A person who expects to spend his whole life in dependency, with no way out, tends to reduce his needs and aspirations to the prescribed measure. He finally learns and internalizes how to react in due form to the expectations, sanctions, and rewards of his masters since this attitude alone secures his survival under the existing circumstances. In the psychological state of mind of South Africa's subject people the same process seems to occur that integrated the former proletariat into a petty bourgeoisie in countries of earlier industrialization. The dependency of the dependents consists no longer only of coercive circumstances but of internalized coercion. In terms of psychoanalytic theory the response known as "identification with the aggressor," tends to be revealed collectively in South Africa. The subjugated group takes over the explanations of its rulers and identifies with their strength. The oppressed rationalize their suffering with the very ideology of their oppressors, since this is the only way out under conditions of overwhelming, one-sided power. The government and many of its strongest critics agree in this evaluation. Thus Laurence Gandar, one of the most astute opponents of *apartheid*, writes: "For so cowed are these sections [nonwhites], so subservient are their leaders, and so preoccupied are the non-Whites generally with the basic requirement of making a living and keeping out of trouble that they now appear as anything but menacing to even the most faint-hearted of White people."[61]

While the majority of politicized and educated Africans are forced into obedience by the awareness of the overwhelming state power, many peasant workers on the white farms lack the consciousness of alternatives although they experience daily the different life of their masters. The ability to project the possibility of such a life for themselves is impaired by their very existence in the system as well as a view of the *apartheid* order as an imposed and inevitable system. To experience *apartheid* as unjust presupposes the idea of a society of equals. Even though the African living conditions are so much lower, this objective difference does not automatically lead to questioning of the system. This fact is clearly recognized by the government, which is suspicious of "agitators" who incite the "otherwise happy natives." The frequent banning of "undesirable" books and films not only reflects an attempt to preserve an isolationist, puritan Afrikaner way of life in the cultural sense, but to maintain the lag in political information on which its domination largely rests.

One of the most powerful tools of social control over the urban African, apart from legal impositions, has proved to be the use of the mass media, some specifically devised to cater for the nonwhite audience. Radio Bantu, established in the early sixties, now broadcasts in seven African languages for a daily audience totaling more than three million. A network of sixty-five FM stations are to be completed in the beginning of the the seventies, two shortwave and twelve medium wave AM stations ensures that 95 percent of the South African population can tune in. In 1970 the South African Broadcasting Corporation proudly announced that daily services to remote groups such as the Ovambos (in both Kuanyama and Ndonga), the Hereros and the Nama Damaras in South West Africa have been added to the program. A number of African broadcasters' enjoy popularity, similar to disc jockeys in Western countries. Radio Bantu receives letters at the rate of five million a year. It considers hundreds of original plays, legends, or songs for Radio Bantu prizes. A famous Zulu drama was broadcast in the original vernacular by several stations in Europe. The few political programs aim at interesting the urban African in the events of his "homeland," such as the Xhosa feature "Today in the Transkeian Parliament." Sometimes appropriate world news is given prominence, especially when they demonstrate "the might of the White man," as in space flights and moon landings. Not less important appears to be the special school program of Radio Bantu which regularly reaches thirteen thousand teachers and six hundred thousand pupils according to the SABC. FM sets for this purpose are supplied by the Department of Bantu Education and booklets are distributed to supplement the programs. The National Readership Survey of 1967-68 showed that over a period of two years radio ownership among the urban Bantu had increased from 26 percent to 48 percent. The conspicuous display of a transistor is no longer a status symbol in the townships.

Compared with the radio, the press has relatively minor influence among the 70 percent urban Africans who are able to read. Virtually no Afrikaans newspapers are read among this group. Thirteen percent read a daily paper in English. The "Bantu weeklies" and magazines which are mostly white-financed apolitical products, focusing on crime, sport, and other sensationalism, have the highest readership. Table 6 indicates the percentage and number of urban Africans reached by the various media.

TABLE 6
Use of Media by Urban Africans

		Percentage	1,000s
Dailies	English daily	13.0	378
	Afrikaans daily	0.7	20
	African daily	11.7	340
Weeklies	English Sunday	15.2	442
	Afrikaans Sunday	2.1	61
	African Sunday	28.0	814
Magazines	English magazines	12.8	372
	Afrikaans magazines	5.4	157
	African magazines	23.8	692
Radio	Radio Bantu	36.0	1,047
	Springbok	2.5	73
	Lourenco Marques Radio	3.1	90
Cinema		7.9	230

Source: National Readership Survey 1967-68 as quoted in STATS (February 1969): 905. Radio use: "yesterday"; cinema attendance: "last month."

The big, and as yet unanswered, question is what political impact the recent introduction of television will have on the rigidly stratified and segmented society. While few Africans can, at present, afford the cost of a television set, communal sets will undoubtedly prove popular entertainment for low-paid workers whose bleak environment predisposes them for projection through the television screen. However, they will have to watch a program made for whites. A separate Bantu television is planned, but launching it seems difficult when the task of creating a homemade or dubbed Afrikaans program is already considered a costly enterprise. Vistas opened by features from other societies will undoubtedly undermine the isolationist tenets of *apartheid*. The programs do not openly need to stimulate black aspirations in order to create appetites, difficult to satisfy for the rulers. In this sense, the warning by extremist Albert Hertzog that "television means the end of the White man in Africa" could prove more correct than the confidence of the censors in their ability to restrict and confine television-initiated black expectations. On the other hand, there seems good reason not to overestimate the short-term political impacts of television in South Africa. A medium which has in other societies on the whole integrated masses into the existing status quo, rather than enlightened them toward changing it, seems unlikely to suddenly lend itself to a revolutionary change, especially when carefully controlled to achieve the contrary.

From an African perspective, furthermore, the "superiority" of a white is not a mere myth. Their "advancement" is not only due to their advantageous environment and better educational conditions. The self-assurance ensuing from membership in a group that enjoys structural supremacy in itself reinforces personal capacities and, hence, encourages achievement. The objects of this authority, meanwhile, blame themselves for their "inferiority," which is in fact caused by the vicious structural circle of crude domination.

The idea of equal chances obviously encounters serious obstacles when transformed from its historical origin in French enlightenment to different circumstances. For many of the South African subject people the idea of equality and dignity for all human beings still remains abstract. Since the various race groups obviously differ on the surface and are not equal, and since the formal dignity now is somewhat respected, there is for many little reason to complain about the unequal though improved living conditions. They continue living passively with God-given poverty and the apathetic dependency they have known from childhood, with any small improvement appearing as progress. Even if they experience obvious injustice—when, for instance, the Group Areas Act drives them out of their family home into a strange suburb—under the peculiarity of South Africa circumstances they are forced to rationalize their predicament instead of fighting the cause. The talk of the awakened masses of the developing countries is based on what has yet to germinate under the influence of education, a higher horizon of expectations, and above all, a higher standard of living, which are the prerequisites of sophisticated political awareness.

Under present circumstances manifest frictions and latent tensions among the subordinate groups occur more frequently than between them and the ruling race. Factors that are irrelevant when compared with the dominant power structure, such as differential economic advantages, differences in the tribal origins, religions, and shades of skin, serve as criteria for distinction among the subordinates, and function as substitutes for the enemy. The assumption that the three nonwhite groups are equally pressed into a united front by the indiscriminate *apartheid* restrictions is open to question. In contrast to this position, van den Berghe writes: "Political consciousness militates against ethnic particularism."[62] Yet in fact there is hardly any realm in which the "success" of racial separation has shown itself more clearly than in the increased significance of a racially defined ethnocentrism. Apart from a few intellectuals in the three nonwhite groups, coloureds and Indians are less afraid of whites than of Africans. The latter, on the other hand, find a substitute for their aggressions in the profiteering Indian trader or the coloured boss workers. In response to their marginal situation, the majority of coloureds have always favored stronger affinities to the whites. The Indians, on the other hand, tend to isolate themselves from other groups by pointing to their distinctive cultural tradition and their relatively higher living standards. Were the Indians faced with the choice of a nonracial state under African leadership, or the continuation of the present situation, it is probable that a sizable majority would opt for white rule. The same applies for coloureds, affiliated more strongly with the whites through heritage and cultural tradition than with Africans. Since most Africans in the Western Province live there without their families, the sexual contacts between both groups have increased, but, at the same time, the sexual resentment of the coloureds against this Africanization has also grown.

The enforced ethnocentric structure and indoctrination of South African neotraditionalism—separate living areas, schools, and finally ethnic universities—pays off for white rule. The policy designed chiefly with the goal of *divide et impera*, but also partly a simple projection of the Afrikaner's own nationalist ideologies onto other groups, is beginning to bear the expected fruit of increased group prejudices, despite the universality of *apartheid* repression.

In summary, it is suggested that rapid economic growth and resulting upward mobility has mitigated the effects of ethnic disprivilege. This does not mean the material aspirations of the Africans are satisfied, but rather that the average African is not sufficiently dissatisfied to involve himself in risky efforts to break down the system. They tend to estimate the future in terms of their present experiences and, hence, do not expect riches, but only a somewhat better standard of living plus a potential upward social mobility. The feeling of being better off than can reasonably be expected is reinforced by the large influx of immigrant workers from the underdeveloped neighboring countries, for whom low South African wages are still far higher than they could earn in their home countries where there are often no employment opportunities at all. A psychological mechanism Herbert Marcuse applies to advanced industrial societies can also be applied to a certain extent in the racially segmented South Africa: "Under the conditions of a rising standard of living, non-conformity with the system itself appears to be socially useless and the more so when it entails economic and political disadvantages and threatens the smooth operation of the whole." Economic advance thus tends to reduce political tensions to a manageable point. On this basis the government is able increasingly to replace coercion with built-in self-policing, self-regulating, and self-perpetuating psychological and institutional controls, by steadily increasing the numbers of nonwhites with a vested interest in the maintenance of the system. Many of those who have been through the fallacy of false accommodation have had to retreat in resignation in the face of stronger antagonists and the failure of their past endeavors.

Resigned adjustment to the inevitable seems at present the dominating tendency among the politically aware nonwhites inside the country. This alone is the success of *apartheid* in moral terms, but this is all the white rulers needed to achieve in terms of political control.

If the latent potential for an alternative system is to be mobilized, then more is demanded than outworn clichés and stale oratory, which the critics of white South Africa have so far profusely displayed. Compared with the ineffective threats of sanctions or resolutions against discrimination, the progressive alternative to *apartheid* remains surprisingly vague. Even the much quoted "Freedom Charter" constitutes a declamation rather than a concrete political program with an indication of how to implement it. What doubtlessly derives its final form from a changing practice and what cannot be anticipated in detail beforehand, however, comprises in itself a potential for change, the more concretely it is anticipated and compared with the existing situation.

It is characteristic of the failure of the nonracial *apartheid* opposition that even the most astute analysts of white oppression are pessimistic about the outcome of an eventual change. Many non-Africans (including Indians and coloureds) fear a reversal of the racial order and are ambivalent about the risk of supplanting a white dictatorship with a black one. In the event of a revolutionary change, Leo Kuper expects "racial radicalism rather than economic radicalism,"[63] especially in light of the fact that common race but not common class would be the denominator for joint action of the African proletariat and the African bourgeoisie. Pierre van den Berghe has probably most clearly expressed this growing and now widespread pessisism about an initial African government: "The end of White supremacy must come in South Africa, and it willl come through revolution and violence. But the end of White supremacy will not mean the end of racism. I have little doubt that the first African government of South Africa will be better than the present government. It could scarcely be any worse. Unfortunately, I am not convinced that it will be enough for an improvement to want to fight for it."[64]

But only when the real and imagined risks of the alternative society are gradually demolished in the perception of non-Africans in the country can their greater susceptibility for and nonresistance to change be expected.

This does not place a naïve hope in the change of heart by South African whites, but stresses that their fear of revenge is a major political factor which blocks African advancement.

Notes

1. Muriel Horrell, *A Survey of Race Relations* (Johannesburg: South African Institutes of Race Relations, 1968), p. 57.

2. Ibid., p. 41.

3. Muriel Horrell. *A Survey of Race Relations* (Johannesburg: South African Institute of Race Relations, 1969), p. 39. Recent estimates put the figure substantially higher.

4. Nadine Gordimer, "Censorship and the Primary Homeland," *Reality*, January 1970, p. 14.

5. Well known among these is Trevor Huddleston and his account, "Naught For Comfort."

6. *The Star*, 15 November 1969.

7. *Die Transvaler*, 3 February 1970. For an analysis of NUSAS, see Martin Legassick and John Shingler, "South Africa," in *Students and Politics in Developing Nations*, ed. Donald K. Emmerson (New York: Praeger, 1968), pp. 103-45.

8. *Die Vaderland*, 19 January 1970. All quotations from the Afrikaans press are from editorials as translated by the Institute of Race Relations, unless stated otherwise.

9. *New/Check*, 7 February 1969, p. 8.

10. Hogarth Hoogh [pseud.] *Sunday Times*, 27 April 1969.

11. *Sunday Times*, 1969.

12. See "The Nature and Aims of the South African Institute of Race Relations," last page of each annual survey.

13. *The Star*, 28 February 1970, p. 10.

14. Ibid., p. 10.

15. Ibid., 11 October 1969, p. 11.

16. Fatima Meer, "African Nationalism-Some Inhibiting Factors," in *South Africa: Sociological Perspectives*, ed. Heribert Adam (London: Oxford University Press, 1971).

17. *The Star*, 4 April 1970.

18. J. E. Spence, *Republic Under Pressure: A Study of South African Foreign Policy* (London: Oxford University Press, 1965), p. 125.

19. Pierre van den Berghe, "Racial Segregation in South Africa: Degrees and Kinds," *Cahiers d'Etudes Africaines* 6 (1966): 408-18, reprinted as chapter 1 of the present volume.

20. B. Gustavson, "Versuch über den Kolonialismus," *Kursbuch* 6 (July 1966): 117.

21. Gwendolen M. Carter, Thomas Karis, and Newell M. Stultz, *South African's Transkei: The Politics of Domestic Colonialism* (Evanston: Northwestern University Press, 1967), pp. 180-81.

22. Barrington Moore, *Political Power and Social Theory* (Cambridge: Harvard University Press, 1958), p. 22.

23. Quoted in E. S. Munger, *Afrikaner and African Nationalism* (London: Oxford University Press, 1967), p. 81.

24. Ellen Hellmann, in a reply to J. J. Rhoodie, *Sunday Times*, 4 January 1970, p. 13.

25. Hajee Joosub, speech as reported in the Indian weekly, *The Graphic*, 27 September 1968.

26. Joosub, *The Graphic*, 27 September 1968.

27. A. M. Rajab, member of the Executive Committee of the Indian Council, *The Graphic*, 23 January 1970.

28. Muriel Horrell, *South Africa's Workers* (Johannesburg: South African Institute of Race Relations, 1969), p. 119. Figures at the end of 1968. Private manufacturing 1967. Public Service excludes the railways administration.

29. *Current Affairs* (South African Broadcasting Corporation), 22 February 1968.

30. Govan Mbeki, *South Africa: The Peasants' Revolt* (Baltimore: Penguin, 1964), p. 137, interprets the motives of Kaiser Mantanzima this way.

31. *The Star*, 14 December 1968.

32. *The Star*, 23 August 1969.

33. *Die Burger*, 11 December 1967.

34. Pierre van den Berghe, "Race Attitudes in Durban, South Africa," *Journal of Social Psychology* 57:55-72; Kurt Danziger, "Self Interpretations of Group Differences in Values," *Journal of Social Psychology* 47 (1958): 317-35; Kurt Danziger, "Value Differences among South African Students," *Journal of Abnormal and Social Psychology* 57 (1958): 339-46.

35. *Die Beeld*, 3 November 1968.

36. *Sunday Times*, 9 December 1968, quoting Dagbreek en Landstem.

37. Dagbreek en Landstem, 3 November 1968.

38. *Die Vaderland*, 21 November 1968.

39. Ibid.

40. *Dagbreek en Landstem*, 24 November 1968.

41. *Die Transvaler*, 26 November 1968.

42. T. M. D. Kruger, *New Nation* (October 1968).

43. Karl Mannheim, *Ideology and Utopia* (New York: Harcourt, Brace and World, 1936), p. 192.

44. *Dagbreek en Landstem*, 29 December 1968.

45. *The Star*, 23 August 1969.

46. Quoted in Ellen Hellmann, "Urban Bantu Legislation," *New Nation*, September 1969, p. 7.

47. *News/Check*, 2 October 1970, p. 10.

48. *Die Transvaler*, 30 April 1969.

49. *News/Check*, 5 September 1969, p. 7.

50. S. P. Chilliers, "Border Industries," *Optima* (September 1969): 164-73.

51. Leo Kuper, *White Settler Societies*.

52. Quoted in Horwitz, *Political Economy*, p. 412.

53. Merton Dagut, "The South African Economy through the Sixties," *Optima*, September 1969, p. 119.

54. Sheila Suttner, *Cost of Living in Soweto* (Johannesburg: South African Institute of Race Relations, 1966) and several other studies.

55. All figures from STATS (February 1969): 901-6.

56. Leo Kuper, *An African Bourgeoisie: Race, Class, and Politics in South Africa* (New Haven: Yale University Press, 1965), p. 363.

57. I. Th. M. Snellen, "Apartheid: Checks and Changes," (London) *Interna-*

tional Affairs, April 1967, p. 303.

58. *The Star*, 10 January 1970, p. 9.

59. *The Star*, 2 November 1968.

60. Bengt G. M. Sundkler, *Bantu Prophets in South Africa* (New York: Oxford University Press, 1961), p. 305.

61. L. Gandar, "Economic Wind of Change," (Johannesburg) *Rand Daily Mail*, 26 August 1967, p. 11.

62. Pierre L. van den Berghe, *South Africa: A Study in Conflict* (Middletown, Conn: Weslyan University Press, 1965), p. 68.

63. Leo Kuper, "Stratification in Plural Societies: Focus on White Settler Societies in Africa," in *Essays in Comparative Social Stratification*, ed. Leonard Plotnicov and Arthur Tuden (Pittsburgh: University of Pittsburgh Press, 1970), p. 92.

64. Pierre L. van den Berghe, "A Reply to Matthew Nkoana," *The New African*, 53 (November 1969): 42.

Chapter 3

Radical Resistance in South Africa

John Daniel

A paradox of South African political history is that a small white minority has been able to resist for so long the political aspirations of a black majority by which it is heavily outnumbered. Despite a continuing tradition of radical resistance—that is, resistance employing illegal or violent methods—the whites have been able to preserve their privilege, and today appear as thoroughly entrenched as at any time in the past. Prophecies of bloody revolution are as old as the first white settlement of Southern Africa, but there has never yet been a remotely plausible attempt to overthrow the regime. My concern in this chapter will be to trace the history of the internal resistance movements and to account for their failure to date.

The history of the radical resistance movement in South Africa falls into two main stages, each characterized by different methods of struggle. In the first, the indigenous peoples engaged in armed resistance against white invaders. As independent tribal nations with their own territories and, in the case of the Bantu-speaking peoples, with their own military organizations, they pitted their *assegais* and shields against the firearms of the intruding Boer and British forces in an ultimately vain defense of their land and sovereignty. This form of resistance had virtually ended by the time the white migrants turned on one another in the war of 1899-1902, a contest for control of the mineral wealth and expropriated lands of the South African interior.

The second stage dates from the early years of this century and is characterized by the attempts of black, Indian, and coloured South Africans, often assisted by small groups of radical whites, to overthrow the political order and replace it with one based on majority rule. Between 1906 and 1949 a number of radical organizations emerged to challenge briefly the white power structure, but all collapsed or declined into obscurity. Each contributed, however, to the slow development of an indigenous radical ideology. From 1949 to 1961, this ideology crystallized into a coherent program that dominated the mainstream of black politics but was translated into political action only in a nonviolent form. Finally, from 1961 to 1965, internally based radical movements used organized violence for the first time. The collapse of this phase resulted in leadership being transferred abroad and the resort to guerilla warfare on the borders of white-ruled southern Africa, a topic dealt with elsewhere in this book. Much internal resistance has, of course, continued since 1965, but it has consisted almost exclusively of disorganized, spontaneous outbursts, easily contained by the authorities. There has been little sign of an organized internal resistance movement for more than a decade.

At no time in this second stage did whites constitute more than 20 percent of the South African population, yet this minority experienced little difficulty in preserving the status quo. In an age of decolonization and international commitment to self-determination this situation requires some explanation. Most of those who have wrestled with the question have provided only partial accounts, because they have tended to focus primarily, if not exclusively, on the failings of the radical movements themselves. What these analysts have ignored is that change, or the lack of it, is the outcome of complex and intricate forces: social systems do not survive simply by dint of the incompetence of their adversaries. They must be preserved, and in the attempt to do so, as Barrington Moore has observed, "human beings are punched, bullied, sent to jail, thrown into concentration camps, cajoled, bribed, made into heroes, encouraged to read newspapers, or stood up against a wall and shot."[1]

What I am suggesting is that any analysis of the continued survival of white rule in South Africa must give due weight to both insurgent and incumbent factors, as well as to the nature of the environment in which the power contest is staged. Comparisons with superficially analagous situations in other countries can be misleading, because no two social environments are the same. Each contains certain natural factors (such as those of geography and ethnic diversity) and certain induced factors (such as settlement patterns, differential access to arms, and degree of distribution of wealth) that render it unique and influence the prospects for success of both insurgents and incumbents. The problem will be addressed, then, in terms of an incumbent-insurgent-environmental paradigm, in which factors within the white power structure—its armed strength, coherence, determination, sense of legitimacy, and superior organizational capacity—and factors within the black political structure—its lack of a mass base and revolutionary consciousness, its disunity, factionalism, and organizational deficiencies—can be examined in the context of environmental factors affecting the radical movements' task.

1652-1906: Resistance to Dispossession

The most critical factor determining the contemporary residence patterns and distribution of power in South Africa has been violence, which continued almost uninterruptedly for two hundred and fifty years after the first migration of white settlers to South Africa in the mid-seventeenth century.

The first indigenes encountered by the early Dutch settlers were the Khoikhoi (Hottentot) and the San (Bushmen). The former were seminomadic pastoralists, living in clans under the severely circumscribed authority of a chief; the latter were hunters and gatherers moving without livestock in isolated and relatively egalitarian bands of approximately twenty-five members each. Within two decades the Dutch had fought two wars with the Khoikhoi, both of which resulted in the surrender of land and cattle to the invaders—a pattern of dispossession that was to become the norm in subsequent black-white interaction. The loss of land led to the disintegration of the Khoikhoi social structure: the clans broke up "into small groups of clients and farm servants, no longer independent and ceasing to speak their own language or follow traditional customs."[2] Alien diseases, notably smallpox, took a heavy toll on a people that lacked a natural immunity to them, and in time the pure Khoikhoian became extinct. The San nearly met a similar fate; only about fifty thousand of them survive today in Botswana and Namibia, and the fact that they still exist at all is a tribute to their tenacious resistance to the violent onslaughts made upon them until the mid-nineteenth century. The San were hunted like beasts. Thousands were slaughtered as they were driven from their lands and mountain ranges into increasingly inhospitable areas, until they eventually found refuge in the sands of the Kalahari desert.

By 1750 white settlers were entering the eastern Cape in a relentless quest for land. The explusion of the Khoikhoi and the San from their grazing and hunting lands had been easily achieved, given their crude weaponry and weakly coordinated social structures. But on the eastern frontier matters were markedly different. Here the settlers encountered a third group of indigenous peoples, the Xhosa, one of several powerful Bantu-speaking nations that occupied southern Africa. These were large polities with hierarchic authority structures; land was farmed, natural resources were exploited, stock was raised, and deep rooted military traditions existed.

> These were no agglomerations of determined but small-scale tribesmen at a neolithic stage of material advancement. There were permanent standing armies, a concept of national service and reserve formations, full-time military officers, and there were practiced tactics for battle and a planned overall strategy of warfare.[3]

Conflict between the indigenous nations and the wave of invaders was inevitable. A Xhosa war broke out in 1779, the first of a series of racial wars that engulfed South Africa for over one hundred years as the Zulu, Sotho, Pedi, Tswana and other peoples successively resisted the encroachment of first Boer and then British settlers. The struggles were bitterly contested but, although the intruders lost occasional battles, in all but one of the wars they were triumphant.

The exception was the "Gun War" of 1880. Two years earlier, the Cape parliament had passed the Peace Preservation Act requiring all private individuals to hand in their arms to the authorities. The intent of the law was to disarm all blacks under the Cape government's jurisdiction. Although the already subjugated peoples of the eastern Cape complied, the Basotho refused and took up their arms in resistance. The white forces attacked in 1880, but after seven months of fighting they were obliged to retreat. Ironically, the Basotho victory has been of little importance in the subsequent history of political resistance in South Africa: it was so complete that the Basotho of Basutoland, now the independent state of Lesotho, were able to break away from the mainstream of South African political developments. But one other feature of the Gun War requires comment, for it contains a lesson lost on most analysts. The Basotho raised eighteen thousand rifles in their defense, and were thus able to match the firepower of their antagonists. All the other wars of dispossession were lost to the more advanced military technology of the whites. Not since the Gun War have blacks been able to equal the destructive capacity of the whites, and it has been the relentless efficiency of gun control laws, of which the Peace Preservation Act was only the first, that has prevented the acquisition of adequate weaponry by the blacks. Gun control must be treated as a critical variable in any consideration of the perpetuation of white minority rule.

By the twentieth century the backbone of armed black resistance had been broken and the process of subjugation completed; the once independent tribal nations had been pushed from their lands into crowded reserves. The 1906 rebellion of the Zulus against a poll tax imposed by the Natal government was the last gasp of armed resistance to white hegemony; nearly two thousand Zulu were killed by Natal troops in this final uprising of the indigenous peoples. There are certain parallels between the experiences of the indigenes of South Africa and North America: living in autonomous tribal units, both succumbed to superior weaponry in wars that exacted a hideous toll, and both were finally encapsulated in isolated reserves, with rigid status distinctions between conquerors and conquered. But in the United States the whites became secure as the majority group, and the distinctions are being gradually relaxed; in South Africa the whites, as a small minority, have felt constrained to constantly reinforce them.

1906-1949: The emergence of ideological radicalism

The British parliament legitimated the white conquest of South Africa in 1910 by granting juridical independence to the country under a constitution that enshrined the principle of minority rule in perpetuity. But by now new organizations were emerging and new methods were being devised to continue black resistance. Four main groups contributed both philosophically and tactically to the slow development of an indigenous ideology and strategy of resistance: the Natal Indian Congress, the Independent and Commercial Workers' Union, the Communist Party, and the Youth League of the African National Congress.

The Natal Indian Congress was founded by the Indian civil rights leader Mahatma Gandhi. He had come to South Africa on a legal brief from an Indian firm in Natal and had intended staying for only a short time. He remained, instead, for twenty-one years, becoming the first professional black lawyer in the country and developing the *satyagraha* strategy of nonviolence that he was to employ so successfully in India in later years. Shocked at the plight of the Indians in Natal, he established the Congress party and led it in two separate passive resistance campaigns; one of them lasted for eight years and ultimately secured some meagre gains for the Indian people. Gandhi departed from South Africa in 1914, but he left behind an enduring legacy: a tenacious belief in the efficacy of nonviolent resistance. The subsequent success of Gandhi's strategy in India reinforced faith in this legacy; it remained a dominant theme in the Indian congress and permeated into other resistance movements for decades thereafter.

The Independent and Commercial Workers' Union (ICU) was the most powerful single mass movement of black workers in South African history. Founded by Clements Kedalie as a union for Cape Town longshoremen, it grew meteorically until, by 1928, it had more than 200,000 members and branches in six African countries. The ICU concentrated on improving the material conditions of black African workers, but it also attempted to destroy the sense of inferiority that blacks had already begun to internalize. Through resort to the courts and more particularly through strike action, it won important reforms in work conditions and pay levels. In the mid-twenties, however, communists in the ICU pressed for the organization to engage in a frontal assault on white power. Lacking any coherent ideology himself and reluctant to assume added political responsibilities, Kedalie resisted these pressures. He was able to gain the expulsion of communists from the union in 1926, but in doing so deprived the ICU of most of its limited organizational talent. Four years later the union was moribund, a victim of both internal dissension and repressive steps taken against it by an increasingly agitated government. But the ICU had shown that the mass of poorly educated blacks could be rallied and that the strike could be an effective political weapon. These lessons were not lost on a later generation of radicals, who came to emphasize the importance of a mass base and the potency of strike action by black workers.

The South African Communist party was established by whites in 1921. These whites were primarily European immigrants who brought with them the ideas coursing through Europe at the time—militant trade unionism, socialism, communism, anarchism, syndicalism. The party concentrated initially on the white working class, but soon opened its ranks to black members and, in 1928, committed itself to black majority rule under a "native republic." This native republic was to be a stage on the road to a workers' and peasants' government. There would be full protection of the rights of minorities, land would be returned to the landless, and wealth would be redistributed. In adopting this position, the party placed itself in the vanguard of the radical movement: no other major group then, or for another twenty years, staked out so boldly radical a position.

In 1929 the Communist Party established the League of African Rights (LAR) as an alternative home for black workers who were leaving the disintegrating ICU. The league attracted thousands of members, but just as it seemed set to become a powerful mass organization, Moscow ordered its dissolution on the grounds that it was a petit-bourgeois reformist group that jeopardized the Communist party's independence. The party leadership was staggered, but nonetheless obeyed the directive. A bitter internal struggle followed, in which numbers of radicals were expelled from the party. Among them was a former party chairman, Sidney Bunting, a revered figure among the African members. His expulsion caused huge defections of blacks from the party's ranks, and by the mid-thirties it had only one hundred-fifty members left. The Communist party thus lost its opportunity to lead the radical movement, but its explicit commitment to majority rule and its willingness to use illegal methods became basic tenets of the postwar radical ideology. Through its urban night schools, too, the party produced numbers of black leaders who rejected the restrained liberalism of other black organizations and who, after 1949, became influential figures in the radical resistance.

It was in the Youth League of the African National Congress (ANC) that the various radical strands of the period crystallized. The ANC itself, despite many myths to the contrary, was not a militant organization at this time; it became genuinely radical only in the last decade of its legal existence, the fifties. At the time of its founding, the ANC was a thoroughly conservative organization with reformist goals; its members were primarily a black professional elite and its objective was an equal share with whites in the fruits of power. The leadership was "restrained, religious, and skilled in handling whites with tact and tolerance."[4] As Fatima Meer has noted, the leaders believed that their problem was essentially that of appealing to the Christian conscience that was considered inherent in the whites, while raising the living standards of blacks. Once blacks had achieved the requisite results, equality would follow as a matter of course.[5] The ANC was quite wrong, and in following this path it undoubtedly retarded the black struggle.

The ANC's Youth League, however, represented an altogether different breed of black politicians. Trained mainly at the universities of Witwatersrand and Fort Hare, they had watched black political rights being steadily eroded, noted the inability of white liberals to prevent the process, and seen the Communist party tear itself to pieces over ideological questions issuing from abroad. They were influenced by the success of the ICU's use of the strike weapon, and by the ideas of the black American, Marcus Garvey, who emphasized pride in blackness and coined the slogan "Africa for the Africans." These young politicans brought to the ANC a more exclusive brand of nationalism—one that emphasized the predominant political position of the African, attacked the paternalism of whites, and rejected foreign ideologies. They had no time for the old tactics of petitions and deputations, and favored mass action, illegal if need be. By 1949 the Youth Leaguers managed to take over the ANC itself, installing Walter Sisulu in the key post of secretary-general. The accession of the ideologues brought a new era to radical politics, for they ended what was essentially a preparatory stage in the resistance struggle: a period of transition and recovery in which a conquered people, traumatized by dispossession and subjugation, attempted to build a new national movement to confront their victors.

1949-1960: The organized use of nonviolence

After 1949 two groups, the Congress Alliance and the Pan African Congress (PAC) dominated the radical movement. Both organizations were willing to use illegal methods in their opposition to *apartheid*, but they continued to shy away from the use of violence. After the general election of 1948, however, they faced an incumbent more determined than ever. The Nationalist party systematically created an environment of repression, reacting swiftly and determinedly against every sign of opposition until it had created a full fledged totalitarian state.

The Congress Alliance was an umbrella organization of five groups: the ANC, the Indian Congress, the Coloured People's Congress, the multiracial Congress of Trades Unions, and the Congress of Democrats, the latter being the white wing of the alliance. The ANC was the largest of the participating groups, but there is little doubt that the most influential members of the alliance were the white and Indian leaders of the Congress of Democrats and the Indian Congress respectively, many or most of whom were communists. The Communist Party itself was outlawed by parliament in 1950, but its members were directed to continue their work in the various radical organizations to which their racial group gave them access. Three years later the party was reorganized on a clandestine basis, but most of its activities continued in the context of the alliance. That the ANC was prepared to work with communists was somewhat surprising in view of the strongly anticommunist stance of many of its new leaders who, while in the Youth League, had regarded communism as a foreign, non-African ideology that diluted the militancy of the liberation struggle. This antipathy moderated as the realization grew that communism was not incompatible with African nationalism and that individual communists were among the most efficient and dedicated members of the alliance.

The alliance was established in 1954, largely on the inspiration of a "program of action" drafted by the Youth League a few years earlier; this document represented in systematic form the radical ideology that had been evolving over the past forty years, and contained a commitment to the use of illegal though nonviolent methods of struggle if such tactics should prove necessary. The first real initiative under this program was the Defiance of Unjust Laws Campaign of 1952. Planned jointly by the African, Indian, and Coloured congresses, it aimed at the repeal of, *inter alia*, the pass laws, and the Group Areas, Bantu Authorities, and Suppression of Communism Acts. In the campaign, trained volunteers were to break *apartheid* laws, submit to arrest, refuse bail, and fill the prisons. The objective was to break down the judicial and prisons system and thus force the government to negotiate with congress leaders.

The campaign lasted seven months and led to the arrest of over eighty-five hundred resisters. Toward the end of this period, acts of violence, many of them provoked by the police, threatened to negate the passive resistance strategy of the campaign. Parliament enacted new and tougher laws to deal with political protest, and the courts imposed increasingly heavier sentences on resisters. The campaign began to lag and was eventually abandoned without any of its objectives being attained. Yet the attempt had its positive aspects. Membership of the ANC rocketed seven thousand to over one hundred thousand, and the organization promised, for the first time, to become a mass party. Political consciousness among blacks was greatly enhanced, particularly in the urban ghettoes, and the advantages of cooperation between the various radical movements was demonstrated.

But there were adverse effects as well. Tougher laws made civil disobedience both more risky and more difficult. The police began to treat the congress movement as a serious threat, imposing bans on many of its leaders and infiltrating informers into the various Congress groups. The failure of the campaign should have served to expose the uselessness of nonviolent protest as a tool for effecting change against a determined and monolithic opponent whose very survival was felt to be at stake, but the congress movement was still led by men who were temperamentally and philosophically averse to violence. The strategists of the movement were in a state of indecision, and the rank and file seemed disillusioned.

In an attempt to overcome the malaise, the ANC decided in 1954 to call "a congress of the people, representing all the people. . .irrespective of race or color, to draw up a Freedom Charter for the democratic South Africa of the future."[6] The other congress movements joined the ANC as cosponsors in this new alliance. The convention, attended by over three thousand delegates, met in June 1955. It adopted a charter affirming that South Africa belonged to all who lived in it and that all racial groups should have an equal share of power. The charter contained a socialist strain in its demand for public ownership of banks, mineral wealth, and other strategic resources, but it was essentially a liberal document. Its adoption, however, was to have two important consequences. The first came 18 months later when 156 Alliance leaders were arrested and charged with high treason, a major element in the state's case being the assertion that the charter was a subversive and treasonable document. The trial lasted for five years and resulted in the acquittal of all the accused, but it severely hampered the functioning of the Alliance by tying up the cream of its leadership throughout this period. The second consequence was perhaps more important, for in the charter lay the seeds of the ideological split of 1958 that led to the formation of the Pan African Congress.

In 1958 a sizeable proportion of the delegates at a provincial convention of the ANC walked out. A few months later the PAC was founded under the leadership of Robert Sobukwe. The new organization represented a reassertion of the "Africa for the Africans" brand of nationalism that had been espoused earlier by the Youth League. The PAC believed that only Africans should determine the future of Africans, and that the considerable influence of whites and Indians in the Alliance merely served to water down its militancy and put a brake on the struggle for liberation. The new organization opposed the terms of the Freedom Charter by which all racial groups were to have an equal share of power, because this could lead to domination of Africans by non-Africans. The nonracial principles enshrined in the charter were rejected as "a pandering to European bigotry and arrogance. . .a method of safeguarding white interests irrespective of population figures."[7] The PAC saw the illiterate and semiliterate masses as the decisive element in the coming struggle, and set out to mobilize the rural peasants and the urban workers in preparation for a general uprising. Any and all means of ending *apartheid* and white domination were considered morally justifiable, but for as long as it remained a legal organization the PAC used only nonviolent methods.

The ANC initially welcomed the walkout, regarding the PAC as "a noisy and disruptive clique. . .not likely to make much progress or maintain much cohesion."[8] The prediction was way off target. Speaking the rugged language of the masses and using the Pan-Africanist rhetoric of Nkrumahism, the PAC generated great support—so much so that it probably developed a larger following in one year than the ANC had in fifty. In 1960, the PAC launched its first major campaign, an attempt to undermine the pass laws; the campaign was the first step in a program intended to culminate in black liberation by 1963. The ANC, which was planning its own anti-pass laws campaign, refused to cooperate with the PAC, and denounced the efforts of the rival body as being sensationalist and doomed to failure. Sensational the campaign was, and it certainly did not succeed, but it changed the course of South African history.

The planned campaign bore many similarities to the earlier Defiance Campaign. Protestors were to leave their passes at home, present themselves at police stations, and demand to be arrested; on being charged they were to offer no defense, refuse bail, and pay no fines. On their release, they were to repeat the process until the pass laws became unenforceable. But there were to be two main differences from the Defiance Campaign: leaders were to be the first to offer themselves for arrest, and only Africans were invited to participate. On 21 March 1960 Sobukwe and his coleaders presented themselves to the Orlando police and were duly arrested. Elsewhere in the country the campaign drew such massive support that even the PAC was stunned. But at Sharpeville, tragedy struck: the police fired on an unarmed crowd, killing 69 people and wounding 180 in the worst, but not the only, instance of violent repression of the demonstrators.

The resulting unrest plunged South Africa into a political crisis, worsened by a sudden flight of foreign capital from the country. A week after Sharpeville, the ANC threw its support behind a national one-day strike in mourning for the victims of Sharpeville. Some 450,000 black workers stayed home, some of them extending their strike for a fortnight. In Durban and Cape Town, some 30,000 blacks staged protest marches, a novel event in South Africa and one that terrified the white population. In Cape Town, where the marchers converged on the Houses of Parliament, the regime averted an ugly scene by the simple expedient of double-crossing the leader of the marches, Philip Kgosana. He was offered an interview with cabinet ministers if he would disperse the marchers. Acting on the advice of white liberals, he did so; as soon as the crowd had left the area he was arrested.

This tactic set the pattern for the government's response. To appease the protestors and defuse the situation, the government suspended the pass laws, only to reintroduce them later when stability returned. A national state of emergency was declared, public meetings were banned, and some 11,503 persons were detained, all but 224 of them Africans. Many who escaped the dragnet fled into exile in neighboring African countries. On 8 April, the ANC and the PAC were banned, and stiff penalties were threatened to anyone who continued to pursue the objectives of the now illegal organizations. An era had ended: the white government's tolerance for lawful radical organizations was exhausted, and the period of nonviolent resistance was over. The next stage was inevitable.

An assessment of this phase of the radical resistance movement compels the conclusion that, far from producing any improvement in the political status of blacks, it resulted only in a severe deterioration of their condition and an intensification of the degree of repression. While the strategy of nonviolence was not wholly to blame, it was in large part responsible for the failure of radical resistance in a period when the resistance movements still had a measure of freedom to organize for change.

As noted earlier, the preference for nonviolence stemmed from two sources: the leadership of the Indian Congress, which still possessed an abundant faith in Gandhi's doctrine of passive resistance, and the leadership of the ANC, whose belief in nonviolence was derived from their deeply held religious beliefs. But the assessment that nonviolence could be a powerful moral force for change was faulty. What the Indian leaders failed to recognize was that the conditions in India that had made for success were absent in South Africa. In India, Gandhi faced an opponent who conceded the legitimacy of the Indian claim to independence and differed only on the question of timing; furthermore, the whites in India never regarded that country as anything other than a temporary home. In South Africa, however, the settlers had come to see themselves as indigenes with a legitimate right to occupy and control "their" land. When blacks mounted a challenge, the whites felt their very survival to be at stake and mounted their own resistance campaign, using their infinitely greater resources to do so. The ANC leaders, on the other hand, believed that the whites could be persuaded to a change of heart and that nonviolence constituted not only the most practical but also the most moral means of doing so. They tended to see discrimination in South Africa as an accidental policy, a moral lapse on the part of the whites, and felt that appeals to the sentiments of justice, morality, an compassion would evoke an appropriate response. But the success or failure of an appeal to conscience depends on the environment in which it is employed. Where the environment is insensitive to human values, where the surrender to conscience also involves the surrender of privilege, and where the powers-that-be are as utterly indifferent to moral precepts as South African whites are when it comes to blacks, then passive resistance must fail.[9]

1961-1965: The resort to violence

Immediately after their banning, the ANC and PAC went underground. Neither was well prepared to assume a clandestine existence, but local cells were formed and decision making was centralized as far as possible. Nelson Mandela assumed active direction of the underground ANC, and Oliver Tambo was sent abroad to establish a branch of the organization in exile. The PAC leadership had all been arrested when they surrendered their passes to the police, and they received sentences of from one to three years imprisonment. Many left the country on their release, and in 1962 Potlako Leballo opened a PAC headquarters in exile in Lesotho, then the British protectorate of Basutoland.

The first impulse of the black leaders after the state of emergency was lifted in August 1960 was to reunify the radical forces. To this end Nelson Mandela planned a three-day strike to coincide with South Africa's departure from the British Commonwealth and assumption of republican status. The strike failed to generate mass support, in part because of PAC opposition but primarily as a result of a massive display of government strength. All public meetings were banned ten days before the strike, and in that time some ten thousand Africans were detained. Military and civilian forces were mobilized, and on the scheduled strike days tanks were stationed around the black ghettoes while military aircraft flew overhead.

Responding to the failure of the strike, Mandela declared: "If peaceful protests like these are to be put down by mobilization of the army and the police, then the people might be forced to use other methods of struggle."[10] Mandela was actually expressing the underground's intentions, for in June the ANC and the clandestine Communist party, led by the Afrikaner lawyer, Bram Fischer, decided to begin a campaign of violence. The launching date was 16 December 1961—the most solemn holiday in the Afrikaner calendar, for on that day every year they celebrate their victory over the Zulus in 1838.

The various acts of sabotage that occurred on that day were the work of Umkhonto we Sizwe (MK), a new organization run jointly by the ANC and the Communist party; the title means "Spear of the Nation." The creation of the organization was part of a three-stage Operation Mayebuye: first, the underground was to be built; second, a sabotage campaign was to be launched while recruits were sent abroad for guerilla training; and finally, there would be a full-scale war of liberation.[11] It was still hoped that it would not be necessary to go beyond the second stage—that the sabotage campaign would bring the government to the conference table where South Africa's future would be negotiated. To this end, only inanimate objects—government buildings, railroad tracks, power lines—were to be used as targets in order to minimize the bitterness of the whites.

Acts of sabotage continued until late 1964, and included successful attacks on a government newspaper, a cabinet minister's office, a security police headquarters, and a variety of public utilities and industrial installations. It soon became apparent that the government had no intention of being forced to negotiate, and plans for the launching of stage three of Operation Mayebuye were actually being prepared when, in July 1963, the security police raided the headquarters of the high command and arrested nine of its leaders. Two escaped from prison and fled the country; one, who agreed to be a state witness and was released on bail, also fled, but the other six, plus Nelson Mandela who had been arrested separately, received life sentences. Ironically, they were defended at their trial by Bram Fischer, whose participation in Operation Mayebuye was unknown to the police until some time later. He was eventually arrested, but due to his eminence in Afrikanerdom—he was the grandson of a former president of one of the old Boer republics—he was granted bail; he promptly disappeared and continued to reorganize the Communist party underground. One other member of the high command had also escaped the police swoop and was able to keep the organization going and to continue the sabotage campaign, although on a greatly reduced scale. Late in 1964 the remaining black leadership of MK were arrested and imprisoned, and the organization ceased to function inside South Africa. In August 1966 guerillas entered Zimbabwe, initiating the war of liberation.

In the latter half of 1961 former members of PAC formed a new organization, Poqo. These members were not among PAC's leaders, almost all of whom were currently imprisoned, and they appear to have acted on their own without leadership approval. Poqo was thus not strictly an underground version of PAC, but its core consisted of PAC members and the term poqo, meaning "pure," was taken from the PAC slogan "Um Africa poqo"—pure African nationalist. The organization had seventeen regional divisions and a large number of local branches and cells. While MK was a purely sabotage organization, Poqo was a terrorist group with "an almost anarcho-syndicalist vision of a massive, generalized uprising throughout the country, led by a relatively small number of cadres that would paralyze the industrial state and sweep away an impotent regime."[12] Poqo recruits were encouraged to engage in Fanonist-type violence—a random killing of whites through which oppressed individuals would gain cathartic relief.

The national uprising never took place, but numerous acts of violence have been attributed to Poqo. These include an attack on the town of Paarl in the Cape, in which several whites were killed, and scattered assassinations of whites and of black policemen and headmen. Several attempts were also made on the life of the chief minister of the Transkei, Kaiser Matanzima. In March 1963, Leballo held a news conference in Basutoland at which he revealed that Poqo would shortly launch an uprising in South Africa. The press conference caused a furor in South Africa, and a few days later British police raided the PAC office and Leballo's home in Basutoland, where a Poqo membership list was found. It is highly probable that this list was handed to the South African police, for within days a drive against Poqo took place, ending in the arrest of 3,246 Africans. The Poqo trials dragged on for five years; some 124 members were convicted of murder charges, of whom 97 are said to have been executed.[13] A few isolated incidents followed the arrests, but the drive was so successful that Poqo effectively ceased to exist.

The final sabotage group was the African Resistance Movement (ARM). The group was small and amateurish, consisting of about sixty members, nearly all of them white and most of them young. Most were disillusioned members of the South African Liberal Party and a number were students; two former presidents of the National Union of South African Students were among the leaders. Like MK, the ARM's targets were inanimate objects. The goals were twofold: to demonstrate to blacks that there were noncommunist whites who would work for black liberation, and to attempt to bring home to the whites the gravity of the country's situation. The ARM had two main branches, in Johannesburg and Cape Town, but organization was chaotic and contact between the branches sporadic. The police seem to have been unaware of ARM's existence for two years, and it was only when sabotage continued after the arrest of the MK high command that they began to seek other underground groups. In July 1964 the police undertook massive raids on known white liberals and radicals, in the course of which they discovered ARM documents. The timing of the raids was poorly coordinated, so that friends of detainees in one area were able to tip off likely suspects in other areas before the police arrived, and a number of ARM members were able to flee the country. The remainder were arrested and given stiff prison sentences.

Thus, by the end of 1964, MK, Poqo, and the ARM had been smashed. Under Bram Fischer the Communist party did make one last attempt to renew the underground, but he was finally arrested in late 1965. Fischer earned a life sentence, and with his imprisonment the regime seemed to have contained the threat of internal subversion. Like the earlier use of nonviolence, the resort to violence had been a disaster for the radical movement. Why was this so?

There are perhaps three reasons. First, while the men who led the political underground were radicals, they were not revolutionaries: not one had been trained in the skills of underground leadership, and few possessed the ruthlessness necessary for success. They lacked what Stone has called "the obsessive revolutionary mentallity"[14]—two of the three organizations decided to engage in limited violence, which suggests that they had learned little from the era of nonviolence. The idea that the sowing of confusion could persuade the privileged class to negotiate a surrender seems, in retrospect, somewhat naïve. Second, the leaders of the underground were overwhelmingly the same men who had led the resistance above ground. This was a serious disability, for it deprived the underground of anonymity. The post—1960 leadership was one with whom the poice were thoroughly familiar, and their task was not to identify it but merely to find it. With their elaborate system of informers and unfettered legal powers, the police were able to do so very quickly indeed. Third, the complete intransigence of the white power structure, coupled with its immense resources, enabled it to overcome the threat relatively easily. What the radical underground should have understood, but did not, was that as it increased the intensity of its reaction to white oppression, so too would the white establishment escalate the counteraction by assuming newer and greater powers, even to the extent of becoming a police state. So much of the period of violence itself. How can we account for the overall failure of the resistance struggle?

Conclusion

First, let us look at the incumbent factors. In a study of people ruled by dynasties of an alien race, G. D. H. Cole has concluded that change is not possible where (1) the ruling oligarchy remains united and resolved to keep power in its own hands; (2) the loyalty of the armed forces is not open to subversion; (3) the oppressed subjects are prevented from possessing arms; and (4) the oligarchy is ruthless enough to make full and forceful use of its power. "Such an oligarchy could retain power indefinitely, provided that it suffered no interference from outside."[15] Cole's analysis seems both plausible and precisely applicable to South Africa.

There can be few ruling groups anywhere more monolithic than South Africa's. In the face of glaring need for compassion and concession, the two white language groups remain intransigent and utterly united on the need to retain white supremacy. Far from producing a climate of compromise, civil disobedience and violent campaigns have only reinforced the determination of the whites. Where necessary, as at Sharpeville and in the face of the 1961 strike, the oligarchy has used its powers with ruthless effect, with the police and armed forces seeing themselves not as the protectors of society as a whole but as the guardians of the whites' way of life. Feit has observed that racial stratification has produced what are, in effect, coexisting nations in South Africa, and that in such circumstances the distinction between a "public" and a "population" drawn by David Rapoport is applicable. The "public" in South Africa are whites and the "population" blacks; conflicts between the two are like foreign wars, and "where the armed forces are drawn from the 'public' they will think no more of firing on the 'population' than they would on the foreign foe."[16] The whites have retained power because they have the strength, coherence, and determination to do so.

It is clear that the inadequacies and mistakes of the insurgent radical movement have contributed considerably to its own lack of success. The movement has been characterized for most of this century by a very low level of revolutionary consciousness and a persistent inability to understand the dynamics of the colonial situation and to deduce therefrom an appropriate offensive strategy. But equally debilitating has been the endemic factionalism and disunity of the movement, much of it a product of deep hostilities toward the communists, and particularly white communists, in the movement. Many black radicals accepted at face value the anticommunist propaganda barrage of the cold war era and failed to see in the South African communists a group with a consistent and courageous record of opposition to the regime matched by no other group at least until the sixties. Moreover, the radical movement was critically weakened by its failure to develop a mass base. The organizations that promised to do so destroyed themselves, while others, such as the ANC, never really tried to reach the masses. The ANC leadership was drawn from the ranks of urbanized professionals who had lost contact with the rural areas and had a low regard for the peasantry. Education had turned them toward the secularism of the urban world and they scorned the conservatism of the peasantry whom they regarded as being unprepared for political mobilization. This failing applies even to ANC leaders who had graduated from the Youth League, where they had earlier proclaimed the virtues of the masses. Finally, the radical movement inevitably suffered from an organizational capacity far inferior to that of its adversaries. Drawing its support primarily from the poorest sector of the population, the movement lacked the resources for effective organization. Operating in the face of a regime that lacked respect for democratic niceties and subjected it to constant harrassment, the movement was often unable to provide full-time organizers, to publicize its programs, or even to maintain effective communication between cadres in one part of the country and another.

Two environmental factors have presented real obstacles to the insurgent forces. One has been the problem of access to arms. The strategists of *apartheid* have created another by reconstructing urban population patterns so that white and black residential areas are now geographically remote from each other. In times of crisis and unrest, black areas can, and have been, rapidly isolated and surrounded with rings of steel. The nationwide urban riots of 1976 were readily suppressed; out of several hundred people killed in these incidents, only three were white.

It is little wonder, then, that the radical forces failed in their task in South Africa and that the prospects for meaningful change generated by radical movements within the country now seem negligible. No new radical group of the pre-1965 type has arisen to fill the vacuum left after 1965. The nearest approximation has been provided by the "black consciousness" movement represented by the South African Students' Organization (SASO) and the Black Peoples' Convention (BPC). The ideology of these movements consists essentially of transplanting the American "black power" philosophy to South Africa and directing it toward the goal of black liberation. While it is encouraging to hear blacks speaking in militant vein in South Africa once more, one is also left with the feeling that their version of "black consciousness" is just another spin of the same old merry-go-round. The goals of SASO and BPC are those of the old ANC, while their ideology is a more sophisticated expression of the "Africanism" of the old PAC. Late in 1973 the regime moved in on the groups and crippled them by banning some thirty-five of their leaders. The "black consciousness" movement, which had hoped to cash in on the government's tolerance of black separatism (because it accords with the basic tenets of *apartheid*) is now learning anew the most important lesson of South African politics: one cannot be simultaneously black, radical, effective, and not in trouble with the law.

A degree of militant rhetoric has been flowing of late, too, from certain leaders of the bantustans. This militancy is in part a response to the rise of black consciousness and, in some quarters, the bantustans are now viewed as an alternative avenue for black liberation in South Africa. I find myself highly sceptical of this view. In the first place, it must be remembered that the bantustans and their leaders are creations of the white government, and as such can be "un-created" by that same government should they seem to be getting out of hand. Second, even should the bantustans be granted independence, they will remain political and economic hostages to white South Africa. The bantustan leaders realize this full well; hence the talk of late of some federation of bantustans that might provide a counter-vailing force to the white power structure.

The federal notion is pie in the sky. To effect it, the bantustans would have to overcome the formidable opposition of the South African government; moreover, it is doubtful that the homeland leaders will really, when it comes to the crunch, want to submerge their nations in a new federal system. What the white government is doing in these bantustans is creating a class of state-sponsored mandarins. They relish their relative freedom as they travel abroad seeking audiences, favors, and respect; but while they speak in terms of freeing their people they are developing a vested interest in their positions and their power. Once this happens, as the dismal history of the Pan-Africanist movement on the African continent reveals, the renunciation of positions and power rarely occurs. To the new leadership of the bantustans, the balkanization of power in South Africa is likely to remain preferable to its alternative, the isolation from power.

Prominent among the bantustan leaders is the Zulu chief minister, Gatsha Buthelezi. He travels the world expressing his opposition to the external liberation movements and international boycott campaigns; he pleads for continued investment in South Africa and for renewed attempts at dialogue with Africa and the world; all this in the cause of his peoples' struggle for freedom. But when one realizes that these are the very sentiments of the white government, one is left with the perplexing question: "Just who here is using whom?"

Notes

1. Barrington Moore, *Social Origins of Dictatorship and Democracy* (Boston: Beacon Press, 1966), p. 486.

2. Monica Wilson, "The hunters and herders" in *The Oxford History of South Africa,* vol 1. Monica Wilson and Leonard Thompson (London: Oxford University Press, 1969, p. 67.

3. M. A. Jaspan, "Race and society in South Africa," *Science and Society,* Winter 1955, p. 7.

4. H. J. Simons and R. E. Simons, *Class and Color in South Africa, 1850—1950* (Baltimore: Penguin Books, 1969), p. 135.

5. Fatima Meer, "African Nationalism—Inhibiting Factors" in *South Africa: Sociological Perspectives,* ed. Heribert Adam (London: Oxford University Press, 1971), p. 126.

6. Letter from Z. K. Matthews to the ANC national executive, quoted in Janet Robertson, *Liberalism in South Africa, 1948—63* (London: Oxford University Press, 1971), p. 74.

7. The Basic Documents of the Pan-Africanist Congress, p. 16, quoted in Richard Gibson, *African Liberation Movements: Contemporary Struggles Against White Minority Rule* (London: Oxford University Press, 1972), p. 86.

8. Walter Sisulu, "Congress and the Africanists," *Africa South,* July-Sept., p. 27.

9. Based on comments by Ndabaningi Sithole and Arthur Wina in *Southern Africa in Transition,* ed. John Davis and James Baker (New York: Praeger, 1966), p. 240.

10. Nelson Mandela, quoted in Thomas Karis, "South Africa," in *Five African States: Responses to Diversity,* ed. Gwendolin Carter (Ithaca: Cornell University Press, 1963), p. 543.

11. Edward Feit, "Urban Revolt in South Africa: A Case Study," *Journal of Modern African Studies* (April 1970): 62—63.

12. Gibson, *African Liberation Movements,* p. 91—92.

13. David Sibeko, "Sharpeville, the Turning Point," in *10th Anniversary of Sharpeville* (Dar es Salaam: PAC 1970), p. 55.

14. Lawrence Stone, "Theories of Revolution," *World Politics,* January 1966, p. 168.

15. G. D. H. Cole, "The Anatomy of Revolution," *Africa South,* April-June 1969, p. 9.

16. David Rapoport quoted in Edward Feit, *Urban Revolt in South Africa, 1960-63* (Evanston: Northwestern University Press, 1971), p. 73.

PART II INSTITUTIONS OF APARTHEID

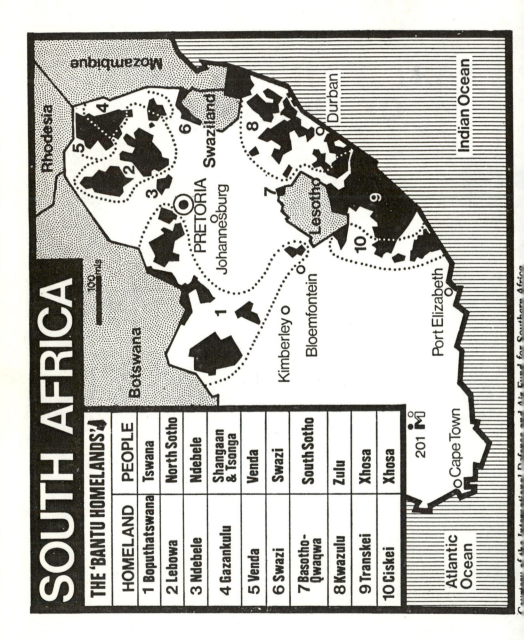

SOUTH AFRICA

THE 'BANTU HOMELANDS'

HOMELAND	PEOPLE
1 Boputhatswana	Tswana
2 Lebowa	North Sotho
3 Ndebele	Ndebele
4 Gazankulu	Shangaan & Tsonga
5 Venda	Venda
6 Swazi	Swazi
7 Basotho-Qwaqwa	South Sotho
8 Kwazulu	Zulu
9 Transkei	Xhosa
10 Ciskei	Xhosa

Chapter 4

The Bantustans

Randolph Vigne

It is more than sixty years since the African people lost their right to live and work on land that, despite two centuries of conquest and resistance, they still occupied as their ancestors had done. As one of the founders of the African National Congress (ANC), Sol Plaatje, wrote at the time, "awakening on Friday morning, 20 June 1913, the South African native found himself not actually a slave but a pariah in the land of his birth." The Native Trust and Land Act of that year took away their right to live on the farms which, in many cases, had been the homes of their people from time immemorial, subjected them to ever-increasing hardships under the pass system, and began the long process which has led to the loss of their title to properties honestly paid for in and around the towns and cities they helped to build.

The grandchildren of the dispossessed of 1913 are the "discarded people" of today, the subject of Cosmas Desmond's invaluable eye-witness account of the resettlement, *The Discarded People*. The lucky ones are those working in factories and mines, albeit at wages below the poverty datum line and without basic workers' rights. The 1913 act and its successor, the Bantu Trust and Land Act of 1936, formally froze African lands to 13.7 percent of the country's area; most of which the Africans had held by resistance or treaty in the face of settler expansion.

*Originally published as "What Are the Bantustans," in the June 1973 of *Third World*, pp. 5-37.

These "native reserves" had existed in the Boer republics and British colonies before union in 1910 and much legislation had been contrived to perpetuate them as reservoirs of cheap labor for the mines, industries, ports, and farms that were now the sole preserve of the white community. The reserves were allowed to stagnate, becoming overcrowded, eroded, depressed areas where women worked and the aged brought up the children. The adult males spent their working lives away from their families, establishing a pattern of migratory labor with disastrous social consequences for the African community.

It is these areas of recurring famine, their original resources exhausted and with few known mineral deposits to tempt the whites to further expropriation, that the promotion of the Bantu Self-Government Act of 1959 has turned into today's "self-governing Bantu homelands." The homelands are the same poverty-stricken places of 1913-36, their citizens are the same migrant workers, ruled by proclamations from the state president as "Supreme Chief of the Bantu," who have paid with the destruction of much of their social fabric for the prosperity of white South Africa today. This is the uniform background of the "bantustans." They differ only in the degree of their ability to ward off chronic starvation; serious consideration of them as viable states has never been possible. The scattered areas, some three hundred of them in ten major groupings, lie in two broken lines that are roughly parallel with the southeast coast and the Marico-Limpopo river to the northwest.

Northern Reserves

Bophuthatswana

The majority of the Tswana-speaking people of southern Africa live outside of Botswana, a former British protectorate, now an independent republic with an uneasy client-state relationship with South Africa. Of the Botswana population of 1.68 million people, just over half are said to live in the nineteen reserve areas scattered across the northern Cape Province, western Transvaal and (at a distance of many hundreds of miles) in the Orange Free State. This is both the largest and, in places, the poorest of the so-called Bantu homelands.

Its 9 million acres include the deserts around Kuruman, Taung, and Vryburg (the "white" towns themselves, as throughout the reserves, remain part of the Republic). Here there are no major industries and scarcely any means of subsistence. "Everyone," wrote Cosmas Desmond, "including priests and teachers, suffers from scurvy. It is not a matter of not knowing what to eat, but simply of not being able to get it." The doctor in charge of the Batlharos hospital wrote in 1969: "The widespread starvation and very real suffering can only be described as a disgrace to the country." Desmond himself saw death certificates at the hospital where the cause of death was given quite simply as "starvation." He writes: "Into this area, rife with scurvy, beri-beri, pellagra and malnutrition, thousands more people are still waiting to be moved, for the sake of tidying up the map of apartheid."

Further north, in the reserve land surrounding the white town of Zeerust, there is almost equal misery, and it is not until the outskirts of Pretoria, the Reef, and Durban are reached that any substantial employment near to their "homeland" can be found by the Botswana. The industrial town of Brits, outside the reserve, will thrive on cheap black labor, while profits will flow back into the Republic and the Tswana worker will take home only the low wages that mass unemployment in the reserves impels him to accept.

As in most of the reserves, road and rail links of importance run through corridors of white-owned land, though they do traverse the reserve to the north of Rustenburg, to the south of Mafeking, and near Taung. Furthermore a two-lane highway is being built at a cost of R10 million (R1 = $1.15) between Pretoria and Mabopane with an R1 million rail link. Thus will ever more labor be ferried to the border industry area of Rosslyn and on to the South Reef.

Other than the platinum mines near Rustenburg, which bring revenue, there are surprising few jobs for the urban Tswana. The main area of development is a complex of light manufacturing industry, at present employing five thousand people, at Babalegi near Hammanskraal; at peak it will employ ten thousand. There are further mining possibilities in the Tswana reserves, where diamonds, crocidolite, manganese, chromium, and other minerals are found; the mines are white-owned, with royalties and a percentage of profits payable to the local authorities.

The fifty thousand Tswana, around Thaba Nchu in the Orange Free State, mainly provide labor to the Free State goldfields and the Witwatersrand. Like their brothers in the western Transvaal and northern Cape, they farm low rainfall lands with insufficient capital. Bophuthatswana held its first elections in 1972, the legislative assembly, under the chairmanship of Chief Lucas Mangope, meeting in November. The capital was, at first, the white town of Mafeking, but is now to be at a spot called Mmabatho. The legislative assembly consist of seventy-two members, twenty-four elected (twenty from the governing party and four from Chief Tidimane Pilane's opposition party) and forty-eight members are nominated by Pretoria. The territory was to be granted full "independence" on 6 December 1977, but at the time of this writing Chief Mangope has refused to accept this status if

Bophuthatswana's citizens are thereby deprived of their South African citizenship.

Lebowa

Northwest and southeast of Pietersburg, in the northern Transvaal, are two blocks of land with an additional small block further west, totalling 4.4 million acres. This is dry *bushveld*, with a very low annual rainfall and periods of intense drought. Over a million Bapedi (or Northern Sotho) live here, with another million permanently outside the reserve. There are also many thousands belonging to other language groups, descendants of tribes once alien to each other, but until recently living amicably together. The Ndebele (of Zulu descent) have nowhere else to go, but the Tsonga and Venda minorities are being removed, often in conditions of great hardship, to the other Transvaal reserves.

These reserves, now grouped together as the Bapedi homeland of Lebowa, have no towns, no industry (though an industrial growth point is scheduled at a spot near Pietersburg) and main roads and railways run through white territory. Eastward lie the huge citrus estates of Zebediela, its reserve neighbors in a state of near destitution, the menfolk at work in the white farms and mines sending remittances that can scarcely contribute to development in the reserves. Crocidolite, andalucite, coal and, more profitably, platinum (at Atoka) are mined in the northern Sotho reserves under the control of the Pretoria-run Bantu Mining Corporation.

Lebowa became the fourth group of reserves to become a self-governing Bantu homeland, in October 1972, with a one-hundred member legislative assembly, forty members to be elected, a chief minister (Chief M. M. Matlala) and five other ministers. Such key portfolios as finance, justice, and defense will continue to be run from Pretoria. A land dispute with the neighbouring Tsonga-Shangaan reserves was settled amicably, but Pretoria vetoed the agreement. The capital is at present Sheshego, in the planned growth point a mile or two north of Pietersburg. The new capital, Leboakgoma, is to be built further south.

Lebowa has a "Bantu university" for the northern Sotho at Turfloop near Pietersburg, which has itself been a growth point of the surviving spirit of African nationalism and resistance among students, and others who also totally reject the homeland policy. Grassroots resistance has long been kept alive in Sekhukhuneland in the southeastern tip of the reserve, which like Zeerust in the Tswana reserves, opposed the *apartheid* policy of the Bantu authorities from its very start in the fifties, with dire consequences.

Gazankulu

The reserves lie adjacent to the western borders of the Kruger national park, peopled by a quarter of a million descendants of the MaTshangana, followers of Sotshangana, a nineteenth century Zulu chief who had settled first in Mozambique; and also by the Tsonga people, over whom he had set up his Gaza kingdom in 1835, and by the BaVenda. A further 650,000 MaTshangana and Tsonga live in the white areas. The area of 1.65 million acres is in four separate blocks of land.

Tsongas, Shangaans, Vendas and Pedis have lived at close quarters in these areas for a century or more, and there has been little or no friction. The *apartheid* blueprint demanded their segregation into separate homelands and the woeful results are described by Cosmas Desmond: loss of livelihood, disorientation, and increasing hostility among the now separated tribal groups.

The most productive enterprise in the area is the Rio Tinto zinc mine at Phalaborwa, where phosphates, copper, iron and vermiculite are extracted from a volcanic pipe south of the white town; but Phalaborwa is not in the reserve. The black miners commute from Namakgale, ten kilometers away, inside the smallest of the separate areas of land comprising Gazankulu. The land is cattle country but the inhabitants, especially after removals, lack cattle. The rainfall is higher near the Lebombo mountains to the east and some mixed farming is possible where capital allows.

The area became a "self-governing Bantu homeland" in April 1972. At the inauguration of the legislative assembly (sixty-eight members, forty-two elected) at the capital, a new rudimentary settlement called Giyani seventy miles northeast of Tzaneen, the chief councilor, Professor Hudson Ntsanwisi, said: "The black man is considered a sojourner not only in the urban areas but in the homelands as well. The homelands still belong to the government, they allocate land and people at will." Separate development, he said, was generating "insecurity, uncertainty and frustration" among his people.

Vhavenda

The Venda reserves total 1.6 million acres in the remotest northeastern corner of South Africa, bordering on the Limpopo River. Here 264,000 Venda have survived absorption by invaders and migrant communities in the past, often withdrawing into the Soutpansberg mountains to do so. There are three blocks of land, much of it mountainous, and the inhabitants grow crops and farm small stock. The white commissioner-general and other white administrators live at Sibasa, and the capital is a tiny new village on the outskirts, Makwerela.

The Venda are thought by the less malleable Pedis, Tsongas and Shangaans to be favored by the government, whose officials do tend to treat the peaceable Venda with some indulgence. Nevertheless, when Prime Minister Vorster visited Vendaland in 1971, the chief councilor, Chief Patrick Mphephu, was greeted with laughter and murmurs of disagreement when he expressed appreciation of the government's help and guidance toward gradual independence. Chief Mphephu was the target of an attempted assassination in 1966. In May 1972, the Vhavenda legislative assembly met for the first time; but elections have not been held for the eighteen elected seats out of the sixty-strong house. The Venda are now technically a self-governing territory within the Republic, entitled, like the others, to their own flag and anthem.

Southern Reserves

Ciskei

When the last Frontier War ended in 1878, the Xhosas south of the Great Kei river remained in possession of twenty to thirty scattered areas on both banks of the Keiskamma river. Across the Kei was what the British called "Kaffraria proper," while the Ciskei had become the overcrowed and exhausted reserves which have been the subject of innumerable distress reports, poverty surveys, and rehabilitation schemes.

The *apartheid* policy has sought to consolidate these areas into only four, but white opposition to the loss of old settler villages like Peddie and Indwe is strong and there are, at the present count, 17 of these areas total-ling just over 2 million acres (though some sources refer to as many as 50 separate areas). They are very overcrowded, carrying, in some areas, over 100 inhabitants to the square mile, with a population total of 600,000; another 400,000 live in the coastal towns and other white areas, and are due for removal into the Ciskei.

All the main towns and villages remain in white control, and some scheduled for transfer (such as Alice, a famous eastern Cape Province educational centre, and Hamburg, the home of the chief minister, Chief Justice J. Mabandla) have been cancelled under pressure from white voters.

The country is mainly dry and scrubby, with mixed farming. The huge herds which were the booty for both sides in the days of the "Kaffir wars" have gone, and some of the land seems incurably eroded. The Ciskei is the scene of some of the most distressing living conditions in the country. The resettlement villages of Dimbaza, Ilinge, and Sada aroused the humane feelings even of the Bantu Administration minister, Piet Koornhof, who stopped the building programme, thus depriving many of their sole possible means of employment. These villages, and a future center at Committees Drift, are the result of mass uprooting of Africans living west of the Kat and Fish rivers. The subjects are, in many cases, members of the Mfengu community (the Fingoes), descendants of nineteenth century collaborators with the government against the Xhosas.

The six thousand Mfengus of Grahamstown are the last group of Africans to hold title deeds on urban property, but these have been cancelled, although most of them date back to 1855 and were the reward for faithful service to the settler cause. The Mfengu are to be moved into the reserve to scenes of even greater poverty than they are subjected to in the notorious Grahamstown location.

There is employment for Ciskei residents in "border industries" in East London and King William's Town, and the black townships of Mdantsane and Zwelitsha (capital of the Ciskei) house the necessary labor. As with all border industry, profits flow into the white area and sub-poverty datum line wages flow into the black areas. The Mfengu support the governing party under the Chief Minister, Lennox Sebe, and there are several opposition groups, including the Ciskei Conservative party which is led by O. Bokwe. The legislative assembly consists of fifty members of whom twenty-nine are chiefs or headmen, one the paramount chief of the Rarabe section of the Ama-Xhosa, and twenty are elected. The Ciskei became a "self-governing homeland" in August 1971. Moves for consolidation with the Transkei (as originally envisaged by the chief theoretician of the bantustan system, Professor Eiselen) have come mainly from the Transkeians and the Rarabe leaders. The government intends to continue to treat the "Xhosa national unit" as two separate states.

Transkei

North of the Great Kei river lies the largest single block of land, with only one other smaller reserve detached from it, that has withstood white encroachment over the centuries. These "Transkeian territories," the home of a cluster of once independent tribes, from the Xhosas in the west to the Pondos in the east, have provided the single largest source of labor for the mines of the Transvaal and Orange Free State (one hundred thousand Transkeians are in the compounds at any one time) and also for the industries, farms and ports of the Cape and Natal.

Of the 3 million Africans who are now registered as "Transkeian citizens," 1.75 million live on the territory's 8,400,000 acres, mainly sub-sisting on maize, herding cattle in the traditional way but gaining very little food thereby, and surviving only by massive maize imports and the cash wages brought in by the migrant workers outside the territory. A few small factories around Umtata, the capital, new shoe and maize-bag factories at Butterworth, and a paper mill, just over the eastern border, provide the only industrial employment. The main road running through the territory and the railway line remain under Pretoria's control, as does the only har-bour, Port St. Johns, and the whole of the coast line.

The Transkei's importance lies in its size, its consolidation and its ad-ministrative and legislative infrastructure, which the Akrikaner Nationalist government inherited from a more liberal administration and changed mainly in the direction of indirect rule through government-paid chiefs. The Transkei was a "self-governing homeland" from 1962 until 1976, when it was formally granted full "independence" at a ceremony ignored by the entire international community. This "independence" is no more than a constitutional fiction (the administrative work is done by white of-ficials on secondment from Pretoria, as shadows to the cabinet ministers, who are mainly appointed to the legislative assembly as chiefs). The legislative assembly consists of sixty chiefs, five paramount chiefs, and forty-five elected members.

The prime minister, Chief Kaizer Matanzima, has perennially called for more land and more powers, and a cessation to the use of the Transkei as a dumping ground for homeless blacks "endorsed out" of the white cities. This both contributes to his electoral successes (his National Independence party's minority of elected seats has been turned into a majority over the three general elections held since 1963) and enables the Republican government to show its power over him by ignoring his demands or rebuk-ing him for making them.

Matanzima is the only Transkeian of any distinction to accept *apartheid* wholeheartedly, though critically where purely Transkeian interest are in-volved. The leader of the opposition Democratic party, K. M. Guzana, lacks grassroots support and is a moderate multiracialist; at the time of writing, he is being detained without trial. The Tembu paramount chief, Sabata Dalindyebo, provides popular leadership for the opposition. Two distinguished sons of the Transkei are Nelson Mandela, serving a life sentence Robben Island, and Oliver Tambo, leader of the African National Congress in exile.

The Transkei was the scene of open insurrection in 1960 and 1961, and was governed under an emergency proclamation until independence; upon independence, Chief Matanzima declared his own state of emergen-cy, which has been in force ever since. Matanzima has been saved from assassination on numerous occasions and he and his closest supporters live under armed guard. He depends upon the South African police and special branch for the control of his state, and has continued to rely on this security since independence.

KwaZulu

The great Zulu nation founded by Tshaka out of numerous Nguni tribes in northeastern South Africa was finally shattered with the defeat of the Zulu forces by the British at Ulundi in 1879. With unintended symbolism, the South African government has decreed that Ulundi will be the new capital of KwaZulu, the name given to the more than two hundred areas comprising the Zulu reserves now under bantustan-style self-government. Their total area exceeds 7.5 million acres, and is populated by over two millions, with the same number again living outside the reserves. KwaZulu is not yet a fully self-governing homeland in the *apartheid* sense, but has its own legislature of 130 members, 55 of them elected. It sits at Nongoma, where the Zulu kings' great palace is situated.

The same conditions of poverty, epidemic tuberculosis, deficiency diseases such as kwashiorkor, and the breakdown of family life due to the migrant labor system obtains in Zululand as in all the other bantustans. There appears to be a greater availability of employment in border industries, since few of the reserves lie far from white settlements with their own industries, but work and pay conditions in these factories if anything worsen Zulu life. There is some revenue from coal and gypsum deposits. All main roads and railways run through white corridors.

Great publicity attended the opening of the R60 million Alusaf aluminium smelter at Richards Bay, the port which (like Port St. Johns in the Transkei) has been excised from the Zulu "homeland." Alusaf, said Prime Minister Vorster, would save South Africa R14 million a year in foreign exchange and would create jobs for the border and Bantu areas. In March 1970, the seven hundred black workers at Alusaf went on strike for an increase of twopence on their pay of 10 pence an hour, and all reports show that the black workers lack minimal facilities of all kinds. A further eight hundred went on strike at Richards Bay, and were met by tear gas and police baton charges.

Other strikes in Natal have involved KwaZulu citizens, and the Bantustan government of Chief Gatsha Buthelezi has championed the strikers' cause against the employers and the Republican government.

This is the outstanding difference between the leadership of KwaZulu and that of the other bantustans. The other leaders seldom express more than the superficial criticism of the *apartheid* policy that is common to the thinking of even the most submissive Africans. Chief Gatsha Buthelezi, since reversing his own policy of nonacceptance of "separate development" in 1968, has consistently challenged the basic assumptions of *apartheid* and claimed to be taking South African government promises of aid and development at face value. "KwaZulu exists by proclamation made by the Republican government. . . . (We) are not participating in the implementation of separate development as free agents. We are doing no more than attempting to exploit the limited political expression within the framework of the policy, for what it is worth," he said in 1972. Buthelezi was an outspoken critic of the government during the urban riots of 1976, when his denunciation of police actions brought him into open confrontation with Pretoria.

Yet Buthelezi recognizes the risks of what irreconcilables see as his supping with the *apartheid* devil, even the risks to his own standing as leader. "It is bad enough that many of my people regard me as a puppet. . .This is made much worse when a minister tells us we are stooges of overseas countries", he complained in response to government charges that he was being influenced from abroad to bring about a black-white confrontation in South Africa.

It is undeniable that Buthelezi's role is seen as support for tribalism, rather than pan-Africanism or multiracialism, and for cooperation rather than intransigence in the face of white *baasskap*. All allow him his complete integrity in the decision he took, but many doubt its wisdom, while being thankful for the focus he has provided on what he has called the hollow dream of the bantustan system.

Buthelezi will survive as a political leader as long as the South African government chooses to tolerate his criticism. An unsuccessful attempt was made to transfer power to the new young Zulu paramount chief and doubtless other courses will be adopted to contain Buthelezi. He does to an extent serve the government's purpose by lending an apparent reality to political freedom in the bantustans and also by the aura of Zulu tradition and history which he carries with him. Government propaganda highlights Zulu pageantry and lore, obscuring the greater reality embodied in such resettlement camps as Limehill, Babanago, and Mondlo, scenes of human squalor and misery the equal of any in South Africa's resettlement camps.

The so-called "black spot" removals (the transfer of blacks into the reserves from farms and villages they have long inhabited, but which they now must leave in the inexorable processes of the 1913 and 1936 Land Acts) are the reason for the establishment of the notorious resettlement camps in most bantustans. They arose simply because the already overcrowded reserve areas could not accommodate newcomers in any other way. Cosmas Desmond, whose own Natal mission residents were sent to

Limehill in 1967 and 1968, thus entered "the labyrinth of broken communities, broken families and broken lives which is the South African government's removal policy." At Limehill, he saw how the homelands policy "makes homeless prisoners of Africans in their own lands, with no escape from the brutality, impoverishment and hopelessness of the system." It is these "prisoners" who are the inhabitants of the self-governing homelands, even the highest of them being rightless Bantu inside the Republic and inheritors of starved, denuded lands at home, which is all that hard-won white conquest left their ancestors in the last century.

KwaZulu has its own legislature of 130 members, 55 of them elected. It sits at Nongoma, where the Zulu king's Great Palace is situated.

There are, of course, numerous other small ethnic groupings which have even less credibility as separate states. The largest are the Swazi minorities in their three northern Natal reserves (which are to be "consolidated" into one, on the Swaziland border); the mountainous Witzieshock reserve, where 250,000 southern Sotho live on the Lesotho border; and the Ndebele minorities in the Transvaal. There are also the Asian and coloured minorities for whom a physically separate state has been ruled out.

The Future

Prime Minister Vorster has said that it was the inalienable right of the Africans to have independence in their own homelands. He told the South African parliament in 1970 that he would prefer it if a request to discuss independence were to come at a time when the homelands were economically viable, but he did not wish to make economic viability a prerequisite. Considering the present and potential resources of these areas in relation to their "citizenry", the sincerity of Vorster's aspirations for the genuine independence of South Africa's African population may be seen in its true light.

Even assuming that the African people of South Africa would consider accepting the final cancellation of their residual rights as citizens of South Africa in exchange for citizenship of the old reserves renamed, the nature and size of the latter would make their rejection of it certain. In 1936, the Land Act defined the future boundaries of the reserves in terms of the African labor needs of the South Africa of those days. The 13.7 percent of the country they would eventually constitute was never dreamed of as living space for the whole African population in independent sovereign states, themselves fragmented into hundreds of black islets. A government minister, Dr. A. Treurnicht, reiterated in September 1977 that "homelands governments could negotiate with South Africa if they felt a more meaningful consolidation of their land area was necessary (but) it would be impossible for all allocated land to be acquired and handed over before independence." Another government minister, Dr. F. Hartzenberg, confirmed that additional land would not be made available to the homelands. However, he said that further consolidation could take place on the basis of exchange of land, although there could be no total consolidation. The "native reserves" of 1936, even with all scheduled areas to be added, are in the last analysis "subsidiary units" of the Republic of South Africa, allowed varying degrees of home rule, which can be abolished by the South African government. Recognizing this, the General Assembly of the United Nations has called on all governments to deny any recognition of the so-called independent Transkei and refrain from any dealings with it and other Bantustans. The call has been obeyed.

Chapter 5

The Churches
in South Africa

Kenneth N. Carstens

In "capitalist" countries, churches usually represent laissez-faire as the
desire of a god who resembles David Rockefeller times a million, while in
"communist" countries with reasonably secure churches, it is generally
some form of communism that an appropriate god desires. This political
versatility of the churches is attested to by an Indian revolutionary who is
alleged to have commented that it is good to have Christians in India: they
may have to suffer during the revolution, he said, but then they could be
relied upon to support the new régime afterwards.

Some may object that this is a caricature of the churches. But a
caricature merely exaggerates recognizable features—not all features, but
some, and usually those that are unbecoming. The fact is that churches are
more political than most other "nonpolitical" organizations; and self-
interest, not morality or doctrine, has all too often been their primary consideration. Even churches that try to avoid questions of public policy give,
by their very "neutrality," tacit support to the prevailing policies: doing
business as usual, whether religious or commercial, serves to legitimate,
reinforce, and perpetuate existing conditions. Those groups and individuals who are not against *apartheid* (or any other prevailing
sociopolitical system) are for it, whenever, whereever and in whatever
·guise they may encounter it. Even those who say they are against *apartheid* in fact support it if they practice it, accommodate to it or do nothing to

oppose it—although they are by no means such reliable supporters as those who don't even profess opposition. That is to say, there are widely varying degrees of support and opposition.

On balance, the South African churches, *qua* institutions, support *apartheid*. Even the English-speaking churches, despite their often vigorous formal condemnations of *apartheid* and their symbolic gestures of defiance, have clearly demonstrated that they will consider substantive resistance and civil disobedience only when their institutional interest and prestige are openly assailed. As far as the white-controlled churches are concerned, these interests are quite compatible with *apartheid*. The black churches continue to suffer severely from *apartheid* but have not broken their pattern of subservience. What is sometime perceived as a growing church-state confrontation in South Africa is in fact a conflict between the government and some extraordinarily courageous individuals and their marginal organizations (representing the "Christian wing"). The churches cling to the sidelines.

Before I outline the basis upon which this judgment has been made and assess some future possibilities, let me pause to clarify my use of a key term. Unlike an increasing number of writers, I refuse to substitute the euphemism "separate development" for *"apartheid." "Apartheid"* means literally "segregation," but as every South African knows, the stark realities and the policy that produced them, which constitute the real meaning of the term *"apartheid,"* are more accurately translated as "white domination." During the 1950s, some influential clerical and lay Afrikaner intellectuals used the expression "separate development" to denote the only means by which whites could both maintain their domination and give it what they considered a less offensive appearance.

When the systematic brutality of *apartheid* could no longer be disputed, a public relations blitz began in the early 1960s to substitute the label "separate development" for *"apartheid."* As a result, even that renowned and esteemed opponent of *apartheid*, Alan Paton, sees fit to refer in all seriousness to "the positive aspects of separate development." The expression is nevertheless a propagandistic euphemism for a cruel and abhorrent system which one of its chief architects, the late Prime Minister Verwoerd, frankly defined in Parliament on 25 January 1965 as follows:

> We want to keep South Africa white. . . .Keeping it white can mean only one thing, namely, white domination, not "leadership," not "guidance," but "control," "supremacy." If we are agreed that it is the desire of the people that the white man should be able to continue to protect himself by retaining white domination. . .we say that it can be achieved by separate development.

The change in terminology was accompanied by a more systematic program of dividing Africans along tribal lines, not only in the reserves or "bantustans," but also in the "white areas"—a program both advocated and practiced by the largest of the Dutch Reformed Churches.

Religious Affiliation

Church history is replete with conflicts over questions that seem and are purported to be doctrinal. One might therefore expect doctrinal differences to determine the churches' politics, instead of more mundane factors such as the interest of the dominant groups, their international links and their administrative structures. But it is these mundane factors that are decisive in South Africa. For example, the two churches that are the least racialist are the Roman Catholic and Anglican churches. Both have strong international links and are administered by authoritarian hierarchical structures—especially the Catholic church, in which the "chain of command" runs from the Pope in Rome through the regional episcopate to the priest in the shanty-town.

In terms of power and influence, the dominant group in all the "established" churches is, of course, the whites, although they are heavily outnumbered by blacks in all but the Dutch Reformed Churches (DRC). The international pressures on the English-speaking churches to hold to the nonracial principle are reinforced by the presence of the blacks in the policymaking bodies of churches whose hierarchical structures are weak, such as the Congregational and Methodist.

The preliminary report of the 1970 census gave the following figures on religious affiliation: Christian: 15,796,590; Hindu: 423,300; Muslim: 255,210; Jewish: 118,120; other (mostly African traditional religon): 4,909,250; total population: 21,402,470.

Among the Christians, the three main DRCs have the most adherents: 3,300,000, of whom about 60 percent are white, over 20 percent African and nearly 20 percent coloured and Asian. About 50 percent of the entire white population claimed to be DRC adherents in 1970, with 40 percent of them in the Nederduitse Gereformeerde Kerk, by far the largest of the DRCs.

Of the 2,141,840 reported to be Methodist, some 80 percent are black and most of these are African. The Catholics had 1,844,270 members, of whom 1,329,980 were African, 304,840 white and the rest coloured and Asian. The figures for the fourth of the four largest churches, the Anglican, whose membership exceeded the Catholic in the 1960 census, are buried among the 5,572,400 "other Christian" in the sources available to me to date. This last figure excluded 110,960 members of the Apostolic Faith Mission and 66,000 Presbyterians.

Finally, the census report showed the African Independent Churches with a membership of 2,761,120, representing 18.3 percent of the African population, down from 21.2 percent in 1960. If correct, this figure would represent the first brake on the spectacular growth in AIC membership, which represented only 9.6 percent of the African population in the 1946 census.

The Dutch Reformed Churches

The three main Dutch Reformed Churches (DRCs) in South Africa are the *Nederduitse Gereformeerde Kerk* (NGK), the *Nederduitsch Hervormde Kerk* (NH) and the *Gereformeerde Kerk in Suid-Afrika* (GK). The NH and the GK were founded in the 1850s in a frontier society; racism was axiomatic in both church and the state from the outset. The GK, however, has since moderated and become the most *verligte* ("enlightened" or "progressive") of the three.

I shall focus on the NGK, by far the largest and oldest church in South Africa (it dates back to 1665). Both the practice of and the rationale for *apartheid* are at their most elaborate in the NGK. There are separate churches not only for blacks and whites but also for the ethnic groups among the blacks: the coloureds, the Xhosa, the Zulu, the Sotho.

For nearly two hundred years, the NGK held to the nonracial principle against mounting pressure for racially separate services. In 1857, the synod finally yielded, declaring that integrated congregations were "desirable and scriptural," but that "the weakness of some" made it necessary to permit segregated congregations.[1]

This drastic change in the policy of the single most influential Afrikaner institution further entrenched racism in South African society. The 1857 decision sanctioned institutional segregation "in the one vital area hitherto unbreached by white prejudice," and the NGK's pattern served as a "blueprint for what was to become the cornerstone of the *apartheid* ideology—*eiesoortige ontwikkeling* (autogenous development).[2]

Political and doctrinal disputes in the NGK during the 1860s ended in victory for the conservatives, with the NGK eschewing both political and theological liberalism and identifying itself with the exclusiveness and incipient nationalism (or, more precisely, tribalism) of the Boers. This process was unintentionally aided by the surge of British imperialism that led to the Anglo-Boer War. Postwar conditions led the church to an even closer identification with the Afrikaners and their Nationalist party, resulting in the fusion of "the twin pillars of *Volkskerk* and *Volksparty* into an organic Afrikanerdom,"[3] by which the church virtually abdicated from its function as a bearer of a universal religion. For the NGK has clearly set the survival and implied dominance of whites in South Africa—with the Afrikaner *volk* as their guardian—above God, Scripture, and the other sources of moral authority by which a church identifies itself with a universal ethos. The NGK judges all societal matters not by a universal criterion but by the criterion of the self-preservation of its tribe, the boundaries of which are now being opened to non-Afrikaner whites (but not Jews and Catholics) by virtue of the need for mere numerical viability.

During World War II, the Federal Council of the NGK declared to the government its "sacred conviction that the only salvation of the people's existence lies in. . .race-separation *(rasse-apartheid)*."[4] In May 1951, the NGK Federal Council adopted and "commended to the political leaders of our *volk*" a document entitled "The Basic Principles of Calvinist-Christian Statecraft."[5] Chapter six declares: "the Christian citizen" must have "more than indirect. . .participation" in politics, otherwise governments can be changed only "by assassination or coup d'état." "The primitive or immature person"—that is, the blacks, referred to as "natives"—"may be satisfied with passive participation. . .because his level of civilization does not justify the vote." For Christians—whom the document consistently presupposes to be white—the vote "is a means of grace" and "a symbol of God's sovereignty." But voteless "natives" "are by no means slaves or oppressed people": they have not "come of age" and cannot use the vote "responsibly before God" and therefore merely "enjoy the full protection of the government."

Every General Synod has reaffirmed the NGK's approval of the South African government as "a servant of God," and of the measures the state has taken to "preserve" the whites. Churches are therefore urged not "to meddle in civil affairs or to fall into critical negativism." A report adopted by the NGK quadrennial General Synod in 1966 and reaffirmed in 1970 expanded on the theme of the "salvation" of the *volk*, declaring it to be God's will that "every people" should "maintain and preserve" itself. This subject, as usual, includes one of the Afrikaner's most persistent obsessions: interracial sex. Although "Holy Scripture contains no direct command or prohibition on the mixing of different races," such "mixing must be resisted with every resource as wrong and sinful," otherwise people's "distinctiveness" would be destroyed, their "culture bastardized" and "then the pure religion of Christianized peoples would be threatened." Thus a "Christian state" should prohibit "racial mixing and mixed marriages."[6] (The fact that some 70 percent of all Christians in South Africa are black would seem to confirm that the NGK's concern is racist, not religious.) Reflecting a reactionary trend in the NGK, the 1974 General Synod advocated an extension of this prohibition to marriage between members of certain *black* ethnic groups. Instead of providing the hoped-for "spiritual legitimacy for the new verligte programme" of the Nationalist Government, wrote the columnist J. H. P. Serfontein in the Johannesburg *Sunday Times* on 27 October 1974, "the NGK has now become more a hindrance than a help to the Nationalist Government in their verligte moves." Serfontein went on to cite a NGK minister as saying after the synod: "Theologically we are strong, but morally we are weak."

The 1974 synod shows the NGK moving to the right of the Nationalist party for the first time. The differences, however, have been exaggerated by the South African press, for they are over short-term strategies, not over the long-term, overriding goal of white supremacy. Moreover, the NGK's subservient attitude towards the state is clear in theory and practice. On the rare occasions that differences with the government have appeared, the NGK has always fallen into line. In 1950 the NGK urged the government to implement total territorial *apartheid* as soon as possible. Prime Minister Malan thereupon delivered a stern lecture on the whites' dependence on "native labour" and the church obediently came to heel. In 1960 the World Council of Churches (WCC) and South African member churches—including the NGK—met in Cottesloe, Johannesburg, to discuss the crisis into which *apartheid* had thrown the country. This Cottesloe Consultation issued a statement, the most daring clause of which espoused the right of blacks living in "white areas" to vote. The assent of the NGK delegates to this clause galvanized the Broederbond-controlled cadres in both church and party into action with predictable results: the repudiation of the Cottesloe statement, the withdrawal of all DRCs from the WCC, and the eventual expulsion of some of the ablest leaders of the "Christian wing" of the NGK, of whom Dr. C. F. Beyers Naudé is the most notable and effective—thus he was canned in October 1977.

There have always been tensions between extreme reactionaries (known as *verkramptes*) and moderate reactionaries *(verligtes)* in both church and party (those extreme *verligtes* whose views approximate those of "Middle America" are generally expelled; those who would qualify as liberals in the United States are banned or jailed as "communists") and the *verkramptes* have always won in the past. This time, however, the lines are drawn differently and if the *verligtes* in the party should continue to prevail, the country's unbroken slide to the right may slow or stop. Since the party is already so far right, this would be of small consequence to blacks: even if those *verligtes* now speaking of extending rights of some kind to blacks domiciled in the "white" area should finally have their way, it would still all be done in the framework of *apartheid*, leaving the country perhaps irretrievabley Balkanized with the whites still on top. What is therefore of the greatest interest is the growing forthrightness with which the black NGKs are expressing their disaffection with the white NGKs continued fervent advocacy of *apartheid* in both church and society. The black NGKs are a product of church *apartheid*, the prototype of the government's policy, but in 1975 they formally condemned and rejected *apartheid* in general. Such condemnations are a routine exercise in the English-speaking churches, but when the black NGKs follow suit, *apartheid's* last shreds of credibility are at the mercy of the bantustan chiefs and the few other blacks with a stake in the system. But unfortunately, *apartheid* has always rested on the institutionalized violence of the state and not on credibility.

The African Independent Churches

The African Independent Churches (AIC), which made their first appearance in South Africa late in the nineteenth century, seem to be a reaction to conditions imposed by "Christian civilization." The AIC recall to mind the fact that most, if not all, of the major religions of East and West began as prophetic movements of renewal stimulated by cultural and social crises; that the major religions have served sometimes as an opiate and sometimes as an indirect form of political protest; and that the AIC and many other "religions of the oppressed" are phenomenologically related to white Western counterparts such as the Jehovah's Witnessess, Mormons, and Pentecostals.

The AIC consist of a sometime overlapping variety of Ethiopian, Zionist, prophetic, and messianic movements and cults.[7] After the formal British withdrawal from South Africa in 1910, the growth of the AICs became as dramatic as the proliferation of racist legislation, and reached a peak (according to not disinterested government statistics) in the 1960s, when there were between two thousand and three thousand AICs with between two million and three million members.

The government discourages the growth of the AIC movement, partly because it is a strange and largely hidden world to the whites, which makes control difficult, and partly because the regime encourages separatism only when it is submissive. Apart from its use of police informers, the government has regulations that exact at least formal obeisance: no African chuch may erect a building nor may its ministers perform legal marriages without government recognition of the church. Recognition has become increasingly rare as the necessary conditions have been made more demanding and applied more strictly. The hope of achieving or retaining recognition no doubt explains the praise for the government found in many AIC documents. The Reverend Danie van Zyl, who has worked closely with the AICs, considers that this apparent poltical docility hides a deep distrust of whites, and that there may be far more political activity than is visible.[8]

In 1967-68, two closely related phenomena began to emerge among black intellectuals, namely, black theology and black consciousness. Not surprisingly, these bear many of the marks of a black version of Afrikaner "Christian Nationalism."[9] As I write, the government is clamping down in its usual manner on the leaders of this young movement. But the movement is already in contact with black workers, and if its ideas catch on with the black masses—whether through the labor unions, the AICs or the more traditional black churches—apartheid may reap the whirlwind sooner than anyone expects.

The Jews

Blacks obviously hold unchallenged first place on the whites' hate-and-fear list, and with all but 140 of South Africa's 118,000 Jews being white one might expect no trace of anti-Semitism. But anti-Semitism has been a persistent element in Christian civilization—an ironic twist of history, since Christianity began as a heretical Jewish sect. Because virtually all gentile whites in South Africa profess some kind of identification with Christianity and—especially Afrikaners—consider themselves, and indeed are, the primary bearers of that brand of civilization (there being a clear distinction between the civilization and the faith called Christian), it is not surprising that anti-Semitism is widespread.

Anti-Semitism is usually more genteel among English-speaking whites, where it takes such forms as excluding Jews from select clubs. However, some of these whites may well have been among the Afrikaner ruffians, elected to Parliament or roaming the streets, who express themselves more crudely by shouting anti-Semitic slogans, painting Swastikas on Jewish property and occasionally beating up Jewish people. The wealth, culture, and education of many South African Jews, and the disproportionately high number of Jews in the resistance movement, have often caused the anti-Semitic embers to flame up. But these flare-ups have always stopped short of the European-style pogrom, probably due to the presence of that other bogey and scapegoat, the blacks.

The leaders of Afrikanerdom, aware of the unacceptability of anti-Semitism in the outside world, have been predictably more restrained than the rank and file in their public utterances and actions concerning Jews. Some leaders—albeit atypically "liberal" ones such as the late General Hertzog—have seen Jews as allies and even as "fellow-Afrikaners." On the other hand, the Transvaal Nationalist party excluded Jews from membership until 1951. A Dutch Reformed Church Synod failed by only three votes to endorse a committee's conclusion that "the Jews were not the chosen people." But powerful figures in the DRC and the Nationalist party, including future Prime Minister Verwoerd, strove to prevent Jewish immigration to South Africa as Nazism waxed in Europe. And the Vorster brothers—Prime Minister B. J. Vorster and the Reverend J. D. Vorster, Moderator of the DRC Genral Synod until 1974—outstripped most in their pro-Nazi fervor. Indeed, the present prime minister was interned for much of World War II for his activities as a general of a pro-Nazi paramilitary organization.

Anti-Semitism, reinforced by the Afrikaners' basic model of the "Christian National State" gives some reason for South African Judaism to remain officially "neutral"—that is, supportive of the status quo—in South African politics. Thus it is that while Jewish individuals are in the forefront of the resistance, the Jewish Board of Deputies, which regulates Jewish affairs in South Africa, remains resolutely neutral and frequently reiterates Jewish loyalty to South Africa. Such reiterations were felt to be especially necessary when Israel was courting the African and Asian countries during the 1960s and generally voting with them on anti*apartheid* resolutions in the United Nations. The Afrikaner press would often ask why South African Jews, whose financial aid to Israel is among the highest of world Jewry, could not dissuade Israel from such policies. The leaders of the Jewish community protested vigorously when it was revealed in June 1971 that Israel would contribute 10,000 Israeli pounds' worth of food, blankets and medicine to the Organization of African Unity for the liberation movements. In retaliation, Pretoria suspended the transfer to Israel of some £10,000,00 to £15,000,000, that had been raised by South African Jews. The suspension was lifted in September 1971 only after Israel diverted the contribution from the OAU to the Education Fund of the UN High Commissioner for Refugees.

The English Churches

There is a distinction between the "pietistic" churches, such as the Baptist and Pentecostal, and those that show some social concern. The former tend to be segregated on the DRC model and believe that the church should confine itself to individual spiritual matters and ignore or evade issues of social injustice. The latter are usually called "English" because they are dominated by English-speaking whites. In fact, however, the overwhelming majority of their members are black and many worship in the African vernaculars.

The major English churches (Anglican, Congregational, Lutheran, Methodist, Presbyterian and Roman Catholic) differ from the DRC in that they reject *apartheid* in principle, and theoretically follow a policy of

assimilation. Although the nonracial principle has survived in these churches, it has been gravely impaired by discriminatory practices and racist attitudes that prevail among the white members. It is these attitudes, not the
moral rhetoric of church assemblies, that are translated into actual practice
in the churches as well as in society. Discrimination in the English churches is most evident in the quality of church buildings provided for the
black and the white congregations, in the differential stipends of the clergy,
and in the disproportionately small number of blacks in the higher positions
in the hierarchies. The degree of discrimination differs, however, within
and between these churches. It is least visible and concrete in the Roman
Catholic and Anglican churches (which actually have some integrated congregations and pay the least discriminatory stipends), while the Methodist
and Presbyterian churches are at the other end of the scale. The
discrimination is partly offset by the English churches' educational,
medical, and other humanitarian services; but the state now restricts most
of these and discourages even the churches' efforts to feed the starving victims of mass removals.

Out of this morass of ambiguity, compromise, and hypocrisy the churches declare the truth they know but lack the will to practise. In their
declarations, they usually confess their own hypocrisy—though not always
with the fervor, and producing few of the fruits, of repentance. But, as I
argue below, some of these statements are not without political
significance. Moreover, as long as the contradiction between their principles and practices is maintained, there will remain the posssibility of efforts to resolve the contradiction by changing the practices—and such efforts occur from time to time—however remote such a resolution may be.
But once the principles have been abandoned, the English churches will
almost certainly go the way of the DRC.

With varying degrees of promptness and vigor, each of these churches
has pronounced clearly and sometimes scathingly on the immorality of
apartheid, of particular laws and the conditions they produce, and of racist
attitudes and practices in society and in the churches themselves. An
Anglican bishop has said that the preoccupation with the "salvation of
white South Africa" is "a shocking betrayal" of Christian values based on
"a blasphemous assumption that God made pigmentation a permanent
sign of subordination, inferiority, and humiliation." *Apartheid* has been
declared "intrinsically evil" (Roman Catholic) and "abhorrent to Christian
and non-Christian alike, both at home and abroad" (Methodist). The
Lutherans have called on the church "to strive actively for justice" and "to
identify itself with oppressed races in all stuggles to achieve justice." Most
of them have called for a nonracial franchise; have deplored the proliferation of restrictions on Africans; have demanded inquiries into police torture

and apparent murder of political prisoners; and have castigated what the Methodist Church has called the conditions of a "police state."[10]

The government has ignored most of these statements; but there are some declarations and certain actions by the churches to which the regime has reacted sharply. Of the events that have elicited the sternest reactions and the public attention of the prime minister, only one could have been interpreted as supportive of revolution: the first of the grants by the World Council of Churches (WCC) to the Southern African liberation movement in 1970. The South African member churches had not been consulted by the WCC before the decision was made, but Prime Minister Vorster threatened to "take action against them" if they did not resign from the WCC. All of the churches refused to resign, and although they deplored the WCC action, they all vigorously condemned *apartheid* for creating the conditions that had driven the WCC to take such extreme measures. The regime lost face but is still having the last word, because the number of church workers deported, banned, and raided by police has since risen sharply.

Other events have also provoked strong government reactions. One was the establishment of the Christian Institute of Southern Africa in 1963 under the leadership of some of the key figures in the "Christian wing" of the DRC. Unlike the South African Council of Churches (SACC), whose membership is confined to organizations, the institute's members are individuals. This enables participation by DRC and Catholic members whose churches exclude themselves from the SACC. The institute's purpose, tactfully stated (as it always is), is simply to serve the churches from a genuinely ecumenical base; less tactfully, it is to challenge the churches to be Christian on the race issue. Led by the Rev. C. F. Beyers Naudé, the institute exhibits the Afrikaners' genius for political organizing. It has established contact with nearly every section of church life throughout the country and has created a dynamic, ecumenical network of coalitions that can mobilize nationally or regionally at short notice. Two days after the institute had been established, Prime Minister Verwoerd deplored the "deviations" into which "communism" had lured these churchmen. He said they were a greater "danger than external threats"—the danger being the "spread of non-racial ideas into politics."

An event that, like the work of the institute, has continuing significance for the churches was the publication by the SACC in 1968 of a document entitled "A Message to the People of South Africa." Many of the churches' own statements on *apartheid* were far more political and vigorous than the message. But the cogency of its theological argument against racism, the forceful coalition that it represented and its wide public impact obviously aroused great consternation in government and DRC circles. An astonishing dispute between the prime minister and a number of church-men over the right of the churches to intervene in political life provided one of the few public debates on the basic issues at stake in South Africa. Moreover, far from being browbeaten into silence, the SACC and the Christian Institute set up the prestigious national Study Project on Christianity in an Apartheid Society, known as SPRO-CAS, to spell out the practical consequences of the message and to present these in some kind of programmatic form to the churches. How such a program might be implemented is unclear; what is clear from the SPRO-CAS report is that the political debate in the churches is likely to be kept alive. And even though noticeable political change for the better seems highly unlikely, it would be even less likely if such debates ceased.

What could become the most dramatic and substantive of all church-state confrontations in South Africa is taking shape as a result of a surprising SACC resolution passed in August 1974. The resolution declared that South Africa's fundamental "injustice and discrimination constitutes the primary, institutionalized violence which has provoked the counter-violence of the terrorists or freedom fighters." The SACC therefore called upon the churches "to challenge all their members to consider. . .whether Christ's call to take up the cross and follow him in identifying with the oppressed does not. . .involve becoming conscientious objectors."

Coming as it did within four months of the Portuguese coup, which assured the removal of two vital buffer states and enhanced the prospect of guerilla war on South Africa's borders the resolution drew an angry response from the government. Prime Minister Vorster called it a "calculated attempt to bring about a confrontation between church and state" and warned the churches that they were "playing with fire." The government followed up quickly by passing in November 1974 the Defence Further Amendment Act, which prohibits, with heavy penalties, anyone from advising another person to become a conscientious objector and also prohibits all rational discussion of the moral implications of military service. If the churches follow the splendid example of the Catholic Bishops, who declared in September 1974 that they would be bound by conscience to disobey such a law, a church-state confrontation of considerable dimensions might at last light some fires in the ecclesiastical twilight.

Thus the English churches continue to assert their commitment to civil liberties and racial principle. Their official posture is, of course, contradicted by their racist structures. The resolution of that contradiction which is being advocated by the institute, the SACC, and others of like mind is unlikely; but it at least keeps the contradiction alive. The great and present danger is that the churches will resolve the contradiction the other way; by abandoning even the formal principle and following the DRC into its isolated and grotesque ethnicalism.

Conclusion

Have the churches any political relevance? Many African nationalists and revolutionaries regard the churches as either irrelevant or simply part of the system that must be overthrown. A persuasive argument can be made for this view. Both the DRC and the English churches are institutions of the dominant group; the racism of the English and the Afrikaner differs only in degree. And the black churches can certainly be regarded as providing either irrelevant or counterrevolutionary spiritual solace and escape from reality. When the crunch comes, the main question will be: will the churches be with us or against us?

But the crunch has not come and should not be regarded as inevitable. While harsh political repression combined with brutal racial oppression produces potential political combustion, events have demonstrated that this combustion can itself be repressed and perhaps partly diverted. We have learned, in short, that sheer brutality and repression do not automatically bring about revolution. I therefore maintain that the churches do hold some political potential that is worth developing, both as an end in itself and in the hope that it may somehow promote means of change.

Optimists can see some such potential even in the DRC, mainly because of the increasingly stark contradiction between "ideal" *apartheid* and brutal reality. But this prospect is heavily offset by the intrinsically evil nature of the ideal itself, by the past role of the DRC, and by its present role of providing *apartheid* with divine sanction and the regime with moral authority among most Afrikaners and even some members of other ethnic groups. Moreover, the DRC's ethnically separate church structures, going beyond the traditional racial caste system, reinforce the regime's strategy of destroying South African nationalism among all blacks by institutionalizing the ethnicalism of the bantustan policy throughout the country.

It is in connection with this ethnic strategy that I foresee another assault on the remaining theological viability of the churches—and also their main political potential. The non-Dutch Reformed churches are among the last remaining institutions that generally relate to Africans on a nonethnic basis. It is of the utmost political (and moral) value that this "trans-ethnic" character of the churches should be preserved and, if possible, extended. This task could prove to be very difficult, for it collides with an unfolding master-plan that will include a concerted effort to conform the churches to ethnicalism. If the churches fail to withstand the regime on this issue, the only potentially formidable institutional obstacle will have been removed.

Notes

1. *Die N. G. Kerke in Suid-Afrika en Rasseverhoudinge* (Pretoria, 1961), p. 10.

2. Susan Rennie Ritner, "The Dutch Reformed Church and Apartheid," *Journal of Contemporary History* (October 1967): 19.

3. Ibid., p. 21.

4. *Die Sendingraad van die Ned. Geref. Kerke in Suid-Afrika: Sy Ontstaan, Doel en Strewe* (Pretoria, 1943), p. 76.

5. *Die Grondbeginsels van die Calvinisties-Christelike Staatkunde* (Bloemfontein, 1951).

6. *Human Relations in South Africa* (Cape Town, 1966), pp. 8f. This is the slightly abridged official English translation of the report on race relations adopted by the 1966 synod and reaffirmed in 1970.

7. See Gengt G. M. Sundkler, *Bantu Prophets in South Africa*, 2nd ed. (London, 1961).

8. Danie van Zyl, *The Political Future of the African Independent Churches* (Christian Institute, Johannesburg, n.d.)

9. See Basil Moore, ed., *The Challenge of Black Theology in South Africa* (Atlanta: John Knox Press, 1974).

10. Kenneth N. Carstens, *Church and Race in South Africa* (United Nations, 1971).

Chapter 6

South African Education

Ian Robertson

The South African educational system has been relatively neglected by students of *apartheid*, largely because the attention of researchers and critics has been diverted by many of the more immediately arresting features of that society. But the regime itself regards education as one of the most important pillars of the entire South African social order, and it deliberately and explicitly uses the schools as a tool for indoctrination and social control. The form and content of South African education are dictated by the traditional ideology of Afrikaner nationalism and are directed toward a single goal: that of preparing each child to occupy a niche in a highly segregated and stratified society, with the relative position and appropriate attitudes of the individual being determined by the criterion of skin color.

An ideology is a belief system that derives from social structure and functions to legitimate the material interests of the group that creates and disseminates it. The dominant ideology in South Africa as in any other society is the ideology of the dominant group, in this case the Afrikaners. This ideology, usually termed "Christian Nationalism" by its adherents, is the product of the Afrikaner's historical experience. Their history, from the time of their arrival on the African subcontinent until the present, has been one of a struggle for survival—against the physical environment, against the indigenous peoples, against British imperialism, and now against all those inside and beyond South Africa's borders who wish to bring about the downfall of Afrikaner hegemony. As Calvinists believing in the doctrine of individual predestination, the early Dutch settlers and their descendants readily came to believe in the predestination of entire peoples as well; they saw the continued survival of their language, culture, and identity as the work of God, and their mission in Africa as that of exercising trusteeship over the heathen. In 1832, Dutch trekkers who had left the Cape Colony in disgust at the British insistence on racial equality before the law faced their climactic battle with the Zulus at Blood River. On the night before the battle they made a solemn covenant with God, promising that if they were granted victory they and their descendants would remember the day forever. The biblical parallels—the flight from the land of oppression, the covenant with God, the battles with heathen peoples, the quest for the promised land—did not pass unnoticed by the trekkers. The day of the battle is now a national holiday in South Africa, on which a small segment of the population duly gives thanks to God for its victory over the major segment a century and a half ago. The text much quoted on these occasions is Genesis 17:7-8:

> And I will establish My covenant between Me and thee and thy seed after thee in their generations, for an everlasting covenant, to be a God unto thee and thy seed after thee. And I will give to thee and to thy seed after thee the land wherein thou art a stranger, all the land of Canaan for an everlasting possession; and I will be their God.

The result of the historical experiences of the Afrikaner has thus been the creation of a highly nationalist, strongly authoritarian, and extraordinarily cohesive group, clinging with a desparate tenacity to its control of a country in which it is a tiny minority, and believing that the slightest compromise may herald its utter destruction. This group has evolved an ideology grounded in the memory of conflict, oppression, and the danger of racial extinction—an ideology characterized by a wary, ethnocentric, defensive attitude to all who are excluded on the grounds of race, language, and religion from the *volk*.

In ideal type at least, the ideology of Christian Nationalism comprises the following related beliefs: (1) The Afrikaners are a chosen people, destined by God to work his will in Southern Africa; this divinely determined task is, in the first instance, to Christianize the heathen; (2) Western civilization is an attribute inextricably linked to white skin color; it cannot be transmitted to other races except in distorted form; (3) the culture of the blacks, although it has some intrinsic merit, is inferior; this inferiority derives from the innate inferiority of the blacks themselves; (4) racial purity is a moral imperative, to be maintained at any cost; (5) fundamentalist Calvinism, as revealed by the Dutch Reformed Churches of South Africa, is the only true religion; (6) as in the past, there are evil forces abroad in the world dedicated to the destruction of Afrikanerdom; and (7) the preservation of the traditional norms of the *volk* is essential if these challenges are to be withstood in the future.

These are not the principles enunciated in South African Information Department publications intended for foreign consumption, but they are echoed again and again in South Africa itself at the very highest levels of public debate. Let me give a few examples. At the Day of the Covenant ceremony in 1970, Prime Minister Vorster declared:

> It should be clear to everyone who has made a study of South African history that the people of South Africa have been placed here with a definite purpose.

> It is not impossible that the people of South Africa might be faced with a situation similar to that of the Battle of Blood River in the future. But no matter what happens, we know that our forefathers had two things on their side. They realized the power of positive prayer and they had the courage to stand alone against overwhelming odds.[1]

At a similar ceremony the following year, the Prime Minister developed his theme:

> Blood River stands as a symbol of hope for South Africa. . . .It is becoming clear that the enemies of a country do not any more depend on troops but on the aid they receive from inside the borders of the country they want to conquer. This is the softening-up process being used by the advance forces of the enemy and we in South Africa must counteract this. . . .The people of South Africa must know that it dare not lay down arms against the enemy forces that are confronting South Africa today. It would not be a laying down of arms, but the grave of civilization here.[2]

Die Kerkblad, the official organ of the Dutch Reformed Church, has editorialized:

> In this dangerous world we are almost totally isolated. . . .Two million Afrikaners stand alone against the world population of about 3000 million. It is to be expected that as the threats approach us like savage monsters, more will have to be spent on police and defense. . . .There is not one of the people [in the world] which, if it suits it, will not simply sacrifice us.[3]

The Reverend D. J. Vorster, brother of the prime minister and at the time, head of the Dutch Reformed Church, has explained:

We are a conservative church, and we have always been and will continue to be. Our only guide is the Bible. Our policy and our outlook on life are based on the Bible. We firmly believe that the way we interpret it is right. We will not budge one inch from our interpretation to satisfy anyone—in South Africa or abroad. The world may differ from our interpretation. This will not influence us. The world may be wrong. We know we are right, and will continue to follow the way the Bible teaches us. . . .

It is true the Bible teaches that all men are equal. But the Bible also teaches that there are differences between men. We believe in the Bible, and thus we believe, accept, and teach both concepts equally. That, in brief, is the racial theology of the Dutch Reformed Church.[4]

And *Die Transvaler,* mouthpiece of the Nationalist party, commented in a typical editorial:

In Britain and America, the spiritual capitulation of the white man is the order of the day, to such an extent that the British people are apparently prepared to become a bastard race within a few generations. . . .The liberalistic sickness will not continue. . . .The liberalistic striving after equality will be rejected. When liberalism disappears and a normal situation rules again, common South Africa will be praised because it did not want to go with the stream.[5]

South Africa's policies do not always reflect this rhetoric consistently; the regime is often more flexible than some critics allow. But the ideology of Christian Nationalism sets the standard against which policies are judged and in terms of which modifications must be justified. Particularly in the field of education, public policies conform with startling fidelity to this ideology. The link between the ideology and actual educational practice is to be found in a document entitled *Manifesto for Christian National Education* (CNE), first published in 1948 after a nine-year process of consultation with "the whole of Afrikanerdom." A few quotations from the document give some idea of its flavor:

Our Afrikaans schools must not be merely mother tongue schools. . . . they must be places where our children are soaked and nourished in the Christian-National spiritual and cultural stuff of the *volk.* . . .We will have nothing to do with a mixture of languages, of culture, of religion, or of race.

By Christian instruction. . .we mean instruction and education given in the light of God's revelation in the Bible expressed in the articles of faith of the three Afrikaans churches. . . .The Bible should shape the spirit and direction of all other subjects.

By National instruction we mean instruction. . .in which adequate expression is given. . .to the National principle of love for one's own. . .so that the child is introduced thoroughly and with pride to the spiritual-cultural inheritance of the *volk*.

The trend of instruction in all subjects must correspond with the Christian and National attutude. . .Every pupil must be moulded into a Christian and National citizen. . .so that each one. . .shall respect, preserve and perpetuate the Christian and National character of the family, the church, the community and the State.

Every people is attached to its own native soil alloted to it by the Creator. . . History must be taught in the light of God's decreed plan for the human race. . .God. . .willed separate nations and peoples.

Higher education should have the same foundation. . . .Institutions must expound Christian science positively, contrast it with non-Christian science. The professors and lecturers must be convinced Christian and National scientists.

The instruction of the Coloured people should be regarded as a sub-division of the vocation and task of the Afrikaner to Christianize the non-European races of our country. . . .This trusteeship imposes on the Afrikaner the solemn duty of seeing that the Coloured people are educated in accordance with Christian and National principles. . . .The Coloured man can and will only be truly happy when he has been Christianized, for then he will be proof against his own heathen ideology and all sorts of foreign ideologies that give him the illusion of happiness but leave him in the long run dissatisfied and unhappy. We believe he can be made race-conscious if the principle of *apartheid* is strictly applied in his teaching. . . .The financing of Coloured education must be placed on such a basis that it is not provided at the cost of European education.[6]

It is difficult to regard this program as being in any sense Christian, national, or even education, but it has become the basis for educational policy in South Africa. CNE has been endorsed by the Nationalist party congresses, by successive ministers of education, by the DRC, by the Afrikaans press, and by all Afrikaans teachers' organizations. The extreme distaste of English-speaking South Africans for CNE, and in particular the vigorous opposition of the predominantly English-speaking province of Natal, has delayed the full implementation of the program for many years. Ever since the Nationalist party assumed office in 1948, however, it has been slowly and systematically applying CNE principles, gradually centralizing control of education in order to do so. This process and its consequences can be seen in three major areas of the educational system: white schools, black schools, and the universities.

White Schools

The application of CNE principles to white elementary and secondary schools has focused on the segregation of English- and Afrikaans-speaking pupils, the centralization of control of education, and the introduction of new, uniform national syllabuses that present "separate development" in uncritical and glowing light.

Education at the elementary and secondary levels was already racially segregated when the Nationalist party took office in 1948, but control of education rested almost entirely in the hands of the four provincial authorities, three of which had previously been dominated by United party administrations. Soon after 1948 all the provinces but Natal fell under Nationalist party control, and the former three began, stealthily at first, to introduce CNE principles into white schools. Thus we find the administrator of the Transvaal writing in the journal of the Afrikaans teachers' association of the province:

> A white consciousness must be fostered in every pupil. . . .The transmission of the policy of Separate Development of white and native is the task of the school. We must strive to win the battle against the non-white in the classroom rather than on the battlefield.[7]

And the general secretary of the same association declared:

> In no era of history did the future of white and Christian civilization look as dark as now. . . .Principals are urged to act as field generals in the campaign against liberalism. . . .No separate lesson is required; inculcate a little with each lesson.[8]

So strong was the opposition of Natal to CNE that the anomalous position of the province was tolerated for almost twenty years, until the passage of the National Education Policy Act in 1967. This act stripped the provinces of most of their control over white education, empowered the national minister of education to determine "general policy," and specified that "the education of schools shall have a Christian character" and that "education shall have a broad national character."

The passage of the act has been followed by the introduction of uniform syllabuses throughout the white schools system. One interesting innovation, introduced in 1972, is a compulsory high school course entitled "Youth Preparedness." Among the items in the syllabus are these:

> Our national heroes and the message of their lives. School heroes. Our national monuments and our duties in respect of them.

> Rules and laws. Their function, origin, and values. Results of disobedience.

> South Africa's task in the world.

> The Bantu. Dangers of detribalization. Our missionary task.

Modern tendencies and their causes. Conservative groups and decadent groups.

Anchors for the ship of life: the Bible, religion, the family, the church, the nation.

Youth and religion. The role of drink, drugs, and decadent music.

Authority and freedom. All authority comes from the hand of God. The place and function of authority at every stage of man's life.

The servitude of dissipation. Planned attempts to cut young people adrift from their anchors. Techniques used. Pseudo-anchors. The rehabilitation of those who have gone astray.

The Christian philosophy of life. Communism and religion. Communism in practice. Ideologies that pave the way for communism. How communism can be combatted by (a) the application of Christian principles (b) education.[9]

The centralization of educational control also enabled the regime to eliminate dual medium schools—schools attended by both Afrikaans and English pupils who were taught in both languages. Earlier United party administrations in the provinces, dedicated to the ideal of white national unity, had encouraged the development of these schools; the Nationalists, committed to mother tongue education by CNE dogma and generations of fears about the survival of Afrikaans, abolished them. All white children are now obliged to attend a single-medium school teaching in the language of the home, irrespective of parental wishes. The Afrikaans child is now educated in the pure, hothouse atmosphere of the CNE school; the English child, taught by English teachers who have little sympathy for the Christian National ideology however hard the regime tries to impose it, is marginally more fortunate. Both, however, grow up with minimal opportunity for social interaction and the development of mutual understanding.

School curricula have been substantially reformed, mainly, by including instruction in *apartheid* in whatever syllabuses—history, geography, civics—can be made to accommodate it. In no text book is there any indication whatever that there are any alternatives to or even reasoned criticisms of "separate development"; it is presented as an ineradicable, noncontroversial aspect of the social order.

School text books for white children make absorbing if disturbing reading. The fetish of race purity, for example, leads to some interesting distortions of history, for the authors have both to assert the purity of the white race and explain away the existence of more than two million Afrikaans-speaking half-castes, the coloureds. One method is to flatly deny the facts:

In some non-white countries that the whites penetrated centuries ago, the whites begain to marry with the non-whites almost immediately, and bastard populations arose. In South Africa this did not happen. . .Our forefathers believed and we believe today that God himself made the distinctions between the peoples of the earth. For that reason it is not good if whites intermarry with non-whites.[10]

Another method, slightly more ingenious, is to befuddle the issue:

The Coloureds are, in the same way as the Afrikaners, an indigenous ethnic group of this country. These two population groups came into being more or less at the same time in the same part of the country.[11]

Several texts emphasize the taboo attached to sexual and even social relations across the color line. One history text declares:

The sin of blood mixture between a white man and a nonwhite woman— or the other way around—falls in great measure on their children and their children's children. Their children are unacceptable to self-respecting whites and are unacceptable to self-respecting bantu. Can anyone have it in his heart to commit a deed that will cast his children and his children's children into disgrace in the years that lie ahead?[12]

And another text states:

Yes, our forefathers believed that like must seek like. Also, the non-whites do not like the bastardizing of their people. During the years gone by the whites therefore remained white and the non-whites, non-white. It has become the traditional principle that. . .there is no blood mixing, and there is no eating, drinking, or visiting together. The principle is also entrenched in various laws. The living together of white and non-white is not only a great shame, but it is also forbidden by law.[13]

Perhaps a little inconsistently, the text also asserts:

Every white. . .surely does not need a law to pledge him to maintain his loyalty to his own traditions and pattern of culture. We whites' traditions must beat in our blood and in our being.[14]

The attitude of the texts to the black population is either hostile or patronizing. One text states flatly that "from the very beginning, the whites and blacks were sworn enemies,"[15] and texts typically treat other population groups as "problems"—one, for example, has chapters on "the Hottentot problem," "the Basuto problem," "the Zulu problem," and the "South African Indian problem."[16] Another text informs its readers:

It is actually not only the white South African's skin which is different from that of the non-white. The white stands at a higher level of civilization and is more developed. The whites must so live, so learn, and so work that we do not sin to the level of civilization of nonwhites. Only then will the control of our country be able to remain in the hands of the whites.[17]

The texts even treat the abolition of slavery in South Africa as a still-controversial issue, and deal almost exclusively with the its personal and financial disadvantages to the slaveowners. One text describes the emancipation of the slaves in the Cape colony as an "unsavory incident," and goes on to say, in outright contradiction of a mass of historical evidence:

> Slavery in the Cape Colony differed radically from the slavery in other parts of the world. . .In the Cape the slaves were handled by their masters in a respectable, civilized, and Christian manner. This must be attributed in the main to the deep-rooted religious sense of the Dutch-Afrikaans colonist. The great blunder that the British government made, was that it took no account of [this fact]. . .The slave laws that were made for the colonists severely curtailed the powers and rights of the slave owners by degrees, and exposed them to all kinds of humiliations.[18]

Civics texts go to great lengths to justify the racial division of labor and the reservation of skilled jobs for whites:

> X Their simple and inexpensive manner of living makes the Bantu much cheaper workers than the Whites, Indians, or Coloureds, and for this reason extensive use is being made of Bantu labor. . .The Bantu love repetition which is reflected in their songs and dances, and they are therefore preeminently suited to the performance of routine tasks and work of a repetitive nature in the factories.[19]

Another text takes up a similar theme:

> Equal pay for equal work, which after all sounds very nice if a person does not think about it, brought it about that the whites had to make do in life with the same wages as those the non-whites are paid. Such a thing was impossible for most whites, seeing that the non-white's style of life requires less money than that of the white.[20]

The text then suggests the following as the basis for a class discussion:

> X Debating point: What characteristics will distinguish a genuinely South African labor union?
>   There will be only white members.
>   It will adopt a Christian standpoint.
>   "White South Africa first" will be its motto.[21]

Several texts present religious dogma as historical fact. The following passage opens a school history text:

> Adam and Eve, the first people, were fully developed and civilized. They had no clothes, cars, trains, streets, and houses like ours, but just as people in 6,000 years will still have the same civilization as ours, so does our outward form of civilization differ little from that of Adam and Eve. They were innately good and civilized, but through their disobedience and the fall of man, they fell into a state of disgrace. From then on, they and their descendants would have an incessant struggle. Adam however obtained from God permission to work the earth. . .It is the command of God that people carry out. The execution of this command, for better or worse, we trace in history.[22]

The divine mystique of the Afrikaner is treated in similar fashion:

> Nations are creations of the Lord God. They did not simply arise at will. Further, we believe that the Almighty also determines nations' existence in life and plan of life. The Lord thus has a goal in the creation of a nation. This is also very decidedly the case with the South African nation.
>
> Taking all the circumstances into account, the coming into existence and the continued existence of the white Christian civilization in spite of the mass of non-whites, can be seen as nothing less than a providence of the Almighty . . . We believe that Providence planted us more than three centuries ago on the Southern corner of Africa because He had a definite purpose with us.[23]

The remarkable aspect of this sledgehammer approach to indoctrination is that it is probably quite superfluous. White children arrive at school thoroughly socialized into the norms governing race relations in South Africa, and the education system has at most a reinforcement rather than a conversion function: it provides for the continuing legitimation of the existing order and the blanket annihilation of potential alternatives. So many other agencies of control operate to serve the same ends, however, that the minute care with which CNE is applied in the schools must be seen more as a manifestation of pathological insecurity than as a political imperative. The very atmosphere of the schools, irrespective of the indoctrination that occurs within them, seems guaranteed to produce a conformist philistinism. The emphasis is on orthodoxy, regimentation, compulsory sports, and rigorous discipline, including public beatings as routine classroom procedure. There is a national system of twice-yearly examinations based on work prescribed down to the minutest detail, even to the particular stanzas that are be studied in a certain poem in a specific anthology. In a high school graduation examination, for example, one question asks the salary of a character in Dickens' *Great Expectations*.[24]

Teacher experimentation or deviation for the predetermined syllabus is utterly precluded. Such an atmosphere offers little opportunity for personal development or critical thought.

Two other extracurricular influences deserve mention. One is the South African Broadcasting Corporation (SABC), a state monopoly that has recently been transferred to the control of the Education Department in recognition of its potential role in that field. The SABC radio services pour forth an incessant barrage of *apartheid* propaganda, and television, recently introduced into South Africa, is to have a "Christian and broad national character" and to be supervised by, to quote the charmless phrase of an SABC commission on the subject, "norm-conscious officials." A second influence is the South African Defence Force, into which all male whites are drafted after leaving school. Draftees are subjected to an intensive indoctrination program, described by the minister of defense in these terms:

> It is not enough merely to take up an anti-communist stand. A positive message must be offered in its place. The best answer is probably the Nationalist Party, which is not simply an anti-party, but which has a positive message for South Africa, and, in fact, for the whole world. It is my intention to give trainees instruction in their spare time to equip them spiritually to meet the dangers of communism.[25]

This "instruction" has included the systematic presentation of literature from the American John Birch Society.

Black Schools

The CNE manifesto stipulated three basic principles for the education of the indigenous African population: that it should be of a special kind, adapted for the supposed distinctive characteristics of the blacks; that is should be in the vernacular; and that it should not be paid for at the expense of the whites. The regime has acted on all three principles.

When the Nationalist party took office in 1948, all black school education was under the control of the provinces and was operated primarily by religious missions. Within a year, the new government had established a commission to "formulate principles and aims of education for natives as an independent race, in which their. . .inherent racial qualities. . .are taken into consideration."[26] In its report, the commission recognized that blacks showed "an extreme aversion to any education especially adapted for the bantu," but recommended a new system of schooling that would provide for "the transmission and development of the bantu cultural heritage."[27]

What this would mean in practice was outlined in Parliament by Dr. H. F. Verwoerd, later to become prime minister but at the time minister of native affairs:

> Education must train and teach people in accordance with their opportunities in life according to the sphere in which they live. . .Good racial relations cannot exist when the education is given under the control of people who create wrong expectations on the part of the native himself. . .Native education should be controlled in such a way that it is in accordance with the policy of the state. . .Racial relations cannot improve if the result is the creation of a frustrated people.[28]

A few months later he elaborated this position in one of the most remarkable utterances of his career:

> The general aims. . .are to transform education *for* natives into Bantu Education. . .A bantu pupil must obtain knowledge, skills, and attitudes which will be useful and advantageous to him and at the same time beneficial to the community. . .The school must equip him to meet the demands which the economic life of South Africa will impose on him.
>
> There is no place for him in the European community above the level of certain forms of labor. . ..For that reason it is of no avail for him to receive a training which has as its aim absorption into the European community. . .Until now he has been subject to a school system which withdrew him away from his own community and misled him by showing him the green pastures of European society in which he was not allowed to graze. . ..
>
> What is the use of teaching a bantu child mathematics when he cannot use it in practice?. . .That is absurd. Education is after all not something that hangs in the air.[29]

The Bantu Education Act of 1953 transferred control of black elementary and high schools from the provinces to the central government, and made it illegal for anyone to establish or conduct schools for blacks without government permission. Syllabuses were drawn up by the new Department of Bantu Education, and schools were required to operate under government supervision. All the religious denominations except the Catholic church and the Seventh Day Adventists declined to maintain their schools under these conditions, and the schools were taken over by the government.

One of the regime's first steps after passage of the act was to introduce the vernacular as the medium of instruction in black schools, which had previously used English (or much more rarely, Afrikaans) after the first four years of elementary school. In part this policy stems from a projection of the Afrikaner's own insecurities about his language onto other groups, but the main reasons for the change lie deeper. The intention is twofold: to imprison blacks within their tribal culture by denying them the window on the world that easy acquaintance with the English language might provide, and to emphasize ethnic divisions among the various black tribes by reinforcing their cultural differences and depriving them of a common *lingua franca*. In its effort to preserve the "traditional culture" of the blacks, the Department of Bantu Education has had to develop a brand new technical jargon—even for the names of the days of the week—because the vernaculars lack the necessary specialized vocabulary. The language used in schools now diverges so markedly from that used in homes that it is scornfully referred to in the black community as "school Xhosa," "school Zulu," and so on. The vernacular was introduced in the face of the strongest opposition from black teachers and parents, and it is noteworthy that as some control of education is being transferred to the new bantustans, the homelands authorities are reverting to English-medium instruction. In the black schools in the rest of South Africa, however, the vernacular is still used.

White teachers have been eased out of the system, although white administrators occupy the upper echelons of power. The supervision of black teachers is both rigorous and paternalistic. The departmental *Bantu Education Journal*, which contains various exhortations and policy pronouncements, is circulated in schools and must be signed by each teacher as an indication that he or she has read and absorbed the contents. The departmental magazine *Bantu* is also distributed free in the schools for the edification of both teachers and pupils; announcing this step in Parliament in June 1955, Dr. Verwoerd commented with pride that the black people were now hearing "the other side." An examination of the relevant issue of *Bantu* in June 1955 affords a most suggestive insight into Dr. Verwoerd's gratification over the matter. The magazine contains the following poem, eminently worthy of reproduction for its content if not for its style:

Dr. Verwoerd: Minister of Native Affairs

Dr. Verwoerd, thou art the shepherd of the black races,
Thou art the defender of the Bantu, our rock, our mountain,
Thou art our refuge and our shield.
The mountain that saves us, our refuge.
The Saviour who rescued us in time of need.
We the Bantu boast and say, "Glory unto thee Dr. Verwoerd,"
And to all who are defenders of the Bantu;
We were amidst the seas of fear,
Fearing the government of malefactors, trapped in the nets of hypocrites. We
    were in fear.
Thou showed us compassion because we have no guilt,
Thou led us because there was no-one to lead us in our works,

We shall never forsake thy laws, for they bring
Plenty, wisdom, and knowledge.
Dr. Verwoerd, thou art with us! Glory unto thee our redeemer,
Praises be unto Dr. Verwoerd, the defender of the Bantu,
He that helped our chiefs by giving them good laws,
He that gave our schools proper education,
Because he knew what we needed and could not manage.[30]

Every effort has also been made to apply the parsimonious principle that education for blacks should not be conducted at the expense of the whites. Before the passage of the Bantu Education Act, black schools were funded from central government revenue. The new school sytem was financed by a fixed block grant from central revenue of R14 million per year (R1 = $1.15), plus a proportion of the poll tax—a tax imposed on all blacks but not paid by any other population group. It became Nationalist party dogma that the block grant was not on any account to be increased, and the sum was pegged at this level for almost twenty years, during which its value was steadily eroded by inflation. Any increases had to come from the blacks themselves. The poll tax was therefore increased, and the entire sum eventually made over to the Bantu Education account. Black children were and still are charged school fees, unlike whites, whose education is free. Black communities are even expected to bear half of the cost of new school buildings; only when the structure stands virtually shoulder-high does the department pay for the roof and fittings—and even so, many applications for equalization grants have been turned down because the department's funds for the purposes are exhausted. Black communities even raise money to pay for extra teachers to relieve the burden on the grossly understaffed schools. Thus the poorest section of the community is obliged to make the great sacrifices for what is the worst education system in the country.

Challenged to justify the refusual to increase the block grant from central revenue, the deputy minister of bantu education replied that he was not even prepared to discuss:

the unhealthy aspect of continually stuffing the Bantu with more money and spending more on their education than they can absorb, of giving him more education than he can need in proportion to his economic position. . . South Africa is doing as much, and more, for Bantu Education than the Bantu can absorb.[31]

Perhaps more to the point, the minister of bantu education admitted: "The money being spent on Bantu Education is not being spent out of love for the Bantu, but for the future of the whites."[32] Yet these fiscal arrangements finally broke down under the impact of inflation, the increase in the black school-age population, and, perhaps most importantly, the demands of an economy that cried out for more workers who were at least semiliterate and semiskilled. Throughout the sixties the department was obliged to engage in permanent deficit funding, and since 1972 the black schools have again been financed from general revenue, although still at an entirely inadequate level.

Every aspect of the system suffers from the continuing lacks of funds. Black teachers earn on average less than a third of the salaries of white teachers with similar qualifications. Lack of teacher training facilities has meant that most black teachers are grossly underqualified: in the early seventies some 70 percent of them had not themselves completed high school, and more than 15 percent had not even completed elementary school.[33] Teacher-pupil ratios have increased from 1:41 in 1953 to over 1:60 today. More than half the schools operate a "double session" system, serving in effect as two schools—one occupying the buildings in the morning and one in the afternoon. Libraries, which may contain only books whose titles appear on lists published periodically by the *Bantu Education Journal,* are almost nonexistent: throughout the sixties the amount of money allocated to school library purchases for the entire system average R5000 per year. Spending on scientific equipment is at a more handsome but hardly generous level: R35,000 per year, spread over more than eight thousand schools.[34] School feeding programs have been cut: in 1953, R1.7 million was spent for this purpose; in 1961, R73,000; in 1966 and subsequently, nothing—although surveys at the time the program was being eliminated showed that 60 to 70 percent of black schoolchildren were recognizably malnourished, while 50 percent needed medical attention.[35] The per capita pupil expenditure dropped from R17 per pupil in 1954 to R11 per pupil in 1962; since then it has increased once more and now stands at around R25, about one-seventh of that spent on a white child.

Education for blacks remains voluntary, although there are plans to make attendance through the first four grades compulsory. In the early seventies over 90 percent of black schoolchildren were in elementary school, more than two-thirds of them in the first years, and about 10 percent of black children between the ages of seven and fourteen were not in school at all. The majority drop out after four or five years of school, after a curriculum consisting largely of religious instruction, singing, gardening, the vernacular, elementary arithmetic, and enough English or Afrikaans to follow simple commands. It is the government's policy to discourage permanent black settlements in the so-called "white" urban areas, and for this reason it is reluctant to establish secondary schools for blacks in these areas. In 1970 there were only twenty secondary schools catering for high school pupils in the urban areas of the entire country, or one school for every eighty thousand youths living in these areas. In many places, notably Johannesburg and its environs, large numbers of black pupils have been turned away from secondary schools because there are no facilities for them. Less than four thousand blacks graduate from the Bantu Education schools each year, compared with more than thirty thousand whites who graduate from the white schools.

What have the few who graduate finally achieved? A report of the department records "aspects where the Department has achieved particular success:"

1. They use clear, neat uniform and easily legible handwriting.

2. They write their mother-tongue fluently and correctly, and speak it faultlessly.

3. They have no need to be ashamed of their knowledge of both official languages in written or in spoken form.

4. Most of them are also able to converse freely in at least one other Bantu language.

5. When they work with figures they are neat and accurate to such an extent that they have gained recognition for the outstanding quality of the work they perform in this sphere.[36]

These are curious claims. To boast neat handwriting as the prime product of thirteen years of schooling is, to say the least, suspect. To assert that the pupils write their language correctly and speak it faultlessly is simply untrue, since the median mark in the matriculation examination is 52 percent. To claim that they need not be ashamed of their command of English or Afrikaans is meaningless. To brag of the pupils' capacities to converse in other bantu languages is rather curious, since no bantu language other than the vernacular is taught in any Bantu Education school; such facility as the pupils may have, has been aquired elsewhere. And the boast about the arithmetic capacity of the pupils is entirely unjustified: the median mark in arithmetic examinations is 35.5 percent.[37]

Education for Indians and coloureds follows a broadly similar pattern. The government took control of Indian education from the provinces in 1964. In the preceding decade, the average pass rate in the matriculation examinations was 75 percent; in 1964 it dropped to 48 percent, and in the following year to 34 percent. The director of Indian education explained that the problem was that Indian pupils were "taking courses not suited to their attributes and abilities and beyond their scope," a statement that heralded the introduction of a more "suitable" curriculum in 1972. When coloured education was similarly being taken over by the central government, the opposition in Parliament attempted to insert a clause in the legislation guaranteeing that coloured children would have an educational standard equal to that of whites. The minister of coloured affairs rejected the amendment: "Many coloured people cannot cope with the education whites receive." The minister declared:

> There are basic faults in Coloured education. We shall give no inferior education, but we shall most certainly give Coloured people differentiated education. It would not help to give them only academic education, and then throw them on the market as frustrated people.[38]

It has a depressingly familiar ring.

The Universities

The university is potentially a repository of critical thought in society. It is not surprising, therefore, that the CNE manifesto urged state intrusion into higher education, or that the English-language universities, one of the most nonconformist elements in South African society, have been continually assailed by the regime. Ever since it assumed office the government has perceived the excercise of academic freedom in South Africa as a threat to its totalitarian designs. Academic freedom involves the right of a university to engage in the free and unfettered pursuit of truth without being subject to the whims and dictates of transient political authority. The concept necessarily implies a high degree of university autonomy in decisions about who will teach, who will be taught, and what will be taught. Each of these pillars of academic freedom has been steadily eroded since 1948.

Two distinct traditions have existed in the universities of South Africa. One is the liberal tradition of the old Cape Colony under British rule—a tradition which, however attenuated it has become, stems directly from the intellectual mainstream of Western civilization and the values of humanism. This tradition is found in the English-language universities, however inconsistent they may have been in their adherence to it; above all, they have never deviated from their view that they should be entitled to admit students of every race. The second tradition is a particularist one, founded on the belief that race is a primary characteristic of the individual and that the appropriate relations between races are segregated and hierarchical. This tradition is deeply embedded in the Afrikaans-language universities, which see themselves as an organic part of the Afrikaans community, a place from which all "alien" influences and ideas are to be eliminated. As the principal (president) of the Afrikaans University of the Orange Free State expressed it:

> The university belongs to the *volk,* and therefore must be from the *volk,* of the *volk,* and for the *volk,* a *volk* university, anchored in the traditions of the *volk* in accordance with its conception of life and the world, and therefore on a Christian national basis.[39]

When the Nationalists took office there were eight universities in South Africa, four Afrikaans and four English; and there was one "university college" an institution that could not award its own degrees—for blacks. The English universities admitted blacks under varying conditions: Cape Town and Witwatersrand universities did so freely, but imposed social segregation on students outside the classroom; Rhodes university admitted only a limited number of blacks; and Natal university imposed both social and academic segregation, admitting blacks freely but teaching them in segregated classrooms.

Throughout the fifties the government became progressively more agitated at the presence of the tiny black minorities in the English universities. In 1958 Dr. Verwoerd, then prime minister, declared:

> We do not want non-Europeans in the same university as the young European students of today, who are the leaders of tomorrow. We do not want Europeans to become so accustomed to the native that there is no difference between them and the natives.[40]

In 1959 the government secured passage of legislation euphemistically entitled the Extension of University Education Act. The act provided for the establishment of a series of ethnic universities for each of the major sections of the nonwhite population, with the new institutions being under the direct control of the central government. This legislation evoked some of the strongest opposition the government has ever faced in South Africa, both outside and within Parliament, where the opposition forced the longest debates and sittings in South African parliamentary history. Since the passage of the bill, no black has been permitted to register at a white university without a permit, granted only if the student wishes to take a course unavailable elsewhere, and even then only in exceptional circumstances.

There are now five ethnic universities in South Africa: one each for the Indians, the coloureds, the Xhosa, the Sotho, and the Zulu; Africans who are not members of the Xhosa, Sotho, or Zulu attend the college of the most closely related group. Each college has a white principal and a predominantly white faculty, and is governed by a council whose members are approved by the regime. The councils, in fact, are packed with officials of government departments and with principals of Afrikaans universities, never previously noted for their concern with black higher education. There are separate dining room and faculty lounges for the white and black faculty, and faculty members are precluded by their conditions of contract from criticizing any aspect of government policy whatever. Control of students is equally strict; the ethnic colleges have almost identical regulations, which provide that no student society may be formed without permission, that a faculty supervisor must attend all meetings, that resolutions to be put to meetings must be approved beforehand by the principal, and that no student may leave the campus area or invite a visitor to it without permission. The particularist emphasis of the Afrikaans universities finds it counterpart in the new ethnic colleges. The principal for example, of the Zulu college has described his institution in these terms:

> It is situated in purely Zulu territory. Its aims are the development of the Zulu community. . .the development of the Zulu language, the training of staff to be expert in the Zulu culture and the problems of education affecting the Zulu. . .and the encouragement of research into problems of importance to the Zulu.[41]

It is of these institutions that the minister of bantu administration and development has declared, "they are equal to all universities, not only in South Africa, but in the academic world as a whole."[42]

South African universities thus no longer have the right to determine whom they will teach. Their right to determine what they will teach and what research they will do is subject to a less formal control. The universities, operate, however, in an atmosphere that is both stifling and fearful. The presence of spies and informers on campus, documented in many instances and publicly complained of by the principals of the English universities, must have an effect in every classroom. The example of the fate of colleagues whose research has ventured into sensitive areas and elicited banning orders discourages critical social inquiry. The banning of books and periodical literature poses a continuing problem to the academic community; the Publications Control Board has banned over 40,000 books, films, magazines, papers, and records since 1965.[43] Even the possession of a Nobel Prize for literature seems to excite rather than allay the suspicions of the board; among the authors featured on its list of undesirable, obscene, blasphemous, or offensive literature are Jean Paul Sartre, Norman Mailer, John Steinbeck, Ernest Hemingway, Bertrand Russell,

William Burroughs, Vladimir Nabakov, D. H. Lawrence, Philip Roth, Karl Marx, Robert Graves, Erskine Caldwell, Leon Uris, Bernard Malamud, William Faulkner, Edna O'Brien, John Updike, Francois Sagan, James Baldwin, Mario Puzo, and Brendan Behan. Political science students learn about communism or African nationalism from anticommunist or antinationalist tracts; faculty members may apply for a permit to keep banned books for scholarly study, but the books must be kept under lock and key and may not be seen by students. A large number of South African radicals, inside of the country and abroad, are banned or listed under the Suppression of Communism Act and their words may not be quoted in print or verbally; their ideas thus remain largely unknown even in the universities.

Even academic associations are segregated. In 1962 the minister of education wrote in these terms to all learned societies that received government grants:

> It has been decided with reference to scientific and professional societies, no mixed membership is allowed and where this exists a separation must be effected immediately. . .Non-white societies should be combined by way of affiliation into national societies, which can appoint one or two representatives to attend periodically certain executive meetings of the national societies for whites. In this way channels can be created not only for the interchange of ideas, but also to pass on to non-white scientists the knowledge which has crystallized out in congresses and conferences of white scientists.[44]

This document becomes even more fatuous in the light of the fact that of the twelve thousand members of the societies concerned, only *eight* were not white—and of these, four were Chinese.

One indication of the way of the mores of the surrounding society can intrude on the university may be gleaned from the fate of the editor of the Cape Town student newspaper when he published a report about a campus debate on religion. One speaker was quoted as having declared that "God is dead." For publishing this quotation, the editor was charged and convicted of blasphemy. The charge sheet alleged that he:

> Did wrongfully and unlawfully blaspheme God, the Supreme Being. . .by spreading or circulating a disbelief in the Supreme Being, and in contemptuously ascribing to the Supreme Being acts inconsistent with His attributes.[45]

The right of the unversity to determine who shall teach and do research has also been undetermined in many ways. The government screens intending faculty and research students from abroad, and has refused entry visas to those whose views might be offensive or whose research might be unwelcome. Faculty at the ethnic colleges may be arbitrarily dismissed for reasons unrelated to their academic competence; one was fired for having suggested that the pace of "separate development" was too slow. Several South African academics, including full professors of some eminence at the universities of Cape Town and the Witwatersrand, have been banned or listed under the Suppression of Communism Act and prevented from setting foot in a classroom, from teaching any person including their own children, and from publishing their research findings, even on such innocuous subjects as endocrinology. Mr. Vorster has explicitly stated that these steps were taken to prevent the "influence" of these scholars over their students. In the ethnic colleges, politically suspect black students are not permitted to do graduate research, and indeed on more than one occasion an ethnic college has expelled its entire student body after it had displayed symptoms of unrest. The English universities cannot admit black research students on the basis of merit, and even those few who receive government permits to study at white universities risk having the permits withdrawn at any time if their work or attitudes offend the regime. Since 1968, the government has prevented the English universities from appointing black faculty. In that year the University of Cape Town attempted to hire a black anthropologist, and was forced to withdraw the offer after the regime had threatened new legislation empowering the minister of education to reduce or cut off the government subsidy—representing the bulk of university revenue—of universities that flouted its wishes. The university complied, but the legislation was passed anyway: South African universities may now be in effect bankrupted if, "in the minister's opinion," they do not conform to "lawful requirements."

South African students are as divided as the universities they attend. Most Afrikaans students belong to the Afrikaans Student Bond (ASB), a fanatically reactionary body that is one of the most right-wing elements in the entire country. The ASB refuses to have anything to do with other student organizations except under the most peculiar conditions; in 1971 its president declared that "contact and dialogue between Afrikaners and Coloureds is not wrong, provided that the contact and discussion is aimed at greater separation between them."[46] Most English students belong to the National Union of South African Students (NUSAS), a liberal organization that attempted to retain a multiracial membership until the early seventies, although it has since recognized that it can no longer speak for black students. The organization has been a favorite target for Mr. Vorster's attacks; he has variously described it as a "breeding ground of adders," "offspring of vipers," "sons of serpents," and, in imagery less serpentine but equally clear in its general import, "a red cancer in our midst," "young pink liberals playing with fire," and "corrupters of our youth whom no decent person would touch with a bargepole." Leaders of the organization have been routinely banned since 1966. Many black students joined the South African Students Organization (SASO), which was formed in 1968 by blacks disillusioned at what they felt was the patronizing stance of the white liberals in NUSAS. Strongly influenced by the American black power movement, the organization emphasized black solidarity and discouraged contact with whites. The existence of SASO posed a dilemma to the regime. On the one hand the organization appeared to advocate black separatism and to reject any multiracial alternative, an approach that the government commends. On the other hand, SASO was militantly opposed to *apartheid*, rejected "separate development," and urged the unity of all the ethnic groups. For five years the government equivocated, but in 1973 it served the entire leadership of SASO with banning and house arrest orders, and has since harrassed the organization to virtual extinction.

In the final stages of their education, then, Afrikaans students have generally turned out as the government wished them to be: nationalist, conservative, and conformist. Black students have developed the sense of racial exclusivity that was intended for them—but not through being led there by their "trustee" so much as through being pushed into this position by bitterness and resentment. English students, escaping some of the rigors of CNE in their elementary and secondary schools and then exposed to the more liberal climate of their universities, remain on the whole mildly critical of the regime, but their outlook is hardly radical.

Shaped by an ideology that is grounded in an anachronistic system of racial privilege, South African education contributes in countless ways to the inexpressible cruelty of *apartheid*. For the blacks, education offers little more than a training for menial roles in a white-dominated economy, and as such it is little more than a preparation for servitude. The black high school children recognize this fact; at the time of writing they have been taking part for several months in a nationwide boycott of their classes, in the conviction that Bantu Education is worse than no education at all. It was the black high school pupils, too, who played the leading part in the protests and rioting that shook urban centers throughout 1976, and who paid dearly in the loss of lives and liberty in the repression that followed. For the whites the educational system offers every material advantage, but at the cost of distorting their intellects and emotions through the organized encouragement of prejudice and bigotry.

The tenets of CNE have been successfully applied, but ultimately the South African educational system will fail in its objectives. Like so many other institutions in South Africa, the educational system prevents communication and understanding among the various population groups; instead, it fosters resentment and hatred. The system recognizes no common nationhood, no shared human needs; it aims rather at the maintenance of white and particularly Afrikaner supremacy through the deliberate reinforcement of cleavages in the population. Yet, it is those very cleavages that may well, in the long run, precipitate an upheaval that will bring to an end Afrikanerdom's stubborn defiance of the twentieth century. If racial tensions in South Africa increase to an intolerable point, leading to a conflagration that tears apart that unhappy society and brings Afrikaner hegemony to violent and wretched end, then "Christian National Education" will surely be accounted as one of the factors contributing to that conclusion.

Notes

1. *Natal Mercury*, 17 December 1970.
2. *Star*, weekly edition, 18 December 1971.
3. *Die Kerkblad*, November 1970.
4. Quoted in *Daily News* (Durban), 29 March 1965.
5. *Die Transvaler*, 29 March 1965.
6. Education League, *Manifesto for Christian National Education* (Johannesburg, 1948).
7. *Onderwysblad*, 1 July 1961.
8. Transvaal Onderwysersunie circular to school principals, quoted in National Union of South African Students, *The Citizen, Politics, and Education* (Cape Town, 1964).
9. Quoted in *Dome* (University of Natal), 23 June 1972.
10. L. C. Bekker, and G. J. Potgieter, *Vootligting vir St VIII* (Johannesburg, 1961), p. 32.
11. Van Jaarsveld, F. A., *New Illustrated History for Senior Certificate, Vol II: General History* (Johannesburg, 1969), p. 296.
12. L. C. Bekker and G. J. Potgieter, *Voorligting vir St VIII*, (Johannesburg 1960), p. 29.
13. Bekker and Potgieter, *Voorligting*, 1961, p. 32.
14. Ibid., p. 31.
15. B. G. Lindeque, *Geskiedenis: Algemene en Suid-Afrikaanse vir St VIII* (Cape Town, 1954), p. 81.
16. A. N. Boyce, *Europe and South Africa: A History of the Period 1815-1939* (Johannesburg, 1960).
17. Bekker and Potgieter, *Voorligting*, 1960, p. 33.
18. J. F. E. Havinga, G. F. Robbertse, and A. G. Roodt, *Geskiedenis vir St VII* (Johannesburg, 1960), p. 120.
19. J. J. Muller, G. H. P. de Bruin, and J. L. du Plooy, *New History for the National Junior Certificate, Part I—Std VI* (Cape Town, 1969), pp. 108-9.
20. Bekker and Potgieter, *Voorligting* 1961, p. 23.
21. Ibid., p. 24.

22. Havinga, Robbertse, and Roodt, *Geskiedenis,* 1960, p. 5.

23. Bekker and Potgieter, *Voorligting,* 1960, pp. 29-45.

24. *Sunday Times* (Johannesburg), 23 August 1970.

25. *Rand Daily Mail,* 3 November 1966.

26. Terms of reference to the Commission on Native Education, in *Report of the Commission on Native Education 1949-1951* (Pretoria, 1951).

27. Ibid., p. 164.

28. *House of Assembly Debates,* 15 June 1959, 8319 ff.

29. Quoted in Brian Bunting, *The Rise of the South African Reich* (London, 1964).

30. *Bantu,* June 1955.

31. Quoted in National Union of South African Students, *Fact Paper on Bantu Education* (Cape Town, 1968).

32. Quoted in National Union of South African Students, *Bantu Education: Education or Indoctrination?* (Cape Town, 1963).

33. South African Institute of Race Relations, *Survey of Race Relations in South Africa, 1971* (Johannesburg, 1972), p. 261.

34. Muriel Horrel, *Bantu Education to 1968* (Johannesburg, 1968), p. 73.

35. South African Institute of Race Relations, *Fact Paper 4* (Johannesburg, 1960).

36. Department of Bantu Education, *Annual Report, 1968* (Pretoria, 1969), p. 104.

37. See also W. G. McConkey, "Bantu Education: A Critical Survey, with Illustrations," *Theoria* 38 (May 1972): 1-45.

38. Quoted in Bunting, *Rise of the South African Reich,* p. 215.

39. Quoted in David Welsh, "Some Political and Social Determinants of the Academic Environment," in *Student Perspectives on South Africa,* ed. Hendrick van der Merwe and David Welsh (Cape Town, 1972), p. 21.

40. *Cape Argus,* 19 March 1958.

41. P. W. Cook, "Some Aims and Objectives of a Bantu University College," in *Education and Our Expanding Horizons,* ed. R. G. Macmillan, P. D. Hey, and J. MacQuarrie (Pietermaritzburg, 1962).

42. *Rand Daily Mail,* 24 August 1967.

43. *Rand Daily Mail,* 5 March 1971.

44. Quoted in UNESCO, *Apartheid and Its Effects on Education, Science, Culture, and Information* (Paris, 1967).

45. *Sunday Times* (Johannesburg), 3 September 1967.

46. *Sunday Tribune* (Durban), 4 July 1971.

Chapter 7

Apartheid Medicine

David Mechanic

The Republic of South Africa is a country of great contradictions and striking contrasts. Differences in medical care between blacks and whites reflect existing inequalities. The most advanced transplant teams exist side by side with widespread malnutrition and starvation among blacks. The white infant mortality rate is comparable to that of advanced nations; but if you are born in some black reserves you may have no more than a fifty-fifty chance of reaching the age of five.

The patterns of disease and health care in the country reflect its social and economic organization. For example, in 1970 the number of white infant deaths per 1,000 live births was 21.1. For Asian infants the number was 37.1, and for coloured (half-caste) infants it rose to 136.2. Registration of births among Africans is incomplete and infant mortality is not reported, but a 1966 survey found that half of the children in a typical reserve die before reaching age five and doctors practicing among Africans in rural areas report that it is quite typical for African women to have lost half of their children.

The Republic of South Africa, according to the minister of health, has one doctor for every 450 whites and one for every 18,000 blacks. There are relatively few nonwhite doctors in the country, with one coloured doctor for every 6,200 coloured and one African doctor for every 44,000

Originally published in *Transaction/Society*, vol. 10 (March-April 1973), pp. 34-44.

Africans. South Africa has four medical schools for whites; these schools exclude Africans but admit a very limited number of coloured and Asian medical students who are given special permission to attend. In 1971 the one black medical school at the University of Natal had 247 Indians, 172 Africans and 38 coloureds. Blacks have difficulty entering medical school because of deficiencies of prior education, lack of economic resources to support themselves, and limited access to medical education.

The legal exclusion of Africans and most other nonwhites from white medical schools relegates them to an inferior social and medical status, and those who become doctors receive lower wages by law than comparably trained whites. Moreover, nonwhite doctors may never be in a position to give orders to whites, thus greatly affecting training opportunities and possibilities of occupational mobility. Further, they may not use white dining facilities at hospitals or participate in other social activities.

The high doctor-patient ratio among whites makes white medical practice in South Africa highly competitive, and the white population receives exceedingly responsive care. Doctors are highly accessible, make house calls and night calls, and their services are relatively inexpensive by American standards. The basic organization of services is private and on a fee-for-service basis; ordinarily hospitalization is provided in nursing homes (somewhat akin to proprietary hospitals in the United States). Highly specialized hospital services are available in government-financed hospitals. Such institutions as Groote Schuur in Cape Town have medical capabilities comparable to those found anywhere in the world.

The vast majority of the white population of South Africa is affluent, well fed and well doctored, and suffers from disease patterns comparable to other affluent Western nations. Studies of peripubertal growth among Pretoria children show nutritional status among whites to be comparable or superior to anywhere else in the world, while blacks are clearly disadvantaged. Such problems as schistosomiasis, trachoma and idiopathic endomycardial fibrosis, which are extremely common in the black population, receive relatively little medical attention.

The organization of health care services in African areas varies from that available in urban areas to rudimentary services in some reserves and nonexistent services or inaccessible services for large parts of the population. In order to understand the differences in organization, it is necessary to consider the differences between the townships and the reserves.

Reserves (frequently referred to as bantustans and homelands) are those land areas in which Africans of various tribes in South Africa have pseudoindependence and some citizenship rights. In most of the country blacks are treated as "guest workers" and have no political rights. The reserves are not economically viable and are an inadequate basis for separate development. The African townships, such as Soweto and Alexandria in Johannesburg, are defined legally as inside white areas, and Africans require a permit to be there. Access to these areas is controlled, maintaining the fiction that the urbanized African's home residence is in one or another of the reserves. Africans living in Soweto are denied citizenship and property rights, and the government at its pleasure evicts populations from areas in which they have lived when it serves the political, economic, or social needs of the white population.

Disease and Low Wages

White society in South Africa depends on African labor, and the Africans, in turn, depend on work in urban areas for their subsistence. Social and economic hardships suffered by Africans in the reserves are sufficiently severe to encourage large numbers to remain in urban areas without permits despite harrassment and a high risk of arrest. Such "illegal residence" is freqently encouraged by whites who desire access to cheap African labor. Conditions in townships are generally harsh and contribute in major ways to disease and social pathology. Africans coming from the reserves to the townships cannot bring their families with them and this results in long separations and family disruptions.

In one township I observed large numbers of malnourished and neglected young children near a day care center. Personnel at the center—in telling me of their work—indicated that they had sufficient places for all of the children who wished to come. When I inquired about the children playing outside, I was informed that since their parents did not have residence permits the day center was prohibited by the government from taking the children despite available places. These children were just some of the many victims of brutal attempts to enforce *apartheid*.

Many of the disease problems arise from economic inadequacies. In the summer of 1972 the first national survey of African wages, made by the Productivity and Wages Association, was released. The survey results came from 1,086 companies, mainly in manufacturing and financial and commercial sectors (excluding mining), involving more than 188,000 employees. The return rate among firms surveyed was only 13 percent, and it is likely that those responding paid somewhat higher wages than those who did not participate. Moreover, since the survey was based on what firms paid rather than on what Africans earned, it excluded the large number of unemployed Africans and those who do a variety of casual work and household work at even more exploitative wages.

Chronic Malnutrition

Despite the conservative nature of the survey, it was found that 80 percent of Africans in the private sector earn less than 70 rand a month (approximately $81 at current exchange rates, which constitutes the poverty line). The Johannesburg Chamber of Commerce has estimated that a family of five in Soweto requires at least a minimum of R82.19 a month to live acceptably. In 1970 the Human Sciences Research Council estimated that the minimum effective income level necessary for a white family of five in Pretoria was R158.90 per month, and if one takes into account the changes in the cost of living, R200 would be a more reasonable figure.

The problem of low wages is compounded by discriminatory wage scales for white, coloured and African workers doing the same job, by the exculsion of Africans and coloureds from many jobs reserved for white labor, and by identured service characteristic of mining and other aspects of the economy. In mining, Africans are paid 50 to 60 cents a shift of eight hours, approximately one-seventeenth of what white miners earn.

The average social pension for an African is about R5 a month (approximately $6). He is expected to pay approximately half of that total for housing in the township. The Reverend David Russell, in attempting to make visible the plight of the African, has tried to survive on R5 a month. I quote in some detail from his letter of 28 July 1972 to the *Rand Daily Mail:*

> I wish to emphasize that these conditions of tearing hardship do not only involve the so-called "unproductive units." The situation is just as frustrating and harsh for the few able-bodied men "lucky enough" to be working as casual labourers for R20.00 per month. For this they must work a 46-hour week, starting at 7:30 am and finishing at 5:12 pm. Monday to Friday, with only half hour for lunch, and no tea break at all. . . .For a casual labourer with a wife and only four children there is a mere R3.34 a month per person for living. These wages and working conditions are shocking. . . . The R5.00 per month I have been living on for the last three months leaves me significantly better off than most Dimbaza inhabitants [an African Resettlement Township near King William's Town]. Nevertheless I am feeling the strain. It is like serving a prison sentence—I hold on grimly counting the days. My life revolves around my stomach! Human joy is shrivelling up: my capacity for giving out is shrinking. My friends notice the difference in me.

The common health problems of Africans are those generally found in the impoverished and underdeveloped world. The Africans are in a chronic state of malnutrition, and this contributes to a wide variety of disease problems and consequences. Protein-calorie deficiency disease is extremely common, and there is a considerable amount of pellagra and other nutritional diseases as well. Stunted physical and mental growth, often a consequence of chronic malnutrition, is also extremely common. There is a very high prevalence of gastroenteritis and pneumonia, diseases which are major causes of death among infants. Tuberculosis is rampant and so are its complications. Severe burns resulting from falling into open fires used to keep dwelling units warm are a very common problem among children in winter. Because of poor penetration of immunization and preventive medicine among Africans—particularly in the rural areas—measles, diphtheria, dysentery, and many other preventable diseases are quite common.

A Great Tiredness

I was told over and over again that malnutrition was a product of the ignorance of the African, of his unwillingness to follow a healthy diet, of his need for health education. This concerned note became the great rationalization used to explain the human deterioration so evident at every clinic and hospital. It is probably correct that Africans with a limited income could eke out a technically balanced diet if they adhered to a standard of austerity and self-denial that few whites could conform to. It is true that the African can eat what David Russell and other outraged people are attempting to eat as a means of protest; a daily food ration of 306 grams of mealie meal (ground maize), 125 grams mealies, 75 grams of beans, 30 grams skim milk, 15 grams margarine and 7 grams salt. But to argue that the failure to follow this diet is primarily a product of ignorance is to engage in the worst type of sophistry. On 14 October 1972 the New York Times reported that the Reverend David Russell was at the point of collapse and planning to end his ordeal. He was quoted as saying "Trying to live on five Rand a month has been long and dreary. . . .I feel a great tiredness deep within me, I just do not know how Africans manage."

It is extremely difficult to obtain adquate figures on the scope of malnutrition in South Africa. At one time kwashiorkor was a notifiable disease, but now notification has been discontinued; thus, the minister of health has remarked to Parliament that there is no malnutrition in South Africa. But a survey in Pretoria suggested that half of the urban African school children studied in the age group seven to eleven are adapted to a suboptimal protein intake although the basis of the estimate may not be fully valid. Dr. Neser of the National Nutrition Research Institute has written on the basis of his survey, that "at least 80 percent of school-going children from Bantu households in Pretoria suffer from malnutrition and undernutrition." These estimates are both conservatively based, since rural children are obviously more malnourished than those from urban areas, and those most malnourished are less likely to be in school.

Identified malnutrition is only a small proportion of such cases existing in the population. One estimate suggests eight or nine potential additional cases for every one recognized, and an assessment made at the University of Cape Town suggests that for every case of kwashiorkor seen by doctors at clinics, there are forty undefined cases of malnutrition. Similarly, it is well known that the occurrence of tuberculosis is related to nutrition, and this may serve as a proxy for estimates of malnutrition. As in the United States, tuberculosis is relatively uncommon among the white population of South Africa. In some African areas as much as one-fifth of the population may have tuberculosis.

Soweto, the major African township in Johannesburg, is served by a large provincial hospital, Baragwanath, which occupies the physical facilities of a restored army barracks. It is a teaching institution of the University of Witwatersrand Medical School. The medical and nursing staff are well trained, concerned about the health status of the Africans, and cope admirably with an unending flow of pathology within considerable budgetary constraints. Despite an enormous number of beds (approximately 2,200), the needs are so great that only the very sickest patients are admitted and they are commonly released sooner than desirable. Particularly impressive is the pediatrics unit which is especially dedicated and is doing extraordinary work despite severe limitations of funds and space.

Unending Flow of Pathology

In the townships, medical responsibility is highly fragmented between curative hospital medicine, preventive and curative clinics, and the social services. They are each under different authorities, making it extremely difficult to develop or coordinate a holistic approach to the problems of the Africans in the townships. The hospital has no authority or funding for preventive work and must deal with an unending flow of pathology with few tools to alter the conditions producing pathology in the community. Physicians often find their efforts futile, having patients return time and time again for the same difficulties that recur on return to noxious community conditions.

The curative clinics in the townships are crowded dispensaries providing limited and superficial care. Waiting periods to see a doctor are long—with patients queuing up early in the morning—and the number of patients processed by each doctor is extremely large. Dental and opthamological services are virtually nonexistent. Despite the fact that I made special efforts to visit pediatric services, day care centers, and preventive clinics, I never saw a black child in the Republic of South African with eyeglasses, but I assume there must be some.

The preventive clinics are worthy institutions but have inadequate financing and manpower to cope with the existing difficulties in the community. They provide immunizations, pre- and postnatal care, health education and birth control services. Staffed by nurse-midwives and health visitors, they make considerable effort to improve prevention, but the inadequacy of financing and staffing makes community penetration difficult. The government subsidizes the availability of skimmed milk powder which can be obtained at the preventive clinics for young underweight children. More subsidy is approved than utilized, indicating a clear inability to reach much of the population in need.

Birth control programs are probably more enthusiastically implemented than any other by the authorities, and wherever I went, this facet of prevention was emphasized. This is no surprise since the white community fears the growing black population and would like to limit its fertility. Although many black women are amenable to birth control, existing conditions make others in the black community skeptical. The main strength of the blacks in South Africa, they maintain, is in their numbers, and they are reluctant to support efforts to control their population. Similarly, women are frequently skeptical about limiting their fertility when so many of their youngsters die. Children are not only culturally valued, but also provide some security in old age since social sevices are almost nonexistent. It is my impression that birth control, without associated efforts to limit infant mortality in the black community and to improve the social situation of the blacks, will be a futile effort. The authorities have not as yet been willing to confront these issues.

In the reserves medical care is within the jurisdiction of the Department of Bantu Affairs, and it is possible to develop an integrated approach to preventive and curative medicine. I was taken to part of the Tswana homeland near Hammanskraal—by the secretary of health and three of his major assistants heading up various aspects of the health department in Pretoria—to see the evolving plan for health services in the homelands which, in their view, was well developed in this specific area. I was told that the population of that particular area was approximately a quarter of a million and that it was fairly widely dispersed with limited access to transportation. All of the hospital services for the population are provided by the mission hospital, having a staff of five physicians.

Mission Hospitals Impressive

The rural African population has depended heavily on the various mission hospitals for the limited medical services available to them. These hospitals are frequently staffed by mission doctors from abroad and vary in their orientations—some mixing religion with medicine as a condition of service, others with a much more secular attitude. The mission hospitals that I visited were staffed by physicians with dedication and concern. Some limit the patients they serve in terms of available space and resources; others never turn away a patient in need, keeping beds in every available place—indoors and on outdoor porches. These hospitals obviously have made and continue to make an important contribution, and without them the health status of the African would be even more dismal.

Mission hospitals sometimes hospitalize young infants with their sick mothers, for their survival is often precarious when the mother goes to the hospital. A common practice in both urban and mission hospitals is to have mothers stay in the hospital with their dehydrated infants, assuming part of their care and having some exposure to health education concerning nutrition and child care. This was one of the few practices I saw in South Africa that we would do well to follow.

Most impressive of the mission hospitals I visited was the Charles Johnson Memorial Hospital in Nqutu, Kwa-Zulu. The hospital has some 338 beds with an average daily case load of approximately 650 people. It administers clinics in outlying areas, has its own schools for training African nurses and deals impressively with an unending flow of pathology and disease. Understanding the basic plight of the region it serves, the hospital personnel does what it can to assist in preventive and community matters; but the task is immense and resources are extremely limited. Although the hospital has made important contributions to the region over the past three decades, it is clear that no hospital or clinic has the means to intervene effectively in the conditions causing disease.

Not far from the Johnson Memorial Hospital there is a settlement of some five hundred people uprooted from white farms and forced to resettle elsewhere. Officially their presence in the area is illegal, and sooner or later they will be moved on again. Food is difficult to scrape together and water is scarce. The people dig holes in the dry earth with the hope that they might collect some underground water, and since their presence in the area is "temporary" (they have been there two years already), the authorities will take no measures to provide a decent and safe water source. *The Guardian* of 23 September 1972 reported that when the director of the hospital took the issue up with the authorities and tried to do something to improve the situation, he was told to mind his own business and that he was interfering with the Bantu. It may be a concidence that at the same time an official telephoned the hospital questioning the permit of its welfare officer to enter the reserve.

The mission hospitals now receive financial support from the government, although they are underfinanced to meet the needs of the regions they serve. The existing plan is to provide primary medical care and preventive services from satellite clinics dispersed throughout the region, but it has not as yet been made operational in most areas. In the Hammanskraal area, where the plan was said to be in practice, I visited satellite clinics staffed by nurse-midwives who provide other than hospital services, and the clinics are visited occasionally by physicians from the hospital; I was told that there was approximately one session every two weeks. These clinics give considerable attention to family planning and immunizations, prenatal care and midwifery, and are the primary site for milk powder distribution. There are no dental or opthamological services at these clinics, and the basic medical care is rudimentary. Staffing is far too inadequate to reach many people in need in the population. Although these clinics provide sites of care which are of value, the character, scope, and quality of service would be totally unacceptable to the white population of South Africa.

Separate and Unequal

In order to get some measure of the extent of inequality of medical care, I visited white, coloured and African pediatric units in the same evening—all funded by the same governmental authority. In the African hospital, the wards were extremely crowded with very limited staffing. In one of the infant units we saw two nurses attempting to feed, change and generally cope with thirty-seven very sick children. We then went to the comparable white hospital where we found two nurses caring for five white children who were less ill. The comparable unit for coloureds in the same hospital was somewhere between these two extremes. Generally the physical facilities and amenities followed the same pattern.

I also visited the major hospital serving the coloured community in Johannesburg—Coronation Hospital—and the various areas in which these persons live. Although conditions are not quite as harsh as in the African community, they are generally comparable. Housing is inadequate and frequently unavailable, community conditions are poor, and malnutrition and preventable diseases are common. Medical services cannot cope with the magnitude of disease and pathology created by community conditions. From many of the coloured areas, transportation is especially difficult to Coronation Hospital, and medical services in the community are rudimentary.

Few medical facilities are available in the African and coloured communities after dark: and should problems develop, it is frequently difficult to get to the hospitals serving these areas. In both Johannesburg and Cape Town, however, there are projects carried out by medical and law students which provide some health and legal services to a coloured community. These projects are carried out by volunteers and deserve to be commended, but it also should be noted that the type of patchwork service provided by a large number of volunteers—each contributing a little time—does not provide first-rate care; and neither is it an ideal educational experience. The clinics tend to be erratic, depending on the academic schedule, and supervision is spotty. The medical schools involved have a responsibility to make such community services part of the overall approach to medical education and to provide the resources and supervision that guarantees a more adequate service. The practice of community medical care should be as much a part of medical education as work in the teaching hospital, and it should be more than a volunteer effort among those students who feel some sense of social responsibility. It must be clear, however, that the medical schools are also a reflection of South African society and are largely meeting the needs of its white elite. The basic problem is much deeper than the social responsibilities of medical education since the health of the African population is determined primarily by social and political policies, and these affect the performance of medical education and all other human services as well.

It is a well-known principle that the assumptions and conditions under which people live have a pervasive effect on their perceptions and behavior regardless of their particular ideologies. Social structures have the capacities to accent the best or worst in people, and under some conditions even well-meaning and idealistic persons come to take for granted behavior they would not condone if they lived in a different social context. In this regard, I often had the impression that people thought they were showing me one thing, but I was seeing quite another.

At one point I visited a landscaped park in Soweto, which is a stopping point for the visitor's bus tour. Sitting on a hill overlooking the township, there is an elegant tearoom plesantly surrounded by flowers and plants. Since I had noticed no parks or playgrounds or any green areas in Soweto, I asked whether Soweto residents used the park. My escort, somewhat embarrassed by the inquiry, indicated that this was to protect against vandalism.

I had similar experiences in my visits to various hospitals. For even among persons of conscience and commitment a certain callousness and disregard of human factors were frequently evident. It was apparent in many little ways. Some doctors who were obviously persons of integrity and compassion would lecture me loudly on the ignorance and superstitiousness of the African as we went from bed to bed. Few thought it necessary to explain to patients, whose treatment was being disrupted by my visit, who I was or why the disruption. When I embarrassedly requested that a patient be asked for permission so that I could take his picture, I was assured over and over again that I could take pictures of anything I wanted and that I did not have to ask anyone.

White Callousness

Disregard for human dignity is found in hospitals the world over and is in no sense unique to South Africa; but in South Africa it would take saintly qualities to be anything but paternalistic and hardened under the social and political conditions that prevail. One falls in with the culture and those with whom one must cooperate in assumptions and behavior. Even in my short stay I could observe the process occurring in myself: by the time I left I was beginning to unconsciously accept conditions that I found shocking when I first confronted them. Human survival depends on steady concessions to the social and cultural milieu. Thus I have come to have the greatest respect for those South Africans in all walks of life who speak out loudly against the brutalities and indignities of the social structure of South Africa. And if they sound paternalistic from time to time, it is not too difficult to understand why. Already Africans are rejecting their more paternalistic white advocates and indeed, the time may be coming when they reject all whites. This reaction is also clearly understandable, a product of the limited options available.

These economic, social, and medical inequalities are already known to informed physicians, government officials and the involved public in South Africa. But existing conditions make it difficult for many concerned persons to speak out without personal risk. Yet, throughout my visit I was impressed by the concern of many South Africans who were struggling to do what little they could within the constraints imposed on them. There were many concerned physicians in the hospitals; but curative medicine, however important, is somewhat of a smoke screen if not complemented by better preventive efforts and improved conditions in the community. Moreover, it is obvious that progress and decency in South Africa must involve more than good will and the concern of individuals; it must be embedded in the social structure and social conditions which are the primary determinants of health and illness in society. Social policies that divide men, disrupt communities, separate family members against their wishes and breed distrust and hate cannot create a healthy society.

Some South Africans maintain that theirs is a poor country, and that it is inappropriate to impose the kind of standard I have in my observations. They point to other starving Africans. I would be less likely to regard this as a grand rationalization if the country were not so rich in natural resources, if the white population did not dominate so much of the country's resources, and if it did not live in ostentatious affluence in the midst of such great poverty. South Africa has had an enormous rate of economic growth, but it has not shared its growing affluence with its black population. The only relevant comparison is an internal one that takes into account the economic resources and capacities of the country and compares the differences in how the white and black populations live and the impact of social policies on maintaining or closing these differences.

Similarly, I would be more impressed with concerns about the ignorance of the African if education among Africans were encouraged, if they were not legally excluded from white schools and universities, and if they did not have to pay from their meager wages for education that is freely available to whites. The fact is that many of the Africans in the Republic of South Africa are highly urbanized, and their disabilities arise not from ignorance or ineptitude but from systematic exclusion from social and economic opportunities enforced by *apartheid* policies. South Africa persists in plundering its greatest resource—the capacities, labor, and potentialities of its people.

Chapter 8

Law and Justice in South Africa

Albie Sachs

Rapid industrialization and modernization of South Africa in the twentieth century accelerated the integration of all sectors of the population into a common society. In a few decades great cities sprang up on what had formerly been stretches of open veld, and quiet colonial towns on the coast burgeoned into busy ports and manufacturing centers. The demand of the urban areas for food and labor soon destroyed whatever economic autonomy the rural regions had once possessed, and an extensive system of internal communications brought all the inhabitants of the subcontinent into contact with each other. Millions of black, brown and white farmers *trekked* by road and rail into the towns, whilst a reverse flow of manufactured goods proceeded into every *nek* and *krantz* of the countryside.

In this setting it was hoped by some and feared by others that increasing industrialization and cultural assimilation would undermine color consciousness and erase legal disabilities based on race. Some would have

Abridged and updated from "The Administration of Justice in a Racially Stratified Society," chap. 6 in Albie Sachs, *Justice in South Africa* (Berkeley: University of California Press, 1973), pp. 161-231.

argued then, as many maintain today, that an industrial economy was essentially color-blind, and that its labor requirements and marketing needs would inevitably subvert archaic racial attitudes. Liberal investors, politicians and lawyers anticipated that the growth of industry would promote the spread of skills and education throughout the population and pave the way for the extension of the franchise, the removal of the color bar, the softening of law enforcement, and the liberalization of race feelings. The test of citizenship would be civilization and not race. The British parliamentary system as adapted to the Cape and then transferred to the north was seen to have implicit in it an intrinsically democratic character and inherent virtue, which, in the benign atmosphere created by industrial advance, would become increasingly attractive even to the most race-conscious members of the South African population. Finally, it was assumed that the existence of a court system modeled on British lines and staffed by a judiciary imbued with a sense of independence and justice, would insure freedom under the law to every individual irrespective of color. This chapter will examine the extent to which all these expectations were contradicted in the sixty years after unification.

In the constitutional sphere, the limited parliamentary franchise of black and brown was progressively eliminated and in its place a variety of racially and tribally constituted bodies were created. At the same time, the entire surface area of the country was racially zoned, with the result that by 1970 approximately 85 percent of the land was reserved to the whites, who made up less than 20 per cent of the total population. Legal machinery was created to enforce large-scale removals of black and brown; discriminatory notices proliferated until no public amenity was left unsegregated; penalties were attached to an ever-widening range of sexual contact between white and black or brown. An elaborate race register was created in order to ensure that every individual was allocated to a defined racial group and thereby made entitled to certain legal privileges and subject to specified legal disabilities. Controls over the movement, residence, and labor of Africans were constantly extended, while exemptions from the operation of restrictive laws were continually removed. Job reservation was increasingly underpinned by statute, and such "mixed" trade unions as emerged were compelled by law to divide along racial lines. Segregation in schools and universities was intensified. All the courts of law save one were segregated, as were the prisons and police stations. What had formerly been regulated by geographical separation or social practice now became enforced by law, and the courts became more not less active in penalizing breaches of differential statutes.

Thus in the sixty years after the unification in 1910, the number of blacks charged under avowedly racial statutes rose elevenfold from ninety thousand per annum to one million per annum. In 1928, fewer than fifty thousand Africans were charged under the pass laws, while forty years later nearly seven hundred thousand were charged under these laws. The number of prosecutions for illegal occupation of land in the same period rose from ten thousand to more than one hundred fifty thousand.

Partly as a result of this growing enforcement of discriminatory legislation, the number of persons received into prison each year rose from less than one hundred thousand in 1911 to nearly half a million in 1967. A comparison with countries that had a similar penal—though different social—system reveals that in the early 1960s more than twice as many Africans were received under sentence in the prisons of South Africa (total population eighteen million) as persons of all races were received under sentence into the prisons of England and Wales, Tanzania, Kenya and Ghana combined (total population sixty nine million). So great has been the recent incarceration of Africans in South Africa that if the level reached at the end of the 1960s is maintained, more than one African man in two can expect to be jailed in the 1970s.

Racial factors have also played a part in the continuing and in some respects increasing severity of punishments handed down by the courts. Thus in the first forty years after unification a total of one hundred thousand offenders were sentenced to nine hundred thousand strokes, while in the next twenty years two hundred thousand offenders were ordered to receive 1.2 million strokes; although the average number of strokes per offender nearly halved, the total number of strokes actually inflicted each year more than doubled. Similarly, the number of persons executed rose from less than thirty per annum in the first decade after unification to nearly one hundred per annum in this last decade. The number of crimes carrying the death sentence increased from three to nine in the same period, and in the early 1960s South Africa was responsible for 47 per cent of all judicial executions reported to the United Nations for a five-year period.

The Franchise

At the time of union in 1910 some twenty thousand or 15 per cent of all parliamentary voters in the Cape were black or brown. Although they had never managed to elect one of their number to the Cape legislature they constituted a considerable force at election time, especially since the rest of the electorate was fairly evenly divided between Englishmen and Afrikaners. The South Africa Act of 1909, which established the Union of South Africa, entrenched their voting rights, but did not extend such rights to the north. A special section of the act provided that none should be removed from the voters roll on account of race except by a law passed by two-thirds majority of the House of Assembly and the Senate sitting together.

In 1930, the voting power of Africans and coloured persons in the Cape was effectively halved when the vote was extended to white women in South Africa.

In 1936, African voters were by the requisite two-thirds majority removed from the common voters roll and placed on a special roll which entitled them to elect three white persons to the House of Assembly and four to the Senate, which between them had a total of nearly two hundred members.

In 1956, coloured voters were placed on a separate voters roll which entitled them to elect three white persons to the House of Assembly. The necessary two-thirds majority was obtained after a long constitutional battle culminating in the reconstitution and enlargement of the Senate.

In 1959, African representation in Parliament was abolished altogether. And, in 1968, coloured representation in parliament was abolished altogether.

Thus the Parliament elected in 1970 contained no representation, either direct or indirect, of black or brown South Africans. Pursuant to the policy of *apartheid* or separate development, the 80 per cent of South Africans who were disfranchised were provided with various councils. Nine separate tribally based authorities were established in the rural reserves with varying degrees of local autonomy to represent the African population of South Africa; the Coloured Representative Council was created to act as official spokesman for the coloured people; and the Indian Advisory Council was appointed to consult with the government on matters affecting people of Indian descent.

Racial Legislation

At the time of unification differential pass, liquor, and tax laws already existed throughout most of South Africa. One of the first enactments of the new Parliament was a law which regulated recruitment of African workers and made breach of service contracts by Africans a criminal offence. This was soon followed by a statute which prohibited Africans from acquiring an interest in land outside of the tribal areas; the eventual effect of this law as amended was to prohibit Africans from owning or leasing property in 87 per cent of South Africa's surface area.

In the 1920s, Africans living in the urban areas were obliged by statute to live in locations subject to the control of white superintendents. The governor-general was declared to be supreme chief of all Africans with power to rule by proclamation. A special court system staffed by white officials was established to hear civil disputes involving African litigants and to try Africans under differential legislation. Taxation of Africans on a capitation basis was made uniform throughout the country, and the failure to produce tax receipts on demand was made a criminal offense. Sexual intercourse between black and white was made illegal throught the country.

In the 1930s, African voters in the Cape were removed from the common voters roll. And, in the 1950s, pass laws inherited from the pre-Union period were consolidated and extended to African women; exemptions from the operation of these laws were cancelled and Africans in the Cape were subjected to the same controls as Africans in the rest of the country. The education of Africans was taken away from the missions and placed under total government control. The authorities were given extra powers to evict Africans from land and to compel them to live in designated areas. Africans were prevented from belonging to registered trade unions, and strikes by Africans were made unlawful.

In the 1960s, government officials were given extra powers to control the residence and employment of Africans. The African National Congress and the Pan African Congress were declared unlawful organizations.

During these decades, Africans were also adversely affected by a number of laws which discriminated generally between white-skinned and dark-skinned persons. These will be mentioned below. The only disabilities to be repealed during all this time were those relating to possession of liquor. The government contends that the creation of tribal authorities in the 1960s opened the way to the exercise of full citizenship rights by Africans in their separate tribal homelands.

General color bar laws were passed from time to time to enforce segregation between whites on the one hand and Africans, coloured persons and Indians on the other. In the early years after Unification these statutes referred mainly to employment; in the 1950s, statutory authority was given for the reservation of public amenities on a separate and unequal basis; a national race register was compiled in terms of a race classification law; intermarriage and any form of sexual activity between white persons and black or brown persons was prohibited; black and brown students were excluded from the universities of Cape Town and the Witwatersrand; all urban and rural areas were racially zoned for purposes of ownership or occupation; the reservation of jobs on racial lines was extended, and "mixed" trade unions were split on racial lines. In the 1950s and 1960s, major African political organizations were proscribed, the nonracial Communist party and Liberal party were forced to disband or go underground, and the multiracial Progressive party was compelled to shed its black and brown members.

Thus by 1970 legal segregation was more extensive and systematic than it had been in 1910. Instead of the Cape policies being extended to the rest of the country, the rigid segregation of the north was extended to the Cape. African women throughout the country were made subject to the same controls as their menfolk, and the class of Africans exempted from the pass laws—only partially exempted, since in practice they had to carry documents—was abolished. At the same time the legal disabilities of coloured people and Indians were considerable increased. Segregation notices appeared on buses, trains, taxis, and ambulances, on park benches, beaches, sportsfields, and swimming baths, in libraries, concert halls, museums, and zoos, in post offices, telephone kiosks, railway stations, and urinals. Interracial conception was forbidden, interracial marriage was prohibited, the sick were treated in separate hospitals, and the dead were interred in separate burial grounds.

The old policy of segregation, which operated unevenly and without plan, gave way to the new concept of *apartheid*, which was enforced in a total and systematic fashion. There was no essential break between the old and the new, in fact it was this very continuity which was novel, since everywhere else in the world legal differentiation according to race was being formally repudiated. *Apartheid* was the modernized form of segregation, justified by Scripture, adapted to industrialization, and implemented by the formidable machinery of a contemporary state.

Law Enforcement and Race

The differential laws referred to above are not self-enforcing. It is not surprising, therefore, that an increase in what will be referred to as race-statutes was associated with an increase in the extent to which the courts were involved in the maintenance of segregation. In the years from 1910 to the end of the last decade, the total South African population increased slightly more than threefold, the authorized establishment of the South African police increased approximately fourfold, and the number of persons charged in court increased approximately eightfold. This section will examine in some detail the way in which the penal establishment was affected by race, and, conversely, the manner in which the judiciary assisted in regulating race relations.

Prosecutions in Terms of Race-Statutes

The total number of prosecutions increased at a markedly greater rate than did the total population, and the number of race-statute prosecutions increased at an even faster rate. Roughly speaking, during a period of forty years when the total population increased by about two and one-half times, the total number of prosecutions increased by about four and one-half times and the total number of specifically race-statute prosecutions increased by about five and one-half times. In proportional terms, the percentage of race-statute prosecutions rose from 33 per cent of the total in 1911 to 44 per cent in 1967.

The term "race-statutes" has been used here to refer to five main groups of laws, namely, those relating to taxes, passes, liquor, masters and servants, and trespass. The tax laws penalized African men who failed to produce on demand annual receipts for poll tax. The pass laws referred to documents of identity and permits relating to work and residence, all of which had to be produced on demand, as well as to curfew laws and location regulations, the latter including such crimes as failure to pay rent. The liquor laws rendered it a criminal offence for Africans to brew or possess so-called *kaffir* beer or so-called European liquor. The masters and servants laws applied almost invariably to white masters and black or brown servants, and related mainly to indentured farm workers. The trespass laws were used almost exclusively to prosecute Africans found without permission on land or premises owned by whites. Although the total figures for prosecutions under race-statutes increased rapidly over the years, the figures for each of these five main categories varied considerably. The vast increase in the number of prosecutions for tax, pass, and trespass offenses was associated with a marked drop in the number of prosecutions for liquor and masters and servants offenses. Thus prosecutions for tax offenses rose four times in the forty years, for pass law offenses fifteen times, and for trespass sixteen times. Prosecutions under the pass laws in fact rose so steeply that they increased in average from less than one thousand per week to more than two thousand per day. Thus statutory controls over the African people were intensified rather than weakened with the growing economic progress of the country. The archaic masters and servants laws which had served a predominantly rural economy were superseded by modernized pass laws designed for an industrialized society, and the liquor laws which were irrelevant to the economy or the administration were jettisoned.

Race Laws and Sex

The increase in race-statutes prosecutions has been brought about through the more rigid enforcement of old statutes rather than through the creation of new offenses. Penal sanctions were invariably attached to new segregation measures, but they were invoked relatively rarely. Thus prosecution under the Group Areas Act of 1950, and for breach of segregation rules relating to public amenities are not frequent. Nevertheless, the social significance of the new race-statutes was considerable, and the ultimate threat of penal sanctions ensured general compliance with them.

One field of increasing intervention by the law was in sexual relationships between persons of different color. In general, pre-Union statutes prohibited sexual intercourse between white women and black men, the severest penalty being in Natal where twenty-five years' imprisonment could be imposed. The Immorality Act of 1927 penalized sexual intercourse between "Europeans" and "natives" of the opposite sex. The Immorality Act of 1950 extended the prohibition to sexual intercourse between "Europeans" and "non-Europeans" and the Immorality Act of 1957 further forbade sexual activity falling short of intercourse, and at the same time increased the penalties to a maximum of seven years' imprisonment.

The number of convictions for breaches of the color bar provisions of the Immorality Act is small in comparison with those for prosecutions in terms of other race-statutes, and standing on their own they fail to convey the importance attached to the sexual color bar in South African life. Whereas prosecutions under the pass, tax and trespass laws usually pass unnoticed save by those directly affected, Immorality Act trials are highly publicized. The more prominent the white person involved and the more salacious the evidence, the wider the press coverage. A secretary to the prime minister, a minister of the Dutch Reformed Church, lawyers, businessmen, academics, policemen, and farmers have all been hauled before court for loving their black neighbors too well, and almost every year the newspapers carry reports of whites who have committed suicide rather than face the ignominy of such a charge.

It is generally agreed that only a small amount of interracial sexual activity is detected by the police, yet the existence of the act and the bringing of exemplary prosecutions helps to promote the concept that the maintenance of racial purity is the ultimate end of government. A sociologist has observed that when, as in South Africa, status is closely linked to racial type, any assimilaton that blurs the obvious physical differences is seen as a threat to the social order. "The dominant group will apply strong pressure to prevent coition between its members and the underlying population." White tribalism, he adds, contributes its quota to the list of sexual taboos (Simons).

Yet if the preservation of white purity is seen as the primary objective of the Immorality Act, in practice it is white men who seek sexual intercourse with black and brown women rather than black and brown men who attempt intimacy with white women. Figures in police reports for prosecutions under the Immorality laws reveal that very few white women have been involved; thus in 1928 a total of 78 white men and African women were convicted, as compared with a total of only 11 white women and

African men, while in 1966 out of 488 persons convicted only 4 were white women and 13 black or brown men.

Race Laws and Residence

One of the immediate consequences of industrialization in South Africa was the creation of large multiracial urban centers. As industry expanded and the population of the cities increased, so did the legislature increase its measures to segregate residential areas according to racial criteria. Far from declining with the onset of modernization, racial zoning became more extensive and grew to involve even greater sections of the population. In the past two decades the machinery of the law has been invoked to compel the removal of hundreds of thousands of persons from one area to another on racial grounds. The removal of Africans was accomplished by a combination of many statutes, some old and some new, and it it difficult to compile accurate figures for the total numbers of persons involved. One estimate put the figure of enforced removals of Africans during the decade 1960 to 1970 at nine hundred thousand. The enforced removal of Indians and coloured persons, however, was accomplished almost solely by one statute, the Group Areas Act of 1950, the operation of which has been more precisely documented.

TABLE 1

Differential Effect of Group Area Proclamations (1950-70)

Race	Numbers of families ordered to move	Number of families actually resettled
White	1,318	1,196
Colored	68,897	34,240
Indian	37,653	21,939
Chinese	899	64

Source: SAIRR, *Annual Survey,* 1970, p. 186.

The basic aim of the Group Areas Act was to divide the country into separate racial areas for ownership and occupation. In practice the act was used mainly to force Indians and coloured persons living in areas close to the center of towns and villages to remove to the outskirts; while being ideologically satisfying to the white electorate, these removals also proved

to be economically advantageous to the government and to serve its
security ends. The differential manner in which the law was implemented
appears from Table 1.

Table 1 reveals that for each white householder obliged by law to make
way for brown people, almost one hundred brown householders have
been compelled to make way for white people. On the assumption that
each family consisted of five members, only 1 in 570 whites in South
Africa would have received orders to move, compared with approximately
1 in 6 coloured persons, nearly 1 in 3 Indians and more than 1 in 2
Chinese.

Increase in Prison Population

The size of the prison population in any society is an important index of
the extent to which the courts are used as instruments of social control. A
growing prison population indicates either an increase in conduct defined
as criminal, or an improvement in law enforcement machinery, or the
emergence of a sterner judicial attitude towards punishment. In South
Africa all three factors appear to have operated in the years since 1910 to
increase the size of the country's prison population. The growth in the total
number of admissions each year is given in Table 2, which refers to
selected years from 1912 to 1969.

TABLE 2

Admissions to Prison for Selected Years 1912-69

Year	Population of South Africa	Total admissions (including remands)	Column 3 as % of column 2	Admissions on sentence
1912	6,100,000	120,894	2.0%	95,822
1932	8,300,000	202,276	2.4%	172,555
1962	17,200,000	461,000	2.7%	347,000
1969	20,300,000	658,000	3.2%	496,000

Two comments should be made about the figures in Table 2. First, the
growth in total admissions and admissions under sentence greatly exceeded the growth in total population, the ratio being approximately five to
three. Second, the growth in unsentenced prisoners who were subsequently not returned to prison was even greater. Thus in the late 1960s,

the already vast prison population was added to by more than one hundred fifty thousand persons each year who were either refused or unable to raise bail and who were subsequently acquitted or sentenced to a non-custodial order.

A very large proportion of persons admitted to prison each year go there to serve sentences of only a few weeks or a few months. Table 3 gives a breakdown of admissions for the year ended 30 June 1969, according to race, sex and length of sentence.

According to Table 3, out of slightly less than five hundred thousand persons received as convicts into prison during the year, as many as four hundred sixty thousand were sentenced to six months or less. Furthermore, nearly half the prisoners sentenced to less than six months were first offenders.

The Prisons Department has in fact evolved two major techniques for dealing with the large numbers for short-term convicts sent to prison each year. The first is to hire out such prisoners to farmers at nominal charge, and the second is to release prisoners on parole subject to their working on farms and gardens at local wage rates.

In the early 1950s the Prisons Department invited farmers' associations in various parts of the country to construct farm jails to which medium-term prisoners might be sent, and by 1956 the movement of prisoners from the cities to the countryside had become so extensive that the director of prisons was able to report that 37 per cent of all prisoners worked extramurally—mainly for farmers, in the highly productive areas where free labor was in short supply. The remaining 63 per cent were employed in state use, the hiring out of convicts to mining companies having been finally ended in 1955.

The release of short-term prisoners on parole proved to be another boon to persons owning land in the neighborhood of prisons, since the usual condition of parole was that the prisoner remain in the employ of a particular landowner for the unexpired portion of his sentence. Thus in the year ended 30 June 1960, more than 100,000 short-term prisoners were released on parole or probation. It should be mentioned that in practice white prisoners are not among those sent to perform menial tasks on privately owned farms or gardens. Segregation runs right through the prison system in South Africa, and results in black and white prisoners receiving different amenities and rations in physically separate institutions. A leading penologist explained, presumably without intentional irony, that "placing the Bantu offender in a correctional institution for people of his own group and race not only recognizes existing ethnological differences but is in accordance with the national policy of differential development" (Rhoodie).

TABLE 3

Distribution According to Race, Sex, and Length of Sentence of Convicted Persons Admitted to Prison in the Year Ended 30 June 1969

Sentence	White male	White female	African male	African female	Asian male	Asian female	Coloured male	Coloured female	total
Death	1	—	83	1	2	—	19	1	107
Life imprisonment	—	—	12	—	—	—	1	—	13
Intermediate sentence	105	6	838	25	6	—	233	10	1,223
Prevention of crime (5-8 years)	91	9	1,132	51	6	—	356	11	1,656
Corrective training (2-4 years)	170	9	2,444	111	13	2	645	37	3,431
2 years and over	280	18	5,680	172	25	4	1,181	49	7,409
Over 6 months under 2 years	669	23	16,092	1,562	119	3	2,850	167	21,485
Over 4 months up to 6 months	661	41	27,094	3,542	104	5	4,181	285	35,913
Over 1 month up to 4 months	1,595	97	116,746	25,719	354	27	11,631	2,312	158,481
Up to 1 month	3,613	346	181,918	40,682	850	87	30,225	7,992	265,713
Periodical imprisonment	122	—	42	2	3	1	31	—	201
Corporal punishment only	26	—	354	—	—	—	59	—	439
Total	7,333	549	352,435	71,867	1,482	129	51,412	10,864	496,071
First offenders under 6 months	1,852	171	149,631	24,830	902	12	9,590	2,878	189,886

Source: Based on annual report of commissioner of police.

The high proportion of Africans in prison is interpreted by some as evidence of government repression and by others as proof of popular lawlessness. Prosecutions brought under race-statutes are undoubtedly responsible for a large number of Africans going to prison, but common law offenses also make their contribution. Thus in the early 1960s more than 70,000 Africans were convicted per annum for offenses against property and approximately the same number for offenses against the person. Nearly a thousand murders are committed in Johannesburg each year compared with about sixty in London and about two hundred in the whole of the United Kingdom. There are indications that many African employees regard pilfering as a legitimate means of supplementing low earnings, and the courts constantly reiterate their determination to suppress such "betrayals of trust" with severe sentences. Thus theft from an employer, even of the most inexpensive article, is almost invariably punished with a sentence of several months imprisonment; first offenders are not exempt, and not long ago two Transvaal judges confirmed on review sentences of six months imprisonment passed on Africans who had respectively stolen a packet of matches and a toilet roll at their places of work.

Hardly any sociological analysis has been attempted to explain the extent of common law crime among Africans. To adherents of racial theory it is self-evident that Africans have an ethnic propensity towards violence and plunder, and criminal statistics are seen merely as confirming what every white man is considered to know from common experience. In the view of such theorists, the only realistic approach towards crime in South Africa is to have strong laws, a strong police force, a strong judiciary, and escape-proof jails. A common variant of this attitude is that Africans in their tribal or "natural" state are basically law-abiding, but that they are unable to resist the temptations of city life and collapse into lawlessness once they enter the white man's world.

Critics of racial theory, on the other hand, attribute lawbreaking to the very controls that are supposed to counteract it. They point to the disruption of communities and the breaking up of families by the law, and to the blatant inequalities of wealth and opportunity that attach to race in South Africa, and argue that what appears to the racist to be an inherited deficiency in the personalities of blacks is in fact a reaction to deficiencies in society. They agree that traditional African societies in southern Africa were generally fairly free of crime (whether defined in traditional or modern terms), but state that the only realistic solution to contemporary law-breaking is to allow Africans full rights and participation in a common society rather than to try to restore a past that vanished irretrievably with the destruction of the tribal armies and the dispossession of the tribal lands.

By the end of the 1960s, approximately three hundred fifty thousand African men were being received into prison under sentence each year, and approximately one hundred fifty thousand of these were first offenders. If this level of imprisonment is maintained in the 1970s, then according to my calculations, within the decade one African man in three will have served a sentence as a convict in South Africa, and if remand prisoners not subsequently admitted as convicts are included as well, probably one African man in two will have been in jail.

Executions

At the time of unification capital punishment was competent in respect of three crimes, namely, murder, rape, and treason. In the case of murder it was an obligatory penalty, but for rape and treason its imposition lay within the discretion of the trial judge.

By 1967, capital punishment had become competent for nine crimes: murder, rape, treason, aggravated housebreaking, armed robbery, kidnapping, and offenses under the "Sabotage" Act, the Suppression of Communism Act, and the Terrorism Act. The death sentence continued to be compulsory for murder, save that since 1935, if extenuating circumstances were found to be proved, the judge could impose a lesser penalty. As far as the other eight offenses were concerned, capital punishment could be imposed at the discretion of the judge.

The addition of the six new capital crimes took place in the decade 1958 to 1968, which was also a time of considerable increase in the number of persons executed in South Africa (see Table 4).

From the figures in Table 4, it can be seen that in the first decade after 1910 the average annual number of executions was twenty-nine, in the fourth decade it was nineteen and in the sixth decade it was ninety-five. Thus an initial diminution consistent with a trend in many countries towards abolition was followed by a sudden rise inconsistent with such trend. The result has been that after being indistinguishable from dozens of other countries sixty years ago, South Africa now has the distinction of occupying first place in a United Nations survey on the rate of capital punishment throughout the world.

The total number of executions reported to the United Nations for the period 1961 to 1965 was 1,033. During the five-year period ended 30 June 1966 a total of 508 persons were executed in South Africa, representing nearly half the world's reported total for approximately the same period.

TABLE 4

**Persons Executed in the Decades 1911–20,
1939–48, and 1960–69**

1911-20	number hanged	**1939-48**	number hanged	**1960-66**	number hanged
1911	57	1939	11	1960	70
1912	24	1940	22	1961	66
1913	24	1941	20	1962	129
1914	23	1942	12	1963	115
1915	29	1943	17	1964	81
1916	36	1944	14	1965	113
1917	23	1945	14	1966	70
1918	23	1946	20	1967	121
1919	32	1947	27	1968	99
1920	19	1948	37	1969	84
Total for decade	290		194		948
Average per annum	29.0		19.4		94.8

Source: Figures collated by author.

The discovery that the hangman in Pretoria was responsible for almost half of all the world's reported judicial executions, prompted discussion on capital punishment in South African legal journals and the press. Nearly all the academic writing was abolitionist in character, and many advocates as well as a few judges declared themselves against capital punishment. Yet when in 1969 a member of Parliament introduced a motion to request the government to consider the advisability of appointing a commission to inquire into the desirability of abolition, she was unable to find a seconder, and the motion lapsed.

The main argument in favor of retention has been essentially a racial one. Thus the 1947 Penal Reform Commission commented that comparisons with abolitionist countries were unhelpful, since they did not have heterogeneous populations in which the bulk of 80 per cent of the population had not yet emerged from barbarism. In 1968 the head of the Department of Criminology at Pretoria University stated in a popular weekly newspaper that the abolition of the death sentence might be regarded by the nonwhites as a sign of weakness and a license to sow death and destruction.

Corporal Punishment

The incidence of corporal punishment in South Africa dropped consistently for a number of decades and then rose sharply again before recently declining once more. In the first four decades after unification a total of approximately 115,000 offenders received approximately 910,000 strokes, while in the following two decades approximately 220,000 offenders received approximately 1.22 million strokes. Thus the number of persons per decade receiving corporal punishment increased nearly fourfold, outstripping the increase in population, while the number of strokes inflicted per decade more than doubled. Table 5 indicates the number of offenders sentenced to corporal punishment and the number of strokes inflicted during selected years from 1911 to 1969.

TABLE 5

Corporal Punishment during Selected Years
1911–69

Year	Numbers of offenders	Numbers of strokes
1911	3,399	34,048
1931	2,981	19,751
1961	17,389	80,949
1969	5,273	25,933

Source: Based on annual prisons reports.

Starting in 1911 with approximately 3,400 offenders receiving 34,000 strokes, the figures tended to drop until they reached their nadir in 1941, when 1,600 offenders received 10,000 strokes. Thereafter the figures crept up consistently until 1952, when Parliament laid down that corporal punishment should be a mandatory sentence for persons found guilty of certain specified offenses. This led to a very rapid rise in the figures which reached a peak of 18,500 offenders sentenced to 94,000 strokes in 1958. The figures then stayed on a plateau before descending once more when judicial discretion was restored in 1965. By 1969 slightly more than 5,000 offenders received slightly less than 26,000 strokes.

The South African Penal Reform Commission reported in 1947 that corporal punishment as a method of dealing with crime had been abandoned by most of the civilized countries of the world, outstanding exceptions being the British Commonwealth and dependencies and parts of the United States. It added that the main argument for its retention in South Africa was that it was a deterrent "of special efficacy especially in a country largely populated by a people the bulk of whom have not yet emerged from an uncivilized state, and that no other penalty would be equally effective in respect of crimes of violence or those crimes which by reason of their diabolical or inhuman character gravely shock the sense of law-abiding community."

The notion of corporal punishment being a special deterrent was developed in Parliament in the 1950s when the law relating to criminal procedure was amended to make whipping an obligatory sentence for specified crimes. Previously corporal punishment had been a competent penalty, either on its own or in addition to any other penalty, for most common law offenses. Now the discretion of the courts was removed, and judges and magistrates were ordered to impose strokes on all persons found guilty of housebreaking, receiving stolen property, theft of motor cars or theft from motor cars, and the more serious crimes of violence. Defending the subsequent large-scale flogging of youths, the secretary of justice said in an interview: "I frequently walked around with what we regarded as honorable scars after I had had a difference of opinion with authority, and I do not think I am any the worse for it. . . Boys being what they are there will always be some who scream and some who will not. . .Such hidings naturally left small wounds but the same happened to boys who were caned at school" (Jansen, *Cape Argus,* 25 June 1955).

The general increase in whippings was considerable, but there appeared to be little corresponding decrease in the specified offenses. Eventually, after twelve years had elapsed and a million strokes had been imposed, the failure of mandatory flogging was officially acknowledged, and the discretion of the courts was restored.

The word "whipping" has been used here interchangeably with "floggings" and "corporal punishment," in the same way in which it has been used in South African legislation. The term covers both lashes with a cat-o'-nine-tails and strokes with a heavy or light cane. The use of the cat has in fact become increasingly rare, and the prisons reports appear to have made no mention of its administration since 1958, when four persons were whipped with the cat. A heavy cane is used for offenders over twenty-one years old and a light cane for those under twenty-one.

Now that the courts have had their discretion restored as to whether or not to impose corporal punishment, the incidence of flogging has dropped considerably. It is still higher than it was thirty years ago, but proportionate to the total population it is lower than it was at the time of unification. Men who are over the age of fifty or else who are medically unfit may not be whipped, and it is never a competent punishment for women offenders. The flogging of white men and youths is relatively infrequent but nevertheless not rare.

The Law and Black Resistance

Modernization of the Union of South Africa did not lead to a relaxation of race domination but rather to an improvement in the techniques of control and greater sophistication in its justification. As the interdependence of black and white South Africans in a common economy increased, and as cultural differences between them diminished, so was the law used in ever greater measure to create statutory differentiation and to maintain black subordination. Thus industrialization did not erode race distinction; on the contrary, it enabled segregation to be enforced with the powerful weapons of a modern state. The courts were an integral part of the state machine. While the higher courts from time to time delivered judgements which softened or delayed the impact of new segregatory measures, the lower courts continuously and on a massive scale punished breaches of established race-statutes.

White lawyers and judges have generally directed their attention to the occasional superior court judgments which have had great constitutional interest but little practical impact, whereas black litigants have generally been more concerned with the extensive number of inferior court cases which have had slender constitutional import but considerable practical effect.

To any litigant the character of neighborhood law depends upon the kind of neighborhood he inhabits. If he lives in a wealthy suburb and works in a thriving city center, neighborhood law signifies to him company flotations, property deals, tax avoidance, insurance claims, matrimonial disputes, embezzlement, motor offenses, and keeping black servants and employees under proper control. If he resides in a poverty-stricken compound or location on the other hand, neighborhood law denotes pass and tax raids, debtors' enquiries, and prosecutions for theft and violence. The legal profession has been overwhelmingly concerned with the welfare of the wealthy white litigant, and the bulk of legal literature has been devoted to examination of nuances of doctrine relevant to his disputes. To the half million Africans who go to prison each year, however, it matters little whether a new chief justice is liberal or segregationist, whether the courts rely mainly on English or Roman-Dutch authorities, or even whether the law adopts an objective or a subjective approach to the question of criminal intent.

If increasing industrialization intensified rather than reduced compulsory segregation in South Africa, it also highlighted the degree to which race differentiation was being artifically maintained. The absorption of Africans into a common society was coupled with their exclusion from civic rights, while the integration of Africans into a market economy was accompanied by the denial to them of the job opportunities and wage rates available to the whites. The very fact that legal intervention was necessary to enforce segregation established that race differentiation was neither natural nor divinely ordained. The more the police, the judiciary and the prisons demonstrated their physical superiority, the more they undermined their moral authority. Large-scale evasion of the law and growing participation in crime constituted one expression of African resistance to the dominant legal order; crowd revolts and clashes with the police were another. More directly, Africans campaigned through a number or organizations, some political, some industrial, for a relief of burdens and an extension of rights. Their enemy was an internal colonialism rather than an external imperialism; they struggled against local masters rather than foreign overseers; they sought political integration under the slogan of equal rights, rather than political secession under the banner of independence.

The Supreme Court for many decades adopted a relatively tolerant attitude towards agitation for social change in South Africa. The judges likened themselves to the guardians of the black people, and delivered strong lectures to white farmers, policemen, and others found guilty of violence to black persons. Thus in the so-called Bultfontein case, five policemen, including a station commander, were sentenced to up to seven years of imprisonment for thrashing, kicking, battering and giving electric shocks to two African suspects, causing one to die.

This benevolent judicial paternalism became increasingly difficult to maintain as social conflict became more acute. By 1960 the law began to lose much of its more tolerant, liberal aspect. Large-scale African protests were met with large-scale repression by the authorities; African movements went underground and began to plan insurrection, while the authorities abandoned normal procedures and counterattacked with specially trained corps of police. Neither the African revolutionaries nor the white counter-revolutionaries conducted their struggle within the formerly accepted framework of the law. Although the combatants were not rigidly divided along racial lines—many of the police were black and some of the revolutionaries were white—the issue was whether or not white rule would survive in southern Africa.

PART III
SOUTH AFRICA
AND THE WORLD

Chapter 9

South Africa In The Contemporary World

Colin Legum and Margaret Legum

Two great changes have been brought by over a quarter of a century of *apartheid* rule in South Africa. Its internal contradictions have been sharpened by the simultaneous attempts to divide the country along even more rigid color lines and to stimulate more rapid economic growth; and its external relations have declined to the point where the Republic today has become the "polecat of the world."[1] These two developments are inextricably linked so that it makes little sense to try and describe the South African situation without focusing on their interrelationship.

South Africa's is not the only tyranny in the world, but it is the only racial tyranny. The rulers of South Africa are officially committed to a racist policy of maintaining a permanent condition of "white supremacy." There are a number of reasons why other countries with tyrannical regimes have not attracted to themselves the degree of world hostility which is reserved for South Africa. The primary reason, of course, is that its policy of white supremacy is being practiced on the African continent itself. Its white electorate chose to vote into power an *apartheid* regime at the historic moment when the African continent and the rest of the international community were beginning to move in precisely the opposite direction. Imperialism

Originally published in *Issue: A Quarterly Journal of Africanist Opinion*, vol. 3, no. 2 (Fall 1973), pp. 17-27. The African Studies Association, Waltham, Mass.

was on the retreat; a new Third World was being born; the old international system which relegated the colored peoples to an inferior status in the world was rapidly breaking down; new centers of world power, no longer so exclusively Euro-centered, were being established; the United Nations had just been born; new relationships, based on a realistic acceptance of all that these shattering changes involved, were beginning to develop especially in the Western world, but also in Russia and China. Yet Dr. Malan's regime chose to swim against this historic tide of change, and his successors have been doing so ever since—with predictably greater difficulties. Instead of accepting changes dictated by a different kind of world, they are committed even more deeply and desperately to their traditional policies. To abandon these policies at a period of growing uncertainty—especially on the African continent—would enlarge the threat to their strenuously held position of white supremacy. Any concessions which might diminish the reality of white supremacy would only strengthen the capacity and determination of the black majority to assert its claims to equality of citizenship, and would encourage the rest of Africa to complete its "unfinished revolution" of bringing majority rule to the entire continent. Shadowy concessions, on the other hand, would neither satisfy nor deceive their challengers for long.

The only choice facing the *apartheid* regime was between abandoning the status quo and stubbornly defending an established way of life. The great majority of white South Africans, because of historical circumstances,[2] were incapable of accepting the first alternative. So the battle was joined on the international field as well as at home.

The decision to defend South Africa's right to maintain its system of white supremacy necessarily conditioned its foreign relations, particularly with the rest of Africa and the Third World. Thus its domestic and foreign policies became inextricably linked. The *apartheid* regime could protest angrily against the unfairness of being treated differently from other countries with unacceptable regimes, or resist attempts by foreign governments and the United Nations to interfere in its domestic affairs, but because South Africa was unique in its commitment to maintaining a tyranny based on race it was bound to invite world attention.

Britain's former prime minister, Mr. Harold Macmillan, had tried to warn South Africa in 1960 in his historic "wind of change" speech of the dangerous course on which South Africa would be embarking if it failed to take sufficient account of changes in world opinion on matters of race and of the rise of African national-consciousness. Dr. Verwoerd's characteristic reply was that "a government must stand by its principles."[3] The die was cast. A few months after Macmillan's "wind of change" speech, Sharpeville occurred; this marked the beginning of a new divide between the *apartheid* republic and the international community.

The choice made by South Africa when it defied world opinion over its racial policies was bound to evoke an angry response from colored people everywhere. Others to take issue with the Republic's intransigence include those whose stand is determined by moral and political principles, political realists (like Mr. Macmillan), and proponents of expediency in the world power struggle. All four elements were drawn into the international controversy over *apartheid*—though with different degrees of commitment.

The decision of South Africa to stick to its guns (and not only in a metaphorical sense) has landed it in a position where no independent state is so completely friendless; none has so many implacable enemies committed to assisting those who seek to destroy its status quo; and none is faced with such continuous pressures to isolate it internationally. Even those nations which maintain economic and diplomatic ties with Pretoria—for whatever reasons of self-interest—join readily in condemning its policies of *apartheid*.[4] Here, however, one comes up against an extraordinary paradox. During this period—especially after 1960, the year of Sharpeville—when the *apartheid* Republic's international fortunes were steadily plummetting, its regime nevertheless succeeded in expanding the country's economy and its military power. There are some—notably the Brahmins of Western diplomatic intellectuals like Dr. George F. Kennan and the late Dean Acheson—who conclude that the threat to isolate countries like South Africa and Rhodesia results only in toughening their resistance to change. From a superficial understanding of the situation their view seems highly plausible. But it is demonstrably wrong.

The error, not only perhaps surprising, is in concentrating too exclusively on only one of the two factors in the situation—the white factor—while showing too little knowledge and/or understanding of the black factor. The two factors are equally important; to give a lesser importance to either in analyzing the strength and nature of the forces engaged in the South African conflict is to misunderstand the situation fundamentally.

The error made by Kennan is reflected in the kind of policies now pursued by all the Western nations (as well as Japan) with the exception of only the present governments of Sweden, Denmark, Norway, Holland, Australia and New Zealand. These policies focus almost exclusively on how to influence white South Africa "to find better solutions" (Kennan's phrase).[5] What makes this approach so attractive is that it offers the most convenient policy for Western governments to adopt since they see their short-term interest as being best served by remaining on reasonable terms with Pretoria and by keeping South Africa low on their agenda of priorities.

It is also a low priority for the Russians and the Chinese—which is one major reason why Western policymakers can afford to relegate it to "tomorrow's problems" rather than today's.

However, if Western policies towards the racial crisis still remain ambiguous (which is how they would wish to keep it for the present), the Russians and Chinese have already made a clear choice. Their diplomacy and long-term strategy can proceed in low-key, but purposeful, support for the challengers of *apartheid*, while the West is still principally engaged in the tactical diplomacy of avoiding active involvement with either side. This diplomacy is hampered by the international pressures for Western governments and business to disengage from the Republic as part of the strategy to isolate South Africa completely.

Western policymakers mostly share the Kennan view that showing a more understanding approach towards South Africa's problems might produce better hopes for change than the application of increasingly hostile pressures. This is the thinking behind the policy of building bridges favored by the United States, Britain, France, West Germany, and Canada. The rationale for such a policy is obvious enough; but the premises on which it is based require careful examination against the background of what has happened since *apartheid* first made its appearance on the world scene.

The Basis of South Africa's Foreign Policy

Like all foreign policies, South Africa's is designed to achieve what the ruling class conceives of as the national interest. Successive prime ministers have explicitly defined South Africa's foreign policy in terms of a commitment to defending in the international community the country's "right and necessity" to maintain its status quo based on white supremacy. From the first prime minister at the time of unification, General Louis Botha, through General Smuts, General Hertzog, Dr. Malan, Mr. Strijdom, and Dr. Verwoerd down to Mr. Vorster, this has remained a constant factor in South Africa's foreign policy. A particularly striking example of how this "national interest" is translated into international practice was offered by Dr. Verwoerd in January 1966 when he defined South Africa's attitude towards the rebel regime of Mr. Ian Smith:

> If I have to judge the situation in Rhodesia, the attitude of the people [sic] and the resistance they will put up, by what we would do in South Africa under precisely similar circumstances—if our way of life were threatened; *if there were an attempt to remove the supremacy of the white man here, even in the course of time;* if we were subjected to sanctions or embargoes or boycotts; and if we had to put up a struggle for survival, in which we would have to conquer or die—then I am quite convinced that the Rhodesians in their own circumstances will show no less determination.[6]

For South Africa's white leadership the crucial problem has always been how to define white supremacy both at home and abroad. The world community is always more sensitive and, for a time, more militant after dramatic events inside the Republic—especially when they produce violence—as evidenced by Sharpeville in 1960, the general strike in Namibia in 1972-73, the wave of strikes by black workers in 1973, and the widespread urban rioting and shootings of 1976. It is on such occasions that one also sees more clearly the dynamic connection between internal explosions and external pressures. On the other hand, when South Africa appears to have its black population under control and the situation there appears stable, the pressures—especially those exerted by the West—slacken off and the temper of even black Africa is noticeably lower. This interrelationship between violent episodes in the Republic and Western responses is an important, if ill-augured, sign for the future, since it suggests that the West will only be ready to commit itself fully when the challenges to *apartheid* become increasingly violent.

South Africa's overriding concern remains with its Western connection, for if the West were ever to abandon South Africa the consequences would be extremely serious. It would bring closer the danger of isolation within the world community—which, in practical terms, would not only mean more intensive external pressures but, more meaningfully, would affect South Africa's trading relationships and weaken its defense system. Considerations of this kind make it essential for South Africa to resist the forces working to isolate the Republic.

South Africa's Strategy For Survival

There are four main elements, or objectives, in South Africa's strategy for survival. The first is the maintaining of a firm base of political control at home to ensure internal stability while pursuing the "grand design of separate development." And the second is rapid economic growth. The first objective requires a strong economy, and a strong economy depends to a great extent on finding larger overseas markets for exports since South Africa's economic policy, based on cheap black labor and consequently a relatively small home market, relies heavily on exporting its "surplus value." Third is the establishment of a powerful defense system to counter local and external threats to South African security and to obtain membership of as wide a military alliance system as possible in case of threats from any of the major powers generally characterized as "communist." For this latter purpose South Africa needs close economic and military ties with Rhodesia in defense of their mutual system of political control by white minorities. Fourth is improved relations with African states for a number of reasons: to reduce the danger of attacks on its frontiers from Black Africa (and to resist Chinese and Russian penetration);[7] to gain greater access to the African market which is its natural trading area; and to make its international posture more acceptable—especially in the West—by demonstrating that not all black people are its enemies.

The success of such a foreign policy strategy is dependent upon the Republic's ability to avoid becoming internationally isolated and completely unrespectable in the West. Those who participate through the South Africa Foundation, or in other ways, to help present a more positive image of the Republic in the Western community therefore contribute, consciously or innocently, towards helping the present Vorster regime to achieve this vital objective; they are in fact, agents of the Republic, however much they might wish to repudiate the attribution to them of such a role.

The manner in which these four elements in South Africa's strategy fit together can best be illustrated by considering their external aspects in more detail.

The Economic Imperatives In South Africa's Foreign Policy

South Africa's foreign relations are crucial to expanding its economy, which is basic to the survival of its political system. Unlike other countries, it must overcome political obstacles as well as face normal trade competition; also it suffers from the disadvantage of not belonging to any of the major international trading alliances.

South Africa's well-developed economy depends for its continuing expansion on a number of factors, for example, the price of gold, industrial peace (especially among its black workers), fresh external capital to complement its own large internal sources, acquisition of new technology, guaranteed supplies of more oil (all of which must be imported) and, above all, expanding overseas markets. By slowing up its expansion—which would carry the risk of political troubles at home—South Africa could make itself less reliant on imports, except in the matter of oil; and by adopting a "siege economy" like Rhodesia's it could become self-reliant for many years—provided it had an assured supply of oil. However, for normal peacetime conditions South Africa's economy depends, like all other developed economies, on large-scale exports. While its gold and other mineral exports have no difficulty in finding markets, it is much less well-placed when it comes to manufactured goods and agricultural exports.

South Africa's manufactured and agricultural exports must compete in the world markets mainly with the major industrial countries and with the African associates of the EEC. Because South Africa has a high cost economy and its exports carry high transport costs, they are not keenly competitive.

The Republic's economy has suffered two crucial setbacks as a direct consequence of its *apartheid* policies—virtual exclusion from the larger part of the African market, and denial of special access rights to the European Economic Community. If it had remained a member of the Commonwealth, it could have qualified for special consideration when Britain negotiated its terms for membership in the EEC, especially over its manufactured agricultural products, sugar, fruit and wine. Its important canning industry, worth $60 million, now faces collapse because of its exclusion from Europe; another consequence of this setback will be much higher prices for canned products on the domestic market.

Not only has South Africa lost its privileged access to its traditional market in Britain, but it has also lost the opportunity of continuing to expand its exports to the vitally important markets of continental Europe. The direct consequence of this is that the Republic is faced with the damaging prospect of a worsening trade imbalance with the EEC countries. Even before the full impact of Britains's entry was felt, South Africa's trade imbalance with the EEC was of the order of $472 million (over R360 million) in 1972. Its attempts to persuade the EEC to grant it special associate status have been resisted by the Yaounde and other African "associate members" of the EEC. For the present, therefore, South Africa's exports to Europe—except for minerals and seasonal fresh fruit—are seriously restricted. Thus it has been losing ground in one of its major traditional markets at a time when it needs to expand its markets.

Much more serious is the denial to the Republic of what, under normal circumstances, should have been its greatest trading area—the African continent itself. In the long-term only the African market can offer South Africa the chance of competing successfully with the major trading nations; but so long as its regime is viewed with strong hostility by the great majority of African states the opportunities for participating in their markets will be severly restricted. This compels South Africa to pursue its efforts to get into the much more difficult markets of North America and Latin America where its high cost economy and expensive transport costs make South African exports (other then minerals) uncompetitive.

South Africa's trade figures show that Africa is the only continent with which it still has a favorable trade balance. But South Africa's trade with the rest of the continent is minimal as compared either with Africa's trade with the rest of the world or with the total volume of South African exports.[8]

The Republic has been able to incease its "backdoor trade" with a number of African states, largely due to the efforts of French entrepreneurs who have become increasingly involved in South Africa since France became an important trading partner of the Republic because of its opportunistic and cynical policy of selling military equipment to the *apartheid* Republic after the Security Council's arms embargo. Working through countries like Gabon and Mauritius, French businessmen are able to conceal the original source of South African manufactured goods to facilitate their entry into other African states. These channels are also being used to develop a backdoor entry for certain South African goods into the EEC, but this is hardly a satisfactory basis on which to develop a vital export market.

South Africa is having to rely increasingly on devising new ways of infiltrating the African and European markets. Much of this effort is directed by South Africa's leading international financier, Mr. Anton Rupert, the "Czar of the tobacco industry," who controls Rothman international and is himself a member of the Broederbond, the secret Afrikaner society. His latest move is the creation of a multinational development bank—Economic Development for Equatorial and Southern Africa (EDESA). Its aim is to promote private capital investment in Africa through a combination of South African, American, and European banks. By providing an international cover for South African capital investment, and by making Swaziland the headquarters for EDESA, Mr. Rupert hopes to expand South Africa's markets in the African continent. Similar institutions have been set up in Latin America, the Far East, Europe, and Maurititius. These developments are an essential part of South Africa's efforts to overcome world barriers to its exports.

The Republic's economic growth under the constraints imposed by its *apartheid* policies and by external factors has deepened its internal contradictions. Thus, although it achieved an average real growth rate of over 4 percent during the past decade, this expansion was accompanied by a current account deficit in the balance of payments of about $480 million annually and by a high rate of inflation.

The Military Imperative In South Africa's Foreign Policy

The Republic's expenditure on military defense has soared since 1948. The major expansion began after 1960 when the threat of isolation first began to cause serious concern, and especially after 1963 when the Organization of African Unity was formed and declared its support for the liberation struggle in southern Africa. Its first intervention in this area succeeded in getting an arms embargo placed on the Republic by the Security Council.

In 1960-61 expenditure on defense was still only $64.4 million; this rose almost fivefold to $294 million in 1964-65; and to over $422.4 million in 1972-73. In 1974-75 the figure was $1,128 million, and it has risen to $1,560 million for 1975-76. The total number of the armed forces was 109,300 in 1973.[9] In response to threats of isolation the country quickly established its own arms industry which in 1966-67 had 1,000 firms engaged in contracts valued at $33.6 million, over $55.2 million in 1968-69, and over $259.2 million in 1972-73. Through the Armaments Board (ARMSCOR), South Africa now produces about 80 percent of all its weapons. It established its own shipping industry capable of producing smaller ships; and it has spent almost $24 million to establish a submarine base at Simonstown. It established an aircraft industry based on the Atlas Aircraft Corporation. Under mainly French and Italian license, it is now able to assemble, and substantially build, Mirages and Aermacchis, as well as its own trainer aircraft. It manufactures its own rocket missiles capable of carrying a nuclear warhead; and it has made great strides in the field of nuclear power. It has refused to sign the Non-Proliferation Nuclear Treaty.

South Africa's success in building up its military strength despite the United Nations and other arms embargoes is largely the result of its ability to exploit its economic strength to acquire new friends in the West. Although a number of Western countries have helped the Republic to defeat the objectives of the arms embargo, the two major culprits are France and Italy, with West Germany and Britain playing a lesser role.

The French connection has been the decisive factor. France saw the opportunity to expand both its valuable arms exports and to profit from greater trade with South Africa at the expense of Britain when the Labour administration declared its support for the United Nations arms embargo. It has cooperated with South Africa (both at government and private levels) in developing the Republic's Cactus ground-to-air missile system; it has supplied submarines and helicopters, and sold Mirages to be built under license in the Republic; and it has been closely involved in assisting with the growth of South Africa's nuclear power program. France has now become one of the most favored countries in South Africa—and this has occurred with hardly any opposition to its policies from within France, where public opinion over South Africa is conspicuously lacking.

This growing friendship between France and South Africa illustrates an important factor in considering realistically the limits of forcing an economically strong country like South Africa (or even a weak one like Rhodesia) into complete isolation. National self-interest, and especially economic interests, often count for more than political considerations. Only when a conflict of national interests exists, is it usually possible to force decision makers to opt for one course rather than another.

The strength of this economic interest in participating in South Africa's great exportable wealth is illustrated by British, American, West German, Italian, Belgian, Swiss and Iranian policies—but it is best exemplified by the Japanese willingness to swallow the indignity of being treated as "honorary whites" for the sake of their trade interests.

It is the consideration of such realities that has increasingly led African countries to develop, however slowly, the idea of forcing on the West a choice between what they have to offer and the benefits of dealing with South Africa. The OAU has, since 1970, paid more attention to considering ways of exploiting this factor. Tanzania, as a matter of policy, recently excluded all French cars from its market. But it is not always in the national interests of African countries themselves to act in a similarly principled fashion. African states do not always behave with more regard for principle than those they criticize when it comes to considering their own immediate economic interests.

South Africa's response to the twin dangers of isolation and growing military insurrection around its borders was to build itself up into a powerful military nation high in the league of the smaller middle powers. It can therefore be argued with considerable force that the threat of isolation has backfired in that it gave the Republic the necessary incentive to divert a considerable part of its resources to arming itself, thus making itself less vulnerable to attack and more effective in defense than it was before these threats began to take shape. But this is only one side of the picture; the other side is provided by the contradictions forced on South Africa's internal and external policies as a result of the need to bring the country increasingly to a state of armed siege.

South Africa's self-confidence has always depended on its ability to point to its state of internal stability—an argument it could also deploy in the past with considerable effect in making itself more acceptable to the West. But this is a claim which can no longer be made. Furthermore, the need to confront Africa in a posture of military defiance undermines its claims of peaceful intentions in its dealings with African governments. These aspects will be considered in more detail later.

In 1961, the minister of defence, Mr. J. J. Fouche, gave three reasons for strengthening the Republic militarily: to preserve internal security; to enable South Africa to make its contribution on the side of the West against communism; and to meet any external invasion.[10]

South Africa has failed to make any progress towards fulfilling one of these objectives: acceptance into any of the Western defense alliance systems, although it has energetically pursued a number of initiatives such as the formation of an African-Middle East Defense system, a South Atlantic Defense system, an Indian Ocean defense system with Australia and New Zealand, and more recently, a naval defense system with Argentina and Brazil. But nothing has so far come of any of these projects, and the Republic still remains effectively outside any military alliance. Its own southern African defense system with Rhodesia remains an informal one.

While no serious military threat has developed internally, anxieties about the possible emergence of effective guerrilla action has continued to grow. This concern centers in five areas. First, there is concern in Namibia where there has been the beginning of successful, if still minor, military operations by the South West African Peoples Organization (SWAPO), and where the black population has developed a new militancy and a capacity for organization—as demonstrated by the first total industrial strike of black workers in the history of South Africa, and by the overwhelming boycott of elections for the Territorial Authority. Second, South Africa is worried about the existence abroad of South African guerrilla organizations and, especially, of the African National Congress. Third, the failure of the Rhodesian rebel regime to win its legal independence, and the emergence of guerrilla activities along the Zambezi frontier is of concern. Fourth, and crucially, the government is anxious about the transfer of power to the liberation movements in the former Portuguese colonies of Angola and Mozambique. Fifth, the commitment of Zambia (backed by Tanzania) to the liberation movements, providing them with friendly territory through which to operate, is another potential problem for the Republic.

The growth of the armed struggle in southern Africa is one of the significant changes brought about by the decision of the white communities of the region to continue to "swim against the tide." Their taking to arms is not—as the late Dean Acheson claimed[11]—the result of their being inspired by outside interference, but is quite naturally the consequence of growing frustrations of black peoples denied effective opportunities to exercise their manhood and rights of citizenship within the charmed circle of white supremacy.

The guerrilla movements of southern Africa have also introduced a major new element with respect to international involvement in the area because of the support they get from the OAU, the nonaligned nations, the communist countries, and from some Scandinavian countries and Holland.

Although the danger of escalating warfare in southern Africa has forced itself to the top of the Republic's priorities, it still remains well down on the list of areas of concern in most Western countries and in the Soviet Union. This is not the place to attempt an evaluation of the likely progress of the armed struggle; but it is important to recall the warnings so frequently given in the past that the present drift of events is towards, rather than away from, race war—the only logical outcome of a confrontation between white societies embattled in defense of their supremacy and black societies unwilling to accept the permanence of such a relationship.

The effects of an escalation of armed violence in South Africa are well described in a recent speech made by the Republic's army chief, Lieutenant-General Magnus Malan. Describing the episodic nature of terrorist attacks in neighboring territories and incursions into South Africa and South West Africa, General Malan said he had reached the conclusion that

> you and I and our country are involved in a type of enemy activity—if you want to call it a war, then do so—which is of low and high intensity. Resulting from this there is one trememdous danger staring us in the face. . . .This is that we are becoming conditioned by circumstances. We are involved in a war. We do not accept that we are involved because we are becoming used to it. . . .The first terrorist crossed our border in 1967, about six years ago. But today we have become used to it. It's everyday news. It is not real any more, we cannot observe it objectively. Actually we can no longer determine the measure of our involvement. Are we involved, or are we not? We no longer possess the realism to accept and to say that we are involved in a struggle. . . .You see it is important to me that we analyze our involvement and determine to what degree this struggle really affects us. . . .The conclusion I must reach, particularly if the internationalistic spirit to be found at present is taken into account, is that African states can fight and lose, recover and fight again. But can we? I am afraid that we can lose only once. And therefore I say that we must be watchful that we do not become conditioned and over-confident.[12]

The Western Imperative In South Africa's Foreign Policy

The West remains a major factor in South Africa's foreign policy calculations because of the Republic's continuing heavy reliance on its links with Western governments for its political, economic and defense systems. Because the present political system in South Africa was originally produced and subsequently buttressed by Western Europe (and by Britain in particular) it is natural that white South Africa should have come to regard itself as an integral part of that Western community. To remain an accepted member of that community—which nobody thought seriously to question up to the time of General Smuts' defeat in 1948—is crucially important to the Republic. While international developments after 1960 weakened South Africa's place in the Western community, it was by no means altogether excluded. South Africa has even succeeded in developing important new relations in Europe—mainly with France and West Germany—and in expanding its links with Japan, Iran, and to a much lesser extent, with countries in Latin America.

So long as it remained a member of the Commonwealth of Nations it could rely completely on the economic and defense system of Britain and its allies. The beginning of a different kind of relationship was signalled by Macmillan's "wind of change" speech in 1960 with its explicit warning that South Africa could no longer expect British support if its own interest might suffer as a result. The exclusion of South Africa from the Commonwealth in 1961 marked the physical weakening of these bonds; this was confirmed by the decision to turn the country into a republic in the following year. But while British and other Western attitudes became more divided, ambiguous, and defensive over relations with the Republic, South Africa had no real alternative but to try to regain and retain as much as it could of its Western connection. It could—and did—make itself more self-reliant militarily while still desperately clinging to the Simonstown Treaty as a means of retaining the Western defense umbrella for itself, always arguing its case on the grounds of its being a mutual Western defense interest. It turned energetically and not altogether unsuccessfully to making its economy less vulnerable to external pressures—partly by strengthening its industrial capacity to make itself less dependent on strategically important imports, partly by stockpiling, and partly by widening its economic links instead of relying so largely on Britain. It recognized that Britain would be unwilling to sacrifice any of its own larger interests for the sake of helping South Africa—quite rightly as it turned out when the Heath administration took Britain into the European Economic Community.

South Africa knows that it can rely on Britain, the United States, Japan and other Western-oriented countries to promote their interests in the Republic for only so long as these interests remain important to them, and providing their promotion raises no serious conflict of interest with other countries—notably, important African countries like Nigeria or Zaire.

The ability of South Africa to survive in a state of near isolation depends largely on the kind of help it can expect from major Western countries for its trade, new capital investment and technologies, sophisticated weapons (especially planes, ships, and submarines), oil (from pro-Western Middle Eastern states like Iran), and resistance to international diplomatic pressures in the United Nations and other world bodies.

There is no doubt about the Republic's capacity for survival over a considerable period of time if it ever becomes totally isolated—but such survival is dependent upon an absence of serious military pressures along its frontiers (pressures which could result from the independence of Angola and Mozambique and the changing fortunes of Rhodesia), as well as an absence of militant black resistance at home. If the Republic's economy were to decline seriously (as it most certainly would if it were completely isolated), if its military security were weakened by a total cut-off of sophisticated military pressures on its frontiers, and if, above all, its white society were to feel a sense of "total abandonment" by its traditional friends, the impact on the Republic would be traumatic. But whether this would lead to a more peaceful resolution of the crisis or to a more violent conclusion would depend on a number of factors about which one cannot be certain.

The African Imperative In South Africa's Foreign Policy

South Africa can never escape from the reality of its geographic position. A regime like the present one can expect to secure itself more effectively only by achieving two essential objectives of its African diplomacy: peaceful frontiers and opportunities to trade in its natural hinterland. The former is essential to its external security, and the latter to its economy. Both objectives depend on the chances of establishing peaceful coexistence between white-ruled and black-ruled regimes. This is Pretoria's key objective. Winning acceptability in a substantial number of African eyes is also important as a means of satisfying its Western imperative, since deepening hostilities between the two African systems must affect Western calculations in determining their own best long-term interests.

The dilemma is plain: how can a regime committed to white supremacy hope to win acceptability in African eyes? South Africa continues to believe it is possible. Africa's collective answer is provided by the Lusaka Manifesto of 1967 which sets out the essential conditions for peaceful coexistence—acceptance by Pretoria of the principle of majority rule through negotiations to achieve a peaceful transition. No mention is made of any time limit. South Africa rejected this offer, leaving the Lusaka Manifesto signatories with the less acceptable alternative of assisting the liberation movement to achieve majority rule through violent means. Thus the lines of confrontation were drawn along the Zambezi River, which has increasingly become Africa's most dangerous frontier.

Despite all evidence of worsening relations between the Republic and the rest of the continent, South Africa remains fixed in its belief that it is still possible to negotiate the "acceptability" of *apartheid* with enough African states to ensure its own minimum objectives. It is strengthened in this belief by its good neighbor policy with Botswana, Lesotho and Swaziland; by the diplomatic recognition it has won from Malawi and, briefly, from Madagascar; and by its success in subtly penetrating countries like Mauritius, Gabon, and the Ivory Coast.

What is thre reality of these relations? Its brief honeymoon with Madagascar ended with the overthrow of the Tsiranana government early in 1973. There is no certainty that this will not be repeated in a country like

Malawi whose policies are dictated by its idosyncratic president, Dr. Banda. More discouragingly for Pretoria has been the decline in its relations with its closest neighbors—Lesotho, Botswana, and Swaziland—whose circumstances demand that they should remain joined with the Republic in a customs union. Dr. Verwoerd once envisaged that the association of these four could one day lead to a new kind of commonwealth "at the southern tip of the continent between neighbor and neighbor, one white and the other black, a Commonwealth in which no state will lord it over the other."[13]

Yet it is precisely because of the Republic's determination to lord it over its three small neighbors that their relations have steadily worsened. When Lesotho became independent in October 1966, South Africa had no more outspoken friend than its prime minister, Chief Leabua Jonathan. Today he and Mr. Vorster are hardly on speaking terms, not having met since Chief Jonathan warned in October 1971 that "a violent confrontation between black and white South Africans would be the inevitable result of apartheid." Following the shooting of twenty-five miners (including some Basotho) in the Western Deep Level mines in September 1973, Lesotho demanded that the United Nations send observers to attend the inquiry into the causes of the shooting. This produced from Mr. Vorster a characteristically paternalistic reply: "I am prepared to make allowances for them (Lesotho and Botswana) because I am aware of their problems, perhaps sometimes more than themselves. But I must seriously request that South Africa not be driven too far in this matter."

His relations with Botswana have become similarly strained —so much so that the South African foreign minister was sent to see its president, Sir Seretse Khama, in 1971 to discover from him his true intentions.[14] This concern was renewed in August 1973 over a joint communiqué issued by Sir Seretse and President Nyerere. Sir Seretse has worked for closer links with neighboring Zambia and for close ties with the OAU, and he remains a militant defender of the Lusaka Manifesto—to which Lesotho and Swaziland are also signatories.

Relations with Swaziland appear far better; but the impression is only superficial. Continuous friction exists between Swaziland and the Republic over the latter's obstruction of Swaziland's efforts to build up its secondary industries, and over other forms of interference in the kindom's internal affairs.

All three countries are deeply dissatisfied with the working of the Customs Union and are currently engaged in talks about removing the causes of friction.[15]. The true extent of South Africa's interference in the affairs of all three countries—particularly with regard to new industries and their misgiving over Pretoria's unilateral decisions in matters affecting all the members of the Customs Union—has not yet been publicly recorded.

If South Africa failed to maintain its initial good relations with these little African states locked into its economy, it is difficult to see why it still believes it can make a success of its "outward-looking" policy towards Africa, particularly after the debacle of its major initiative to establish "a dialogue" with black Africa.[16] The moment chosen in 1971 for this initiative was exceptionally propitious since ten OAU members—with the Ivory Coast's President Houphouet-Boigny, Malawi's President Banda and Lesotho's Prime Minister Leabua Jonathan forming the nucleus of a "dialogue club"—were willing to challenge their colleagues over the issue of entering into negotiations with Pretoria. Their initiative also had sympathetic backing from Britain, France, and the United States.

The conflict over dialogue was the first decisive challenge the OAU had to face over its policy of isolating South Africa. The 1971 OAU heads of state meeting ended in a rout of the dialogue club; it broke up soon afterwards—partly because of internal differences of opinion between those, like Lesotho, who wanted a dialogue within the framework of the Lusaka Manifesto, and the Ivorian leader who favored unconditional talks about diplomatic links to safeguard peace in the continent by "keeping out the Communists." Chief Leabua later criticized Mr. Vorster for scuppering the initiative through his rigidity; this marked the beginning of deteriorating relations between the two men.

For South Africa the defeat of this initiative—which it had been carefully preparing since 1969 to promote its outward-looking policies—was especially serious for two reasons: it blocked the way towards achieving a substantial diplomatic and economic breakthrough against the African boycott; and it exploded the highly optimistic forecasts that the Republic was on the way to breaking out of its continental strait-jacket which its friends in the West felt was essential if they were to adopt a more forthright policy in support of the Republic's struggle to fight off international isolation. The result of the controversy over dialogue was to stir up even more African opposition to South Africa in countries previously lukewarm about their commitment to the struggle against *apartheid*.

The failure to understand, or to accept, the central reality about the aims and nature of South Africa's foreign policy led some governments—both Western and African—to welcome the dialogue initiative as evidence of a change of attitude towards more enlightened policies in Pretoria. American, British, and French policymakers were so far out of touch with the Africans' mood that they actually believed the dialogue debate would seriously divide the OAU and result in the development of less rigid positions towards an "enlightened" South Africa. It would be interesting to read some of the confidential documents prepared in Washington, London, and Paris on the chances of South Africa's strategy succeeding. What these Western policymakers failed to grasp—or conveniently chose to ignore—was that Mr. Vorster's outwardlooking policy (originally conceived by Dr. Verwoerd) was not a change of policy but of tactics, designed primarily to strengthen South Africa's capacity to resist change at home and to reduce the impact of international pressures. It required the combined efforts of African leaders in the Republic and in the independent African states to expose and defeat this sophisticated strategy.

Far from improving its position inside Africa through its outward-looking policies, the Republic's relations continued to decline. Apart from the worsening relations with its three small neighbors, its setbacks include the political eclipse of some of its friends like President Tsiranana of Madagascar and Dr. Busia of Ghana; the evaporation of its expectations that Zambia's President Kaunda would fall and that his successors would block the completion of the Chinese-built Tanzam railway line between Tanzania and Zambia; the continued rejection by black Rhodesians of proposals for a settlement; and, most importantly, Portugal's withdrawal from Africa.

The failure to curb the southward push of the guerrillas and the attempt to frighten Zambia into abandoning its commitment to support them led Mr. Vorster into extending his commitments further north to offer open military confrontation with the guerrillas and their supporters in the frontier states, especially Zambia and Tanzania. He had earlier committed his so-called police units (actually military units with Panhard armored cars, helicopters and aircraft) to Rhodesia in 1967. To Britain's official complaint about interference in the affairs of its colony, he simply turned a cold shoulder.

In 1967, too, he had issued the first of his blunt warnings to Zambia's President Kaunda that if he dared to carry out his threats against South Africa "we will hit him so hard that he will never forget it." He also gave an open commitment to fight against guerrillas in any area where his help was sought—meaning the former Portuguese territories.

These developments marked the beginning of a new phase in which South Africa's military presence was pushed right up to the Zambezi frontier and strengthened in the Caprivi strip, a phase that culminated in the brief military incursion into Angola. In this situation offers of dialogue were bound to fail.

The African imperative in the Republic's policies is as strong now as it has always been; but the prospects of fulfilling the necessary conditions to develop a détente between the Republic and the African continent have receded rather than improved.

Conclusions

The main thesis of this paper is that change in the Republic will come primarily through effective black militancy posed against white supremacy, which will sharpen both the internal and external contradictions in the apartheid society, and that this will increasingly weaken the status quo. In terms of this thesis international pressures have played an important role—although not as important as the role of *apartheid* itself in radicalizing black attitudes.

South Africa's present position, internally and externally, is far less secure than it was in 1948 when the rallying cry of *apartheid* brought the diehard defenders of the status quo to power. International isolation has become more than a mere threat; but external pressures have so far produced only limited results. The most important are that the Republic has been locked out of most of Africa; it has come to be considered an increasing liability to its best friends in the West; and there is much greater international understanding of, and support for, the aims of black and white opponents of *apartheid* inside the Republic and for the externally based liberation movements.

These developments have not weakened South Africa's determination or capacity to defend its system of white supremacy; its ability to defend itself economically and militarily has become stronger. Indeed, *apartheid* is being pursued with rigorous disregard for any considerations but those thought to be in the best interest of the white economy and to safeguard white power. South Africa has radically adjusted itself to changing circumstances, but without changing the fundamentals of its internal policies.

While resisting proposals to grant independence to the former British High Commission Territories in 1953, Dr. Malan was still asking:

> Can we in South Africa, who are a free and independent State, permit Negro States, Bantu States, to arise within our borders—States which are free and independent and which can lay down their policies in every respect? We cannot possibly do so.

Now these "Negro States" exist within and around the Republic's borders and they have shown that, within the limits of what is possible, they refuse to become *apartheid*'s client states. Dr. Malan's successor, Dr. Verwoerd, opened the way for the creation of Bantu states within the Republic itself. This marked no change in the bedrock policy of *apartheid;* it was the logical extension of separate development. But it also sharpened the internal contradictions by providing some kind of legal political platform which the bantustan leaders could use not as stooges but as increasingly confident articulators of black demands and grievances.

Four years after Dr. Malan had spoken, his foreign minister, Mr. Eric Louw, no longer saw any danger in the emergence of independent black states; by 1957, he actually looked upon this development as a possible impetus for South Africa to become an African power. He was enough encouraged by his contacts with Dr. Nkrumah to predict the opening of diplomatic relations with Ghana, and he confidently forecast that the African states would come to realize that *apartheid* was no threat to them and that they would all combine to "counter external influences."[17] Only six years later, the Organization of African Unity—formed largely on Nkrumah's initiative—put the continent firmly on the side against *apartheid,* and established its African Liberation Committee to give practical support to activists engaged in seeking to destroy the Republic's status quo.

A continental divide had opened up between South Africa and the rest of Africa. Talk about "minding one's own business" now falls easily only from the lips of old-style diplomats wildly out of touch with the dangerous realities of Africa; even Mr. Macmillan warned South Africa that its business was the world's concern.

Each of these major developments—the emergence of a hostile Pan-African governmental organization, growing exclusion from the African market, withdrawal from the Commonwealth, the emergence of armed violence with international backing, concentrated pressures at the UN and in other world bodies to isolate the Republic—forced on the *apartheid* regime the need to develop a counter strategy which, as has been shown, deepened the internal and external contradictions inherent in the defense of the status quo based on white supremacy.

Yet, the question still remains how much have these developments and international pressures actually influenced South Africa? It is possible to build a case on the facts that the *apartheid* system is still being ruthlessly applied and that the machine which runs it is stronger now than twenty-five years ago, to prove that the whole international effort has not only been wasted but that it has contributed to hardening rather than softening white attitudes? This is true, but only superficially.

South Africa has been changing, though not in the way those who look for significant evidence in the liberalization of Afrikaner attitudes would suggest. (These more progressive attitudes, when they occur, are of course important; but they can easily be exaggerated to suit a particular political approach.) The mood of white South Africa is complex: its public attitudes mostly exude confidence and resolute determination; but its private doubts show through in repeated warnings coming from its leaders about the dangers now confronting the Republic. To consider these elements in isolation can be completely misleading.[18]

Changes in the attitudes of whites in fact have been much less significant than the growth of militant black consciousness over the last five years; this radicalization of the black mood may, in the long run, be seen as the most important outcome of *apartheid;* it would be surprising if it were otherwise.[19]

The growing contradictions produced by a rapidly expanding economy subject to rigid restraints on the full use of black manpower have forced themselves into the center of white politics. Evidence of the failure of *apartheid* to stem the increasing growth of "black cities," or to create acceptable "homelands," can no longer be disguised. Instead of the country able to present itself to the world as a "model of stability in an otherwise unstable black continent," we now see a country where the chief of the army refers to the Republic as being in a "state of war"; where strikes by black workers have become regular occurrences; where the brutal repression of urban demonstrations is almost routine; and where black leaders defiantly challenge the inequities of the white-dominated society in even more militant terms than those employed by the old Congress leaders.

How many of these changes would have occurred even without international involvement is arguable. There can be no serious doubts, however, that if South Africa had not been forced into the center of the international stage, or if the OAU and the United Nations had decided to give a lower priority to the affairs of the Republic, the morale of the black and white opponents of the regime would have been considerably lower. Some would see this as evidence of the fact that the opposition in South Africa has been encouraged by outside support—especially from Africa; others would say they have been incited.

What positive evidence is there to show a more direct causal relationship between international pressures and changes of attitudes or of policies? The evidence can be found in two places: Namibia and the world of sports.

If it were not for the role of the United Nations and the International Court of Justice at The Hague, there is not the slightest doubt that South West Africa would long ago have been absorbed into the Republic as a fifth province. When the Rev. Michael Scott first went to the United Nations in 1947 as the emissary of the Herero Chief, Hosea Kukako, he found it hard to get a hearing to prevent General Smuts from carrying through his policy of taking over South West Africa. If ever there seemed to be a lost cause this seemed to be it. But the patient efforts and gradually increasing pressures developed by the Namibians themselves to involve the international community more actively in the future of the Trust Territory, culminated in 1966 in the General Assembly agreeing by 114 votes to 2 (South Africa and Portugal) with 3 abstentions (Britain, France and

Malawi) to terminate South Africa's mandate, to declare Namibia independent. Not only was South Africa stopped in its tracks by the UN, but it found itself in the dock with almost no support to defend its illegal occupation before the World Court; an action which in the end it lost. Although the world community had not been able to agree on means for enforcing its decision, the result of its activities was to strengthen the position of SWAPO and to encourage Namibians to adopt a militantly defiant stand against the Republic so that today the Vorster regime is compelled at least to go through the motions of negotiating with the UN, whereas when the Afrikaner Nationalists first came to power their declared aim was to annex the territory without any discussions at the UN.[20]

The success of the campaign to isolate South Africa in the world of sports shows that when South Africans are directly affected by collective international action they are not nearly as inflexible as is usually supposed. Since athletics—next to the commitment to maintain white supremacy and to expand the economy—is the third most important element in the lives of white South Africans, it was the most obvious point for the testing of their resistance to change.

In 1962 when Dennis Brutus, poet and militant, helped launch the South Africa Non-Racial Olympic Committee (as it was then called), many believed this action was the dream of a poet rather than the practical politics of a militant campaigner.[21] Yet, only ten years later with the help of Chris de Broglio and a handful of supporters, and assisted by Peter Hain's "Stop the Springboks" campaign, Brutus's idea had succeeded not only in isolating South Africa from world sports, but also in bringing about changes in white attitudes which have divided even militant Afrikaners from the government they support.

In an attempt to retrieve its position in world sports, the Vorster regime has agreed to certain changes which are in direct conflict with the strict application of *apartheid* in all other aspects of national life. Now, for example, it is permissible for black sportsmen to wear Springbok colors; "international sport" with mixed competitors is allowed—but not yet "multiracial" sport: another of the Republic's growing contradictions.[22]

White sportsmen—formerly conspicuous by their commitment to keeping politics out of sports—are now openly challenging the government in their efforts to promote interracial events which, if they were to become accepted practice, would entitle South Africa to be readmitted to international sporting events.

The significance of the sports campaign is that when white South Africans were actually confronted for the first time with effective action to exclude them from the international community, they changed their attitudes quickly and, in some respects, radically. If they have not yet been able to get the South African government to capitulate completely to their demands to take politics out of sports, a reversal from their earlier demand to keep sports out of politics, it is not because of their own unwillingness to cross the color barrier but thanks to the effectiveness of the Broederbond's campaign to pressure Mr. Vorster into refusing to go as far as even he was willing to go.[23]

The challenge over sports is the most immediate refutation of the Kennan type of argument; it shows that at this crucial level of social activity white South Africans did not become more, but significantly less, resistant to world pressures. This is, of course, a far cry from suggesting that they would be equally flexible if it came to pressures to abandon white supremacy; they wouldn't. But then nothing short of shaking the white citadel to its foundations by an effective black challenge stands any chance of producing meaningful change.

Those who believe it is possible to achieve fundamental changes—not just ameliorative reforms—by making it easier and less dangerous for white South Africa to remain entrenched behind its siege mentality have not yet reached first base in understanding the South African situation.

Notes

1. This description was first used by the progovernment newspaper *Die Burger* after the Sharpeville shootings in 1960.
2. Colin Legum and Margaret Legum, *South Africa: Crisis for the West* (London and New York, 1964), pp. 6ff.
3. Republic of South Africa, House of Assembly Debates, 10 April 1961, col. 4184-85, and 5 February 1965, col. 610-11, quoted by Gail-Maryse Cockram in *Vorster's Foreign Policy* (Pretoria: Academice, 1970), pp. 13-14.
4. No single member of the UN has failed to join in condemnations of *apartheid*; even Portugal has disassociated itself from South Africa's racial policies.
5. George F. Kennan, "Hazardous Courses in South Africa," *Foreign Affairs*, 49 (January 1971).
6. Republic of South Africa, House of Assembly Debates, 25 January 1966, cols. 46-70.
7. For example, Mr. Vorster justified opening diplomatic relations with Malawi in 1967 on the ground that it was necessary to prevent the communists from cutting Africa in two. "That is why I found it necessary to establish diplomatic relations with Malawi" (Republic of South Africa, House of Assembly debates, 23 April 1969, cols. 4577-78.
8. For a useful discussion of this question, see Robert Molteno, *Africa and South Africa* (London: The Africa Bureau, 1971).
9. *Africa Contemporary Record 1972-73* (London, 1973), p. 384.
10. Republic of South Africa, House of Assembly Debates, 6 June 1961, cols. 7378-79.
11. Remarks to the American Society of Newspaper Editors, Washington, D.C., 16 April 1969; as reproduced in *Dean Acheson on the Rhodesia Question* (Washington, D.C.: Rhodesian Information Office, 1969), p. 30.

12. (Cape Town) *Cape Times,* 12 September 1973.

13. Republic of South Africa, House of Assembly Debates, 9 March 1960, col. 3019.

14. *Africa Contemporary Record, 1971-72,* (London, 1972), p. B305.

15. Cf. South Africa's "Good Neighbour" relations with Botswana, Lesotho, and Swaziland; Africa Bureau Fact Sheet 31 in *X-Ray on Southern Africa* (London, October 1973).

16. For a full account see Colin Legum, *Dialogue: Africa's Great Debate, Africa Contemporary Record Current Affairs Series* (London 1972).

17. Fact Sheet Paper 33 (April 1957); South African Information Services.

18. Cf. Colin Legum and Margaret Legum, *South Africa: Crisis for the West* (London and New York, 1964), p. 74ff.

19. For the growth of African black consciousness, see *Africa Contemporary Record 1970-71,* pp. B489ff; Ibid., *1971-72,* pp. B330ff; Ibid. *1972-73,* pp. B367ff. Also see Peter Randall; *A Taste of Power* (Johannesburg, 1973).

20. For a fuller account see Colin Legum: *The United Nations and Southern Africa,* Institute for the Study of International Organization (Falmer, Brighton: University of Sussex, 1970.)

21. Dennis Brutus, "Year of the Olympics;" *Africa Contemporary Record 1968-69,* (London, 1969). pp. 59-63.

22. For the latest position of sports in South Africa see Africa Bureau Fact Sheet 26 in *X-Ray on South Africa.* (London, March 1973).

23. *Africa Contemporary Record 1972-73* (London, 1973), pp. B398-99.

Chapter 10

Foreign Investment in South Africa

Reinier Lock

A South African cabinet minister once lamented that his country was "the skunk of the world," and it is certainly true that the public stance of the Western governments toward South Africa reflects the odium in which that country is generally held. But the economic relationships between South Africa and many Western nations belie their attitude of political disdain. The volume of foreign investment in South Africa is growing steadily, and the proliferating economic links between the South African and Western economies inevitably have an affect both on the prosperity and stability of the Republic, and on the willingness of the respective investor nations to give teeth to a principled offensive against *apartheid*.

The controversy over foreign investment in South Africa has lasted for more than a decade and seems likely to persist for many years to come. There is no question that the substantial involvement of foreign capital has significant direct and indirect effects on South Africa's social and political system, a fact which must raise many serious moral and practical questions. And because corporate investors are at least potentially answerable to stockholders, consumers, and government, they offer a target for critics and pressure groups that are otherwise virtually impotent to effect change in the policies of a distant country.

Throughout the Western world there is an increasing demand for greater corporate accountability to the public interest. Corporate involvement in South Africa has frequently been cited as the outstanding example of the way in which these private institutions are able to depart at an international level from the prevailing political morality, often doing so in a manner and to a degree that would not be countenanced at home. At the same time, the issue of corporate investment has become a central theme in the international campaign against *apartheid,* and criticisms of Western involvement have become a recurrent feature of debates in the United Nations and other international fora.

The controversy, though complex in its details, revolves around a single dilemma: should foreign investors attempt to disengage from South Africa—or should they maintain and even increase their role in the South African economy, perhaps using their influence to erode the *apartheid* system? Given the necessary commitment and determination, either of these strategies could be put into effect within an acceptably short period of time. The issue consequently poses an immediate moral and political challenge to the corporations concerned, and to the societies in which they are based.

To assess the virtues of these policy alternatives, we must look at the role played by foreign capital in the South African economy, at the various interests involved in the controversy, and at the arguments that have been proposed to justify either course of action.

The Role of Foreign Investment

Foreign investment, British in particular, has been fundamental to South Africa's economic development ever since the country's transition from a purely agricultural economy in the nineteenth century. It was largely the capital and enterprise of British and other European fortune-seekers that opened up and developed the diamond and gold mines, most of which were located in the essentially rural Boer republics—inconveniently for the hated "uitlanders," as the Boers termed the foreigners. When the "inconvenience" became overwhelming, British military power overthrew the republics in the Boer War, and British colonization assured the flow of Western European (and later, American) capital and technology into the development of South Africa's modern industrial economy. It was on this basis that huge mining consortiums such as the Anglo-American corporation grew up, locked centrally into the British and American investment markets.

Almost every major economic development in South Africa was generated by this combination of British, American, and other foreign investment and expertise until the government's crucial moves of state capitalism in the late thirties. These initiatives, notably in the iron and steel industries, allowed the economy to take off into a stage of partially self-generating growth that was no longer entirely dependent on foreign investment. Reliance on foreign capital was further lessened by the rapid growth of local enterprise in which the control of investment capital shifted to South Africa.

When the Afrikaner Nationalist party came to government in 1948, it assumed greater local control of the economy. Harboring Boer War and Great Depression resentment against foreign and local English-language business interests alike, the new regime was determined that foreign investment should continue only on South Africa's own terms: it was to be directed wherever possible toward the political ends of *apartheid* and away from the possibility of foreign influence in domestic policies. While strategic new economic advances by foreign enterprise were not discouraged, they were generally executed in close collaboration with government agencies; where foreign initiatives threatened locally controlled strategic enterprises (as was the case with the Klipfontein munitions factory in 1963) they were headed off. Many new manufacturing plants, most notably those in the automobile industry, were required to progressively increase the "local content" of their product. In this new era of Afrikaner self-assertion, Afrikaans entrepreneurs such as Anton Rupert, magnate of the Rothman cigarette empire, broke through into big business for the first time. New Afrikaner enterprise in manufacturing and banking began to challenge the economic establishment, hitherto dominated by English South Africans and their international allies.

Yet as late as 1960, the profound significance of foreign capital in South Africa's economy and polity was dramatically affirmed in the wake of the Sharpeville massacre of black protestors. Fearing that South Africa was on the brink of revolution, Western investors panicked and withdrew liquid investments as quickly as possible. The flight of capital threw South Africa into a short-lived but serious recession, starkly underlining the economy's potential vulnerability to the whims of the foreign investor. The government was obliged to make some local political concessions—later withdrawn when stability returned—and it abandoned its earlier tolerance for the free movement of capital. Rigid controls, which are still in force today, were placed on capital leaving the country.

The fact that the economy recovered so rapidly and entered a new era of remarkable growth in 1965 does not negate this vulnerability. A major factor in the recovery was the continued confidence of most of the older Western investors, especially those with established or expanding plants in South Africa. United States financiers organized a $150 million loan from the International Monetary Fund, and U.S. banks, led by Chase Manhattan, extended a $40 million "revolving credit" agreement to help South

Africa out of its balance of payment difficulties. The largest U.S. investor in South Africa, mining magnate Charles Engelhard, formed the American South African Corporation to attract investment back into the country. All these actions provided a crucial token of confidence and greatly helped restore South Africa's international credit. The end result of the Sharpeville crisis, ironically, was to lock foreign investment more irretrievably into the South African economy.

Today there is a high level of cooperation between government and big business, both local and foreign, in achieving an overriding common goal: a thriving economy based largely on the maintenance of the status quo. Most disagreements, in fact, stem from changes that result from the policy of "separate development"; in particular, the regime is frequently and strongly criticized for threatening the supply of cheap black labor by constantly repatriating workers to their "homelands." For this reason there is still some distrust of big business, even Afrikaner big business, on the part of the government, but the joint enterprise between the two is otherwise working quite well. The government's general preparedness to avoid advances in "separate development" that might hinder economic growth resolves most disputes.

The South African economy of the late seventies based as it is on an abundance of raw materials and of cheap labor, is vigorous and, in the largely amoral climate of international finance, extremely attractive. The volume of foreign investment is considerable, and the rate of investment has shown no signs of slackening since the post-Sharpeville recovery.

By the end of the last decade, total foreign investment had topped the $7 billion dollar mark, increasing by 70 percent in the years 1965-70 alone. During those years foreign investment added, on average, 11 percent to the gross domestic investment—a rate that, taken alone could double total investment every eight or nine years. Foreign investment stepped up South Africa's annual foreign liabilitiy increase rate from an average of 3.4 percent in 1956-67 to 14.2 percent in 1972. Despite one or two years of economic overheating, this impressive acceleration has continued in the present decade. In 1971, net capital inflow in South Africa reached an all-time record of nearly $1 billion. Of the total foreign investment in South Africa, 88 percent is privately owned, and some 73.6 percent is direct investment—that is, in new enterpises rather than stocks or shares. This is a fact of potential importance, since the direct investor, unlike the stockholder, has a sufficient degree of direct control of the investment to materially influence company policies.

The Sterling Area still has the major share of foreign investment in South Africa—58 percent, or about $4.8 billion, in 1970. Nearly all this capital is British; but after a remarkable growth of some 700 percent during the sixties, the British share of investment is declining relative to that of Europe—now 24 percent—and to that of the dollar area—now over 15 percent. Current Western European and American investment is proceeding at a much faster rate than the British, but Britain still has substantial interests in a quarter of South Africa's top one hundred companies—twelve of which are direct subsidiaries of British firms.

The British stake in South Africa is of considerable importance to the domestic British economy; it accounts for about 9 percent of total overseas investment and 14 percent of total overseas earnings. The return on investment exceeds British investment in South Africa, and thus has a significant effect on Britain's endemic balance of payments problem. The hard facts of Britain's economic plight make it much more difficult for British than American corporations to disengage or to implement costly improvements in black wages and conditions. It is no coincidence that British companies were exposed, in a series of articles in the London *Guardian* in 1973, as paying some of the lowest wages in South Africa.

Other Western European involvement is also achieving new dimensions. From an original role as money-lenders, Swiss and German corporations are now involved in a very substantial direct investment. French investors, who until recently had negligible interests in South Africa, have been expanding their holdings rapidly throughout this decade. France has plugged important gaps left by Britain and the United States, which have joined the U.N. embargo on the sale of offensive weapons to South Africa (although such equipment as "light jet aircraft," very useful against guerillas, still gets in). French arms, aircraft, and technical assistance are vital in developing South Africa's military effectiveness. A secret West German agreement on nuclear cooperation with South Africa was exposed in 1975 and fell through in consequence, but there are strong rumours of a nuclear deal between South Africa, which has very large uranium deposits, and France. Given the contempt that France displays for international opinion and the utter cynicism of French foreign policy, this persistent rumor may prove well-founded. A three way oil-uranium-technology axis between France, South Africa, and Iran is also a distinct possibility.

United States investment has grown from $140 million in 1950 to $1.46 billion by the end of 1974; it almost doubled in the latter half of the last decade, and a massive $289 million was added in 1974 alone. The rate of investment has been increasing sharply—by 20 percent in 1973 and again in 1974. At present, over three hundred American corporations have investments in South Africa. The names of many of them are found in *Fortune's* annual list of the top five hundred industrial corporations in the United States—the investors include twelve of the top fifteen companies, and fifty-five of the top hundred. Many corporate names that are household words in the United States are household words in South Africa too—Mobil, Ford, General Motors, Firestone, General Electric, ITT, IBM, and even Holiday Inns.

American investment has been crucial to the main growth sectors of the economy in the sixties and seventies. Ford, General Motors and Chrysler have led the way in the development of an indigenous automobile industry, and provide 60 percent of the cars in the country today. American companies are also in the forefront of oil exploration in South Africa. Oil is the one natural resource that South Africa lacks, and a guaranteed supply of the commodity has been a major goal of the regime since the first pressure for economic sanctions against South Africa started at the United Nations in the early sixties. The UN has tried to mount an oil embargo against South Africa, but the attempt has failed as a result of the total lack of Western cooperation. Since the discovery of small oil deposits off the South African coast in 1969, twenty U.S. oil companies have joined in a major oil hunt, providing an experience, expertise and technology that would take South Africa years to muster. Four U.S. companies have established refineries in South Africa; Mobil and Caltex now refine over half the country's imported oil.

United States corporations have also been dominant in other growth areas that advance the industrial base of the economy—including petrochemicals, steel, computers, and nuclear energy. American technical assistance and an American reactor have made possible South Africa's development of new uranium enrichment techniques, and the country is now believed to be fully capable of making an atomic bomb. American investment has been particularly important in South Africa's drive for economic and military self-sufficienty—a drive which, if ultimately successful, will further buttress the regime through its strategic, political, and even psychological consequences.

By American standards, none of the large corporations has really substantial holdings. General Motors, probably the largest single U.S. investor, has only 4 percent of its overseas and 1 percent of its total operations in South Africa. Yet to the Republic, even so small a stake is significant—GM is the country's eleventh largest company in terms of total assets. South African holdings account for just over 1 percent of total U.S. direct foreign investment, but this investment means far more to South Africa than it does to the companies concerned. Return on investments has generally run to well over 20 percent (even after a 41 percent tax to the South African government). This figure compares highly favorably with a worldwide average return on U.S. investment of about 11 to 12 percent.

The Conflict of Interests

An inherent limitation on corporate willingness to improve employment practices is the fact that low wages and tight control of black workers' industrial bargaining are the cornerstones of the high profitability of foreign investment in South Africa. Yet substantial improvements in these two areas are the very minimum demanded of investors. The difficulty of reconciling the pursuit of profit with the erosion of *apartheid* is doubtless why American corporations have been so tardy in improving the position of black workers in South Africa; much of their effort has been channeled instead into sophisticated public relations campaigns on the home front. Most of the thrust for more enlightened employment practices, in fact, is coming from local South African managers, who foresee industrial unrest ahead. A market survey in 1969 revealed that most American businessmen in South Africa approved of *apartheid;* only 20 percent expressed opposition to it, and only 10 percent felt it was "altogether incorrect."

Only the most intense pressure in the United States, filtered down through head office directives, is likely to generate substantial reform. Perhaps the best that might be expected is the development among the corporations of a form of enlightened self-interest—exercised even at the expense of short-term profitability in order to ensure the long-term security of investments. Such security implies the maintenance of industrial peace and political stability, through industrial concessions if need be, to ensure the continuance of the present power structure. An approach of this kind is not far out of line with that adopted by South African businessmen, or even of the government itself, whose flexibility and pragmatism is often underestimated.

Minor or gradual changes, however, are unacceptable to most of the interests that are calling for an end to corporate involvement in South Africa. And the intensity of their campaign is growing. No longer confined to moral protestations by churches, student groups, and special lobbies, it has finally reached the upper echelons of the corporations and the federal government. The issue has attracted the attention of the media. It became a major concern of the Carter administration. Black American organizations have become involved. A rash of investigating teams from churches, foundations, Congress, colleges, and even the corporations themselves has visited South Africa. The picture that has emerged, and been endorsed by many impeccably "establishment" sources, is one of American businessmen making full use of South Africa's exploitative wage structure, discriminating between black and white at every turn, and profiting mightily by it.

The usual response of the corporations to this kind of criticism is that the *apartheid* laws give them no option to act in any other way. This is often simply untrue. There are no legal or, in many cases, labor union barriers to paying a living wage, or to increasing fringe benefits, or to creating "separate but equal" facilities. Even when such barriers as job reservation do theoretically exist, they are often waived by the government in the face of a well-argued application; in fact, over 70 percent of such applications are approved. Many of South Africa's racial laws function under considerable adminstrative discretion, with a surprising leeway for flexibility and negotiation. The fact is that most American businessmen have never bothered to investigate the possibility of change.

One of the early attempts to ameliorate the conditions of black laborers in South Africa was the much-publicized program of the Polaroid corporation. Under strong pressure from its black American workers, Polaroid sent a multiracial team to investigate its South African operations. The team—or most of them—concluded that Polaroid could best serve the interests of black South Africans by remaining within the country and trying to improve working conditions through wage hikes, new fringe benefits, and educational assistance. This conclusion was based largely on the finding that local black workers preferred improvements in their position to company withdrawal, which would have put them out of work. The fact that some members of the team were less than happy with the report was lost in a smokescreen of public relations advertising as Polaroid justified its continued involvement to the American public.

In one sense Polaroid's initiative, cosmetic or not, was a real advance: it was the first clear admission of corporate complicity in *apartheid* and corporate responsibility to do something about it. Other corporations, including IBM, General Motors, and Mobil, all announced in rapid succession that they too would be changing their employment practices; they even made proclamations about equal pay for equal work, disingenuous though this seems in the context of a racially stratified employment system. It is possible that some real changes may come about, setting off a spiral of rising aspirations among South African blacks that will be difficult to resist. It is equally possible that the corporations' promises are merely a sop to public pressure, and that any changes will be largely symbolic and designed to pacify a domestic constituency rather than improve the conditions of black South Africans.

In another sense, however, Polaroid's initiative may not be an advance at all. The triumph of the public relations of Polaroid and the other "enlightened" corporations is they have confined debate to the issue of their employment practices, totally diverting attention from the more profound question of whether they should be involved in South Africa at all.

Will their presence, even with improving employment practices, finally help break down *apartheid*? Or will it serve to strengthen and maintain the status quo, leaving the corporations as continuing accomplices in a still durable *apartheid* system? These questions remain largely unaired and unanswered in the corridors of corporate and governmental power.

At the executive and legislative levels of national government, the question of total disengagement is scarcely raised. Congressional interest in corporate involvement has centered around the House Subcommittee on Southern Africa, chaired by black congressman, Charles Diggs. Like Robert Kennedy in 1966, Diggs began with an initial inclination toward withdrawal, but later changed his approach to one of requiring socially responsible corporate practices: that is, the same standards of equal opportunity should be applied in South Africa as are required by law at home.

Adopting much the same approach, the State Department issued in 1963 a "guideline" booklet detailing the improvements that U.S. firms could and should make in South Africa. The poverty datum line is "suggested" as the absolute minimum for wages; the minimum effective level—50 percent higher—is recommended as being more acceptable; and a "fair wage" is offered as a "reasonable goal." Where possible, the department urged, equal pay should be given for equal work. Rather more boldly, the document urges "strong leadership" to "change the institutional framework when the framework limits or threatens progress." In other words, the confines of the system should not be accepted as absolute: if necessary, they should be stretched and perhaps even broken. This suggestion reaches the hub of the Polaroid controversy. If firms do no more than take up the slack in the *apartheid* system, then they can scarcely be considered active agents in changing it, as Polaroid claims to be doing. Unsurprisingly, Mobil reacted strongly to the State Department suggestion, deeming it "unrealistic."

Should the corporations stay in South Africa, and can they achieve any measure of reform by doing so? Or ought they to get out, and will their doing so bring any benefits to South African blacks? Let us look at the arguments for each position.

Arguments for Continued Investment

The "stay-in" approach is presented in two rather different versions. The first argues that continued investment will benefit all South Africans, because economic growth will inevitably generate not only prosperity but also the breakdown of the *apartheid* system—primarily for the reason that a thriving, high-technology modern economy cannot be based on an ascriptive division of labor. The second version is a more activist one: corporations can and must use their influence to bring about reforms that will undermine and perhaps contribute to the destruction of *apartheid*.

The first approach was originally put by the more progressive elements in the South African business community, who detected signs of growing black earning power and some breakdowns in the racial laws that hinder both black and general economic development. Economic growth, they argued, was already creating scarcities of skilled labor; the demands of the economy would inevitably create upward mobility for blacks and smash artificial *apartheid* barriers in the process. Obviously, this approach presents a very attractive panacea to anyone profiting from the South African economy yet feeling or purporting to feel moral qualms about the inequities of *apartheid*. The impersonal hand of economic growth will cure all ills, given time; and the faster the growth, the shorter that time will be. The logical conclusion is that investors should pour more money into South Africa, not less. Withdrawal, it was argued, would merely create massive black unemployment and do little to bring about a more just society. This viewpoint was soon picked up by foreign corporate public relations personnel and disseminated abroad. The approach had the added advantage that it did not offend local managers of U.S. firms, since it did not require them to make any reforms—they were merely to continue making money, and the more of it the better.

An analysis of the facts, however, gives little support to the view that economic growth per se will undermine *apartheid*. Neither the economic nor the political history of the prosperous years since 1948, when the Nationalist party first took office, show any significant black gains. Politically, the years of Nationalist rule have been characterized by increasing racial separation, authoritarian control, and outright repression. White economic prosperity has been accompanied not by political liberalization but by a frightening trend toward totalitarianism.

Far from removing the already staggering gap between black and white incomes, economic growth has widened it substantially. In the short run, the economic barriers of *apartheid*—job reservation, apprenticeship restrictions, and repression of black unions—serve to prevent substantial black gains. While blacks have been slowly taking over some skilled work, this has usually meant a spectacular drop in the wage rate for the job, with accompanying savings to the employer. Since virtually the entire economy relies heavily on the cheapness of black labor, the need to hold down black wages has seemed utterly imperative to the whites.

There is little sign that even in the very long run—and some proponents believe that a period of fifty years or so is a realistic time span in which to test their hypothesis—the government's cheap labor policy will break down. But fifty years—or even twenty or ten—is surely an unacceptably long waiting period for any genuine promotor of black interests, let alone the blacks themselves. Moreover, the implementation of the policy of "separate development" may be so advanced in the next few decades that forces within the South African economy will be largely bypassed. "Separate development" aims at creating a state of permanent migratory labor between independent black "bantustans" and an industrially developed "white" South Africa. What job reservation and influx control achieve at present—a supply of cheap labor that can be turned on and off like a faucet—"separate development" is likely to achieve in the long run.

To point to the historical development of the Western economies as a prototype is therefore misleading. A closer analogy would be those authoritarian states that have experienced economic growth without allowing political liberalization or a more equitable distribution of wealth. What this version of the "stay-in" argument really calls for is a more efficient economy in which wealthier blacks are a useful ingredient and a nice, but not essential, humanitarian by-product. The argument has less to do with equality and freedom in South African than with making the status quo more stable and efficient.

The second version of the "stay-in" argument, the reformist or "constructive engagement" approach, is a relatively new phenomenon that has arisen as a response to intense domestic pressure on foreign corporations, particularly in the United States and Britain. The assumption is that corporate investors can help change the *apartheid* system, both by changing their employment practices and by applying pressure to the regime.

Like the earlier version of the "stay-in" approach, the argument looks suspiciously like an ex post facto rationalization of existing involvement. It has obviously pragmatic corporate aims to avert pressure at home and to provide some means of handling the rising discontent of the black South African labor force. Skeptical as one might be about the motives, however, the policy does promise progressive action that may have some short-run benefits to black workers.

The real test of the "reformers" is whether they understand and are prepared to take the measures required to undermine the *apartheid* system. To date, they have promised and partially implemented a few improvements—some cosmetic, some real. But these will not change *apartheid*. They will not even annoy the government. What will be needed, if corporate measures are to have the promised effect, is sustained and concerted pressure on the regime to make significant structural changes, irrespective of their effect on white supremacy. Serious efforts in this direction might include:

1. Open or covert financial and moral support of black political opposition. There is ample precedent for such a step, of which ITT's contributions to opponents of Salvador Allende's government in Chile is the best-known example.

2. Pressure for black industrial rights and for recognition of black unions, and insistence on effective black representation in industrial bargaining.

3. Promotion of black employees coupled with affirmative action hiring to all positions, regardless of white labor union opposition or government disapproval.

4. Concerted efforts and lobbying in South Africa to have racially restrictive economic laws and regulations changed, and a willingness to ignore the law if it is not changed.

5. Use of skill and expertise, especially in areas relevant to South Africa's drive for military and economic self-sufficiency, as leverage for political change.

6. Strategic investments in areas that will benefit blacks and increase black economic and political stability and power.

7. The provision of a range of services and facilities for black workers and their families—decent residential communities; long-term, secure employment; education that offers an alternative to the system of the "Bantu Education" department; and medical facilities.

If the corporations are not prepared to attempt these or similar reforms, then their argument is without real substance and constitutes a mere rationalization for their continuing enjoyment of the fruits of *apartheid*. It is not enough for the corporations to cry that such steps are "impractical"; American corporations have never displayed a reluctance in the past to influence the domestic policies of the countries in which they operate, neither have they been unwilling to seek the aid of federal government agencies in their efforts to do so. A concerted campaign by foreign investors, blessed by the U.S. government, might have a good chance of at least partial success. And willingness to undertake such a campaign would provide a genuine test of the much-proclaimed sincerity of the corporate "reformers."

If, however, those who promise reform have more limited ambitions, then it is time that they made this fact clear. Chase Manhattan's lofty promise that it will "bring all of the energy and imagination" that it commands to "expand the broad and promising horizons" of "all South Africans," for example, is surely hypocritical verbiage. The modest proposals for reform that most corporations have made constitute, at best, a plea that since they are in South Africa anyway, they may as well stay there. Their arguments hardly constitute grounds for actually increasing investments.

Arguments for Withdrawal

The essence of the arguments for withdrawal centers on the historic and continuing role of foreign investment in the South African economy. Though greatly diminished, this role remains crucial in strategic areas—nuclear development, oil exploration, and weapons production. The argument for withdrawal is thus both moral and practical. The moral component focuses on the complicity of foreign investors in one of the most repugnant social systems of the modern world. The practical component focuses on the possible effect that withdrawal, or even the threat of withdrawal, might have on *apartheid*; it is argued that the resulting damage to the economy might either force the regime to modify its policies, or create a revolutionary climate in the country.

The withdrawal argument has encountered a good deal of opposition, not all of it from those with vested interests in the status quo. The most compelling criticism is that withdrawal would in fact do nothing to change the regime's policies, but would throw large numbers of blacks out of work. Whites might regret the economic losses resulting from withdrawal, but they would regret substantial modifications to *apartheid* even more, and given the choice would rather retain their peculiar institutions. The contention that withdrawal would lead to black unemployment is one much used by the corporations, in a rather dishonest attempt to manipulate the victim's needs into a justification of the corporate role. But others with less suspect motives also oppose withdrawal on the grounds that it offers no immediately forseeable end to *apartheid*, that it would remove a potential force for reform, and that it is sheer arrogance for liberal opinion in the industrialized world to decide, on behalf of South African blacks, that a worsening of their wretched conditions might be to their long-term advantage. Unless the proponents of withdrawal can offer detailed and realistic assessments of how disengagement is likely to improve black conditions in South Africa, or enhance the prospects for a successful revolution, they risk the charge of moral posturing at the grievous expense of others.

Another argument against outright withdrawal is an essentially practical one: that given the losses corporations would face, withdrawal is highly unlikely, perhaps impossible; and that the focus on this issue displaces energies that could more usefully be directed against *apartheid* in other ways. If withdrawal is to have any real effect, it must take place not gradually or sporadically, but rather on a massive, multinational scale. Clearly, such withdrawal would require the collaboration not only of corporations but also of governments. Corporations are unlikely to accept the financial losses involved unless they can be compensated from governmental or other sources. Such a scenario is difficult to visualize, and would be more difficult still to execute.

Recognizing this problem, some proponents of withdrawal have suggested that disengagement and refusal to make further investments should be applied primarily at the strategic areas of the South African economy. If efforts were focused on firms and industries that are central to South Africa's goal of military and economic self-sufficiency, the Republic might have to sustain a delay of years, even decades, in achieving this urgent objective. Such a delay would deeply alarm the whites, for it would leave them vulnerable to the weapons of international pressure, including arms and oil embargoes.

The selective withdrawal suggestion has considerable promise, and not only because it is relatively practical. The white minority is surprisingly sensitive to tough pressure from the West—a fact that is little appreciated because that pressure has so rarely been applied. While years of internal attempts on the part of blacks did nothing to change the country's pass laws, the intense world reaction after Sharpeville did. For years sports boycotts of South Africa were opposed in the West on the grounds that they would merely harden the attitude of the whites. Yet shortly after a fairly uniform boycott was applied, South Africa was willing to field multiracial teams abroad and to allow some interracial sport at home. For a long while South Africa would not admit foreign blacks to the country; but when the black caucus in Congress mobilized for punitive action, the whites adapted readily and now allow visiting blacks to stay in all-white, luxury hotels. In short, the plausible threat of withdrawal, especially in strategic industries, might well provoke significant modifications in *apartheid*—although it would certainly not be enough to end white supremacy.

Conclusion

Each side of the debate tends to assume the conditions necessary for its strategy's success. In fact, the ideal conditions will probably never exist for either approach, and I believe that neither of them, taken in isolation, offers much prospect of bringing about major changes in the political structure of South Africa. However, adherents of each approach tend to neglect possibilities offered by the other. Most "stay-in" proponents seldom ask whether it is really possible to overturn *apartheid* without some form of revolutionary change. Most withdrawal proponents, in their anxiousness to precipitate conflict in South Africa, neglect some real evolutionary possibilities. The prospect of some fruitful interaction between the two approaches, and between evolutionary and revolutionary forces, is seldom considered, perhaps because its dynamics are so hard to predict. But there are some possibilities for change that involve this kind of interaction:

• History, if not dogma, teaches that most revolutions are initiated not by an oppressed proletariat but by a rising new class, whose aspirations are frustrated by an antiquated political and economic order. It is precisely this situation of rising but frustrated aspirations that characterizes the contemporary black South African experience. Even before the Soweto riots, it was clear that black industrial and economic conditions were starting to take center stage politically. Black industrial action may yet prove to be the cutting edge of social liberation in South Africa.

Effective "reformist" or "constructive engagement" policies by investor corporations, especially if they trigger a chain reaction of reforms by local industrialists, could provide black South Africans with the measure of full employment and economic stability they need for successful industrial bargaining and political organization. An effective reform policy by investors might do more to enhance the prospects for revolutionary change (violent or otherwise) than withdrawal, although the investors themselves may draw little comfort from this fact. Of course, the aim of "separate development" is to foreclose this possibility by keeping blacks in a state of utter economic dependence on the whites and by isolating them into a separate social and ultimately geographical realm, thus preventing the formation of the permanent urban proletariat and disaffected middle class that has historically provided the breeding ground for revolution. The "separate development" policy thus faces a race against time that it may already be losing; there are already signs that many of its professed goals are being quietly abandoned. The real question for investors—critical to the withdrawal debate but not easily answered—is whether they reduce the time to achieve revolutionary change more than they accelerate "separate development" by strengthening the *apartheid* system.

• A possibility that has been almost entirely overlooked is that investors could, if allowed to and if prepared to take the risks involved, alter the mening of "separate development." For some years, white South Africans debated whether or not they should allow "white" capital to be invested in the bantustans. The bantustans' own inability to generate capital developments is so obvious and acute that the government has finally agreed to allow "white" capital in, although under restrictive conditions. But the leaders of the new bantustans are now openly mooting the possibility of soliciting foreign investment. If "constructive engagement" is to be the policy in South Africa, investors should seriously consider expansions and relocations of existing plants into the bantustans themselves. By giving the bantustans a measure of economic independence, investors could markedly alter their dependent status and give black "nationhood" some real meaning. Many young black militants feel that a series of eight economically viable bantustans within South Africa's borders could provide as good a springboard as any for the ultimate overthrow of white supremacy in the Republic.

• A crucial element in the development of a revolutionary consciousness among black South Africans is the development of their own sense of identity and dignity. The most significant influence of the United States on South Africa has perhaps not been its dollars, but rather the impact of political comparison. Black South Africans have followed avidly the civil rights and subsequent black power movements in the United States, and the new swell of black self-assertion in South Africa is unquestionably greatly influenced by this example. U.S. involvement could accelerate the development of this consciousness by providing living examples of equality and integration; corporations could promote black South Africans to top positions and fill managerial offices with some of the new black American executives about whom they are so inordinately boastful. The presence of even a few hundred black American corporate officials, to whom the usual laws of *apartheid* could not be applied, would provide a real and provocative glimpse of the disparity between the status of blacks in the two countries.

These possibilities all involve some element of "staying in." But they will not be effective without the reality of a very convincing threat of withdrawal. Furthermore, no investments should be made that enhance South Africa's independence in strategic areas such as oil, nuclear power, and weapons development. U.S. investments in these areas should be withdrawn, and new investments should certainly be proscribed. If corporations are genuine about improving black conditions in South Africa, they should not be jeopardizing one of the West's major points of leverage. And however genuine and enlightened some corporate investors may be, their role will be negative if they act as a precursor for American military involvement—overt or clandestine—aimed at maintaining the status quo in order to protect U.S. financial interests in South Africa. Until the U.S. government is able to formulate a sensible foreign policy, corporate investment in South Africa must remain suspect. To be effective, in fact, corporate practices—whether of constructive involvement or of selective withdrawal—would probably have to be policed by government, as cor-

porations are intrinsically concerned with profits rather than people or principles and simply cannot be trusted on their own.

In short, certain conditions are essential for the success of any approach—not least the backing of a government with an intelligent foreign
policy. Moreover, no single approach will be a panacea for changing *apartheid*, if indeed outside forces will ever affect the situation that profoundly.
Most successful would be a flexible but coordinated approach, including a
credible "make changes or else" element that seeks to undermine *apartheid* on many levels. If we opt simply for continued investment or outright
withdrawal, we will probably have minimal effect on South Africa's future,
and the forces of history will pass us by.

Chapter 11

External Liberation Movements

Randall Stokes

Depending on what one reads, it is possible to form radically divergent opinions of the current state and future prospects of black resistance to the South African regime. If one reads the official organs of the liberation movements or the pronouncements of the resistance leaders in London, Lusaka, Dar es Salaam, or Addis Ababba, violent liberation often appears just around the corner. A number of respected social scientists, such as Pierre van den Berghe, have made similar prognoses.[1] The opposite view is equally prevalent and has been aptly summarized in the title of a recent work by a leading scholar of South Africa, Lewis Gann: "No Hope for Violent Liberation."[2] The purpose of this chapter is to make a sober survey of the current activity and future prospects of the exile organizations aiming at the violent liberation of South Africa.

A Brief Background on the Resistance Movements

Although the early years and development of South African resistance movements are discussed earlier in this volume, a brief review is necessary here for an understanding of the current situation. The commitment to violent liberation on the part of black leaders and organizations dates back only to the late 1950s. Until that time, black organizations were remarkable for their forbearance and pacifism. Their aspirations were for racial equality before the state and law, and their methods were those of peaceful demonstration, petition, and noble example. For most of South Africa's history, blacks have been willing to settle for gradual and evolutionary change in these directions.

A combination of dispair over the ineffectiveness of peaceful means and the stirring example of newly independent black nations to the north began to change the peaceful orientations of the South African resistance movement after 1959. Disillusionment with nonviolent protest spread as a result of the actions of the South African Police (SAP) during a series of "antipass law" demonstrations in March of 1960. The African National Congress of South Africa (ANC) and its offshoot, the Pan Africanist Congress (PAC) proclaimed 21 March (PAC) and 31 March (ANC) as antipass days, during which Africans were urged to disobey pass regulations and present themselves for arrest.

At Sharpeville, several thousand Africans answered the call and gathered unarmed at the local police station. Faced with the mass, the police panicked and fired indiscriminately into the crowd of men, women, and children. Sixty-nine were killed and many more wounded. Similar, though less brutal, events occurred in other parts of the country. Altogether, nearly a hundred Africans were killed by the SAP and many hundreds were seriously injured. No SAP fatalities or serious injuries were reported. The government justified the actions of the police and praised them for their quick response, and proceeded to ban both the ANC and the PAC on 8 April 1960. The two organizations responded first with efforts to carry on their struggle underground within South Africa, but soon assumed their current status as liberation movements in exile.

Another major factor in shifting the goals of the black movement was the "year of Africa" in 1960. During 1960, eighteen African nations achieved independence and another dozen did so in the next few years. These nations were an exciting example to the national aspirations of black South Africa. Also, the black nations offered the promise of aid and support in the liberation of South Africa, and so made violent overthrow of the regime seem a practical possibility for the first time.

South African Liberation Movements

The ANC and PAC remain the major organizations dedicated to liberating South Africa. Of the two, the ANC is older, better funded, and more widely recognized by the international community. The ANC dates from 1912, when it was established as the South African Native National

Congress.[3] From its creation until after World War II, the ANC maintained a low profile in South Africa, restricting its activities largely to resolutions and brief symbolic demonstrations. Younger members, led by Walter Sisulu, Oliver Tambo, Nelson Mandela, Robert Sobukwe, and Anton Lembede, sparked a new militancy in the 1940s which greatly accelerated the level of ANC activity. During the 1950s, the ANC embarked on a campaign for civil rights, much like that which was to later emerge in the United States. Depite often brutal repression, the ANC was able to enlist thousands of Africans in work stoppages, "sit-ins" in white facilities, and strikes. The fact that eighty-five hundred of the ten thousand persons who were requested to disobey racial regulations in the June 1952 demonstrations voluntarily went to jail is an indication of the depth of commitment mobilized by the ANC during this period.

From 1950 onwards, the ANC fell increasingly under the influence of exmembers of the outlawed South African Communist Party. In 1953, the ANC formed an alliance with several other resistance groups made up of coloureds, Indians, and whites. The Congress Alliance, as it came to be known, was dominated by Soviet-oriented communists and was able to largely determine ANC policy. This group drafted the so-called "Freedom Charter" which was to later fragment the African resistance movement. A central part of the Freedom Charter was its insistence on multiracialism, which implicitly denied the "one man one vote" principle to which many ANC members were deeply committed. "Multiracialism," as opposed to the simple majority rule of the "one man one vote" principle, represents an attempt to balance political power among racial blocks. The debate within the ANC over accepting the charter, the increasingly great influence of whites in the ANC's leadership, and mistrust of communist intentions combined to split the movement into two factions.

In 1958, a large group walked out of the Transvaal Congress and, in 1959, formally created the Pan Africanist Congress. The dominant ideology of the PAC was, and remains, African nationalism. Led by Potlako Leballo, Peter Molotsi, and Robert Sobukwe, the PAC quickly captured the loyalties of many Africans. In the brief period before their banning in 1960, the PAC organized demonstrations against the pass laws which drew great support. It was these demonstrations which led the government to outlaw both the PAC and the ANC.

Immediately after their banning, both organizations sent selected groups of members for guerrilla training in other African nations, including the UAR, Ghana, and Tanzania. In addition to these preparations for eventual guerrilla warfare, PAC members and supporters stimulated a brief period of intense antiwhite violence. Altogether the Poqo, as these groups were called, killed perhaps a dozen whites in scattered locations around the

Republic. The speed and effectiveness of SAP reactions, however, soon convinced ANC and PAC that any hope for liberation lay in the formation of armies in exile.

The Southern African Context

Before the character, activities, and prospects of these liberation armies can be assessed, some mention needs to be made of other liberation organizations in southern Africa.[4] The liberation front in Southern Africa has been a maze of competing and affiliated groups, complicated by cross-cutting international affiliations. In the outline which follows, the South African movements are placed in this larger context.

In Angola, the new government is the most successful of the organizations which engaged in armed resistance against the Portugese; it is the Moviemento Popular de Libertacao de Angola (MPLA). MPLA headquarters were in Zambia and most of its military efforts were directed against the eastern regions of Angola, thereby providing for quick retreat into Zambia. MPLA is estimated to have had from five thousand to seven thousand trained fighters in the field, and enjoyed a great deal of popular support. Along with FRELIMO's successes in north and west of Mozambique, the MPLA's domination of eastern Angola was decisive in Portugal's change of policy towards her colonies. Neither MPLA nor any of the smaller Angolan liberation groups have been directly allied to either ANC or PAC forces.

The situation in Mozambique, where the liberation movement FRELIMO (Frente de Libertacao de Mocambique) has become the new government, is far more important to the fate of South Africa. FRELIMO and its allies have over ten thousand trained guerrillas with active combat experience. Furthermore, FRELIMO has given support to ANC and PAC in the past. The PAC, for instance, has shared infiltration routes through Mozambique with the Mozambique liberation forces, and FRELIMO has reportedly assisted in the training of ANC guerrillas. It is widely predicted that the liberation movement in Mozambique will intensify its aid to the South African resistance movements now that it has come to power.

The struggle for Zimbabwe (Rhodesia) is also highly significant for South Africa. There are two major revolutionary movements, ZANU (Zimbabwe African National Union) and ZAPU (Zimbabwe African Peoples' Union). These groups have several thousand trained fighters. Thus far, their military success has been limited. From 1967 to the present, ZANU and ZAPU forces have periodically infiltrated from Zambia and engaged in skirmishes with Rhodesian forces, but they control no secure territory within Rhodesia. They do, however, appear to be gaining greater support among the African population of Rhodesia and seem likely to increase their level of activity in the future if efforts to achieve a settlement with the white government are not successful.

Rhodesia is significant for South Africa's future in two primary ways. The first is symbolic. With the Portuguese withdrawal from Africa completed, Rhodesia is now the only other white government in southern Africa. If Rhodesia were to fall because of increased vulnerability along its long eastern border with Mozambique, this would be a psychological blow to South Africa. Second, and more important, the survival of a white regime in Salisbury is strategically useful to South Africa. Rhodesia is now an effective buffer against infiltration, and her conflict with Zambia serves to make Zambia economically dependent upon South Africa. Zambia's efforts to participate in United Nations sanctions against Rhodesia have forced her to rely heavily upon South Africa for transportation and essential imports.

Also, there is a close alliance between the ANC and ZAPU which would seem to assure a strong position for ANC should ZAPU come to power. Since 1967, ANC forces have fought alongside ZAPU guerrillas in the north and west of Rhodesia under a unified military command. Both groups profess to see the liberation of Southern Africa as a single effort and have pledged to continue fighting until both Rhodesia and South Africa are liberated.

Despite the possible threats which would be posed by a black dominated Rhodesia, South Africa has increasingly qualified her support of Smith's regime in recent years. Prime Minister Vorster has made it evident in public statements that he has no intention of allowing South Africa to become embroiled in an endless war in Rhodesia. Neither does he wish by his military support of Rhodesia, discreet though it is, to attract renewed world attention to South Africa's own racial policies. For these reasons, Vorster has put considerable pressure upon Smith to reach a compromise with Rhodesia's black leaders, even though this would lead to majority rule in the near future. Part of Vorster's change of policy is undoubtedly due to the realization by South African military strategists that a ring of poor and politically weak black nations around South Africa may serve her interests just as well as "expensive" white allies. At the least, South Africa appears determined to play a more passive role in Rhodesia's conflicts than has been the case in the past. Since mid-1974, South African soldiers and police have played no part in the sporadic antiguerrilla activities of the Rhodesian forces.

Nonetheless, it does not appear likely that South Africa will completely abandon Rhodesia should compromise fail and fighting begin again in earnest. South Africa seems prepared to extend economic support, as she has done throughout the international boycott of Rhodesia. As of 1975, two new rail lines from Rhodesia to South Africa have been completed with South African aid. These are intended to serve as the main arteries for Rhodesian trade, should Rhodesian traffic through Mozambique be blocked. Furthermore, Vorster is under intense pressure from the right wing of his own party and from splinter parties not to "betray" Rhodesian whites. On the whole, South Africa is likely to continue a somewhat reluctant support of Rhodesia's struggles against ZANU and ZAPU.

It should be noted here that even the collapse of the Smith regime is not likely to improve materially the prospects of the South African liberation forces. Any government emerging from such a collapse is apt to be a fragile affair and more concerned with domestic troubles than with aiding the liberation of South Africa. As will be seen, the forces which seem destined to make a black Mozambique no threat to South Africa apply equally well to Rhodesia.

In Namibia (South West Africa) there is only one currently active movement, SWAPO (South West Africa People's Organization). Although SWAPO has over a thousand trained soldiers, its military activity has been negligible. The few engagements that have taken place with South African forces have been largely due to accident and chance encounters. Such success as SWAPO has achieved has been through less direct action as, for example, in stimulating the Ovambo miners' strike of 1972 which led to significant concessions by the government. In addition to the formidable forces arrayed against them, SWAPO has been hindered by a lack of support among many Ovambo. Until very recently, South Africa's efforts to stem Ovambo political discontent with economic and other favors have been relatively successful. Growing unrest among Ovambo miners, however, suggests these tactics are losing their effectiveness.

Neither ANC nor PAC has established strong ties with SWAPO, despite the fact that they are fighting essentially the same enemy. The only existing formal link emerged from the Russian-sponsored "Khartoum Conference" of 1969, which was attended both by SWAPO and by representatives of the joint ANC-ZAPU military command. The resulting alliance has not produced any joint action and remains purely symbolic.

In addition to these liberation movements, there are several other international forces with an interest in southern Africa. Among these is the Organization of African Unity (OAU), a loose and sometimes factious association of African states, which established an African Liberation Committee (ALC) in 1963. The ALC's role in the struggles in southern Africa has three facets. Most importantly, the ALC extends a highly influential formal recognition to resistance groups that meet certain criteria, particularly those of demonstrated success in the field or a popular following.

Recognition by the ALC provides a group with legitimacy which is widely recognized in the international community and which is useful in obtaining a public hearing and funds. With the exception of SWAPO, all of the organizations mentioned above have been long recognized by the ALC. Recently, however, ALC withdrew its sanction from PAC because of the organization's ineffectiveness and continued refusal to form a united front with ANC. A second function of the ALC is to provide the resistance movements with funds raised from a levy on member states. The total funding by the ALC, however, constitutes only about ten per cent of the resistance groups' expenditures, largely because of refusal by many states to pay their full annual levy. The final significant activity of the ALC is to mediate the endemic dissension between competing liberation groups. A condition of OAU financial assistance is the willingness to establish "common fronts" with other liberation forces that have the same target area. The success of the ALC in this endeavor has been minimal, although several "alliances of principle" have resulted.

A number of nations and agencies outside Africa are also important to the struggle in southern Africa. The most significant by far is the USSR, in terms of training, material support, and ideological guidance. ANC, SWAPO, ZAPU, FRELIMO, and MPLA have received the bulk of their weapons and funds directly from the Soviet Union. With the possible exception of the ANC, which remains relatively western oriented, each of these groups is heavily influenced in its policies and external relationships by the USSR.

For the past decade, the Chinese Peoples Republic has competed with Russia for influence over the various resistance movements. Even though some groups, such as the ANC, receive funding from both the USSR and CPR, there is strong pressure upon the liberation armies to affiliate themselves predominatly with one or the other. At the present time, PAC and ZANU have rejected Soviet ties in favor of Chinese support and guidance. As Russia moves closer to the West, it is likely that the more radical orientation of the CPR will find favor among the resistance movements.

Cuba, North Korea, and other communist nations have also provided various kinds of support. Cuba intervened militarily in the Angolan conflict, and Cuban troops fought pitched battles with the South Africans in southern Angola. Support from communist nations has otherwise been limited to guerrilla training. Virtually all of the active liberation groups have members trained in both Cuba and North Korea. Cuban political theory and military strategy appear to be particularly attractive at present.

The Contemporary Situation

To the present, neither ANC nor PAC has achieved any appreciable success in its war against South Africa. Neither controls any territory within South Africa and they have engaged in only fleeting and largely disastrous skirmishes with South African forces. In 1969 and 1970, for example, a total of thirteen SAP officers was killed in Rhodesia, Mozambique, Angola and South West Africa. From 1970 to 1974, South Africa admitted to only fourteen additional fatalities, and at least half of these took place in Rhodesia. There is some debate over whether South Africa accurately reports fatality and casualty figures. The ANC argues that the figures are systematically reduced or not reported at all. On the other hand, there is some reason to believe that South Africa might exaggerate the figures in order to maintain a state of alarm and readiness among her white citizens. In either case, it is clear that South Africa is far from violent liberation. Indeed, both the ANC and PAC have recently stated that the liberation of South Africa is going to be a protracted affair, the critical stage of which may lie decades in the future. Both have largely ceased efforts to infiltrate fighters into South Africa in accord with their recognition that the time is not yet ripe.

The pressing question is why the resistance movement is in such a depressed state. Africans and other nonwhites outnumber whites by at least five to one; by the standards of the continent they are well-educated and literate; and the degree of their oppression would seem more than sufficient to stimulate militant action. Furthermore, South African blacks have in the past been both organized and active in militant political action. With seemingly less reason for revolt and with far fewer resources, revolutionary struggles in Portuguese Africa, Kenya under British rule, Algeria, and other African states have achieved far greater success. Why then should resistance to the South African regime be so ineffectual?

The most direct answer to this question is the overwhelming power of South Africa's military forces. Counting fully trained reserves, citizen militia, and the SAP, South Africa has over two hundred thousand men ready for combat on short notice. Moreover, South Africa has the industrial infrastructure and financial resources to equip their forces with highly sophisticated weaponry. Since the embargo on arms to South Africa, the Republic has embarked on a massive and successful program to achieve military self-sufficiency. At present South Africa manufactures short-range tactical missiles, fighter planes, tanks, artillery, and a full range of smaller arms. Indicative of the economic power behind this military effort, the 1976 military budget was $1,128 million, a figure greater than the total budget of any state south of the Sahara and far more than the combined military spending of all the black nations in southern Africa.

In addition to relatively enormous material and military manpower resources, South Africa maintains a far-reaching and efficient undercover network both at home and in surrounding nations. Before PAC and ANC gave up infiltration in 1969, for example, it was common for their guerrillas to find the SAP waiting at the border, fully informed of their place and time of arrival. Although of course there is no official information available on the matter, it is generally accepted that South Africa maintains agents in all the exile headquarters and guerrilla camps in Zambia, Tanzania, and elsewhere.

More elusive, but equally important, is the will of South Africa to survive as a white nation. This determination is shared by virtually all white South Africans and is rooted in the fact that South Africa is not a colonial state. As noted elsewhere in this volume, Afrikaner history in Africa began in the seventeenth century. Ties to Europe have long ago been severed and the white South African, particularly the Afrikaner, feels he has no alternative to the unwavering defense of his African homeland. In contrast to British, Portuguese and other European colonists elsewhere and at other times in Africa, the South African's will to resist is not vitiated by the awareness of a European sanctuary to which he can return. The stark conviction that they must win or die in the struggle against African "terrorism" lends South Africa's resistance an unyielding character unprecedented in the history of white rule in Africa. This determination, in combination with the ample resources at South Africa's disposal, is a potent contribution to the failure of black resistance.

Other factors of a tactical nature, however, are also important. Chief among these is the absence of guerrilla staging grounds adjacent to or within South African territory. Because of South Africa's economic and military dominance of southern Africa, nearby black nations are highly reluctant to give overt support to military action against South Africa. Furthermore, Portuguese Africa and Rhodesia have in the past proven effective buffers against infiltration along almost half of South Africa's land borders. Finally, South Africa's geography is such that there are few areas within the country that are suitable for secure guerrilla bases. Given the extreme importance of staging grounds in guerrilla warfare, these points call for further analysis.

There are six at least nominally independent African nations not including Mozambique or Angola, which could potentially serve as launching areas for raids against South Africa: Botswana, Swaziland, Lesotho, Zambia, Malawi, and Tanzania. Of these, only Zambia and Tanzania have in fact given overt assistance to the ANC and PAC, and then only with great caution and an eye on South Africa's reaction. The reason for their caution, and for the total inactivity of the others, is fear of South Africa's military might. Indeed, to an outside observer, the extent of black Africa's respect for South African military capacity sometimes appears oddly inflated and even hysterical. President Kaunda of Zambia, for example, has stated that South African forces could easily defeat the combined armies of all the rest of Africa. An even more exaggerated assertion has been made by Dr. Banda of Malawi, who claimed that South Africa could fight its way to Cairo "tomorrow" if she so chose. Chief Jonathan of Lesotho has said South Africa, if attacked, would overwhelm Africa in six hours.

Allowing for the exaggerated quality of these claims, it is still clear that fear of South Africa is fully justified. Prime Minister Vorster and other South African officials have repeatedly warned African nations that harboring guerrillas or otherwise supporting the violent overthrow of South Africa may be grounds for direct military action against them. Israel's raids into Jordan, Lebanon, and Uganda have been approvingly cited by Vorster as examples that the African states would be well advised to note. Because of its relative accessibility and great strategic importance, Zambia has been a particular target of such warnings. In a vividly explicit threat, Vorster has warned Zambia that if she persists in giving aid to South African "terrorists" "we will hit you so hard you will never forget it."

The South African military threat is the most extreme to the former British High Commission Territories of Swaziland, Lesotho, and Botswana. Almost encircled by South Africa and totally dependent upon her sufferance, these nations simply cannot afford to aid the liberation struggle in any fashion. To the contrary, each has on occasion returned fleeing guerrillas to South Africa. With no defensive forces at their disposal, they have little choice but to cooperate with South Africa. On the rare occasions when one or the other has pursued an independent course, Pretoria has shown no compunction in resorting to extralegal means and the threat of force. Thus, for example, it is widely assumed that a group of political refugees who fled to Swaziland in 1968, and a year later turned up for trial in Pretoria, were illegally spirited back to South Africa by undercover members of the SAP. The arrest within Botswana of Ramotse, a leader of the liberation movement, is a similar case.

Tanzania, because of its distance from South Africa, has been somewhat more aggressive in its support of South African liberation. Most ANC and PAC guerrilla training camps are openly maintained in Tanzania, for example, while Zambia officially denies the existence of such camps in her territory. Yet, the same distance which allows Tanzania a certain freedom of action also makes it an unfeasable staging ground for raids against South Africa. This is a pervasive problem for South African partisans: nations which are sufficiently distant to be relatively safe from South African reprisals are too distant to be much use, and nations sufficiently close to be of use are too close to dare overt aid.

South Africa's economic power provides a more routine means of insuring tacit cooperation from surrounding black nations. To greater or lesser degrees, the economic lifeblood of all southern Africa is in South African hands. Vorster's "Outward Policy" is explicitly aimed at extending the already great economic dependency of the rest of southern Africa upon South Africa. The Republic is in a particularly strong position inasmuch as her economic relationships within Africa are asymmetrical; South Africa is far more important to the African nations than they are to her.

Once again, the former High Commission Territories are in the most precarious position. Each uses South African currency, transports its goods on South African railroads, and derives the major share of its federal revenue and foreign exchange directly from South Africa. Botswana, Lesotho, and Swaziland receive, respectively, 22 percent, 48 per cent, and 47 per cent, of their total federal budgets from their share of South African customs revenue. Each, furthermore, sends more than one-half of its total exports to South Africa and large numbers of workers to the Rand mines.

Malawi imports in excess of 12 per cent of its total exports from South Africa and, in addition, earns a substantial portion of its foreign exchange by contracting mine labor to South Africa.

Zambia is now in the process of reorienting her international economic relations northward, but has made little progress thus far. Approximately one-quarter of all Zambian imports are from the Republic and the extent of this dependence seems destined to grow in light of the cooling relations between Zambia and Tanzania. Zambia's lack of direct sea access further increases her dependency on white dominated states. Well over one-half of all Zambia's imports and exports are transported through South Africa to South African ports, or through Rhodesia to Mozambique ports. It had been expected that the recent completion of the TanZam railroad northwards through Tanzania would ease Zambia's dependence on white transport, and thus allow more overt aid to South African liberation efforts. This has not yet become evident, perhaps because of the growing realization that the TanZam is insufficient to meet more than a fraction of Zambia's transport needs. Current estimates are that no more than 35 per cent of Zambia's needs can be met by the TanZam.

On the whole, the black states' support for guerrilla activity against South Africa remains severely limited. Zambia and Tanzania allow the liberation movements to maintain guerrilla training facilities and headquarters, but Zambia will not allow raids against South Africa to originate from her soil. Tanzania is perhaps more willing to support direct action against South Africa, but as noted earlier, is too distant to provide adequate staging areas. Botswana, Lesotho, and Swaziland limit their support to harboring political refugees, so long as they do not do anything to antagonize South Africa.

Like Rhodesia, the Portuguese colonies were, of course, full partners of South Africa in the regional struggle against "terrorism," and they proved highly effective barriers against infiltration. The independence of Mozambique may well alter this situation, but Rhodesia is likely to remain as a buffer state for some time to come. Despite some public ambivalence, it is not likely that Pretoria will easily abandon Rhodesia. As the South African minister of defense has stated, "If a neighbor's house is on fire, we will certainly go to his aid."

Staging grounds within the Republic present even more formidable problems. South Africa, particularly in the crucial northern regions, does not have the isolated and remote areas which have proven indispensable to guerrilla warfare elsewhere, as in Cuba and Vietnam. White settlements and communities are spread throughout South Africa, and linked together by efficient communications systems. Whites also know the countryside fully as well as do Africans.

Nor does South Africa provide "urban jungles" to conceal and support guerrilla activity, as was the case in Algeria. African urban areas have been systematically created with strategic concerns in mind. They tend to be compact, in flat terrain, encircled by barriers, and well patrolled; and they are usually several miles away from the white cities. Even if the larger locations such as Soweto in Johannesburg were able to conceal guerrilla concentrations, the logistical problems of supplying them would be insurmountable.

Another broad reason for the ineffectuality of the ANC and PAC has to do with their internal character and their relation to the African masses within South Africa. It is a truism of guerrilla theory that partisan groups must be internally cohesive and must also establish an underground parallel to their own organization within the target territory. Neither of these conditions has been met by the ANC or PAC.

The ANC and PAC are in severe conflict with each other and also internally divided. Reasons for the hostility between the ANC and PAC are many, but include personality conflicts between the leadership of each group, and ideological differences dating back to the days of the "Freedom Charter" and the Sino-Soviet split. As noted earlier, the ANC is closely allied to the Soviet Union, while the PAC is in alliance with China. The net effect is to debilitate both groups by directing energy away from more important goals. Despite prolonged efforts by the Liberation Committee of the OAU, hostility between the two groups persists.

In addition to intergroup conflict, both organizations are plagued by intragroup strife. Such dissension has been most visible within the PAC, and centers around its controversial leader, Potlako Leballo, who appears to evoke hostility from other PAC leaders as readily as he does devotion from the rank and file membership. Conflict among the PAC leadership has frequently led to dissension among their followers in the training camps in Zambia and Tanzania, occasionally erupting in violence. Because of its lack of cohesion, and also because Leballo was thought to be interfering in domestic politics, Zambia has withdrawn all support from PAC.

The most fundamental sources of conflict within the ANC and PAC stem from the inherent difficulties of exile politics. Faced with an absence of any visible success and with overwhelming odds, there is a strong tendency in such groups towards the displacement of external goals (i.e., the liberation of South Africa) by internal ones (i.e., self aggrandizement and personal power politics within the organization). To do otherwise in such conditions requires an extraordinary degree of selflessness and discipline. Displacement of goals is only one of a series or organizational problems to which South African resistance movements are prone. John Marcum has catalogued a number of others, including internal aggression and apathy.[5] It should be emphasized that such internal problems are not the cause of the failure of the exile movements, rather they are a symptom.

A more fundamental limitation on the future potential of the ANC and PAC is their great distance from the African masses in South Africa. To an increasing degree, both groups are becoming "heads without bodies." Although rudiments of an underground still remain, as witnessed by the recent explosion of several "leaflet bombs" in Johannesburg and the occasional organized nature of the 1976 urban riots, the once extensive following of the resistance movements seem to be no more.

Several factors lie behind this development. Once again, the major factor is the power, efficiency, and determination of the South African security forces. Often playing upon ethnic rivalries, the SAP has managed to infiltrate and destroy virtually all organized internal resistance. Potential leaders are ferreted out and either restricted, jailed, or forced to flee the country. The unrestrained ruthlessness of the SAP in dealing with suspected subversives, as illustrated by the common reports of physical brutality, has made the costs of such activity excessive for most Africans. The total lack of any visible successes by the ANC and PAC, furthermore, has severely reduced their credibility within South Africa. Indeed, the affluent life styles of the leaders and their endless round of seemingly fruitless meetings, conferences, and speeches appear to have engendered a certain contempt for them among Africans in South Africa.

Paradoxically, recent advances by Africans on the labor front promise to further limit the internal following of the exile movements. Recent strikes in

Durban, the Rand, and the Cape have succeeded in gaining significant concessions from the government. Most importantly, the new Bantu Labor Relations Act gives a limited right to strike to African workers. Success breeds success, and it thus seems likely that increasingly large amounts of energy will be channeled at least in the short term, into the pursuit of evolutionary change within the industrial sector and away from violent liberation. This shift will be most consequential for the ANC and PAC because it is likely to result in the loss of a new generation of leaders. The current leadership of the exile movements is aging, and the best of the younger generation is apt to be drawn into the revitalized union movement. Faced with permanent exile and hopeless odds, on the one hand, and the new promise of union activity, on the other, the choice of the latter by newly emerging leaders is highly likely.

The government's policy of "separate development" also shows signs of gaining some support among Africans, which is apt to progressively reduce the following of the liberation movements. Despite their ultimately racialist character, the bantustans or "Bantu Homelands" do offer at least the trappings of political participation and power. It is also believed by many educated Africans that the bantustans have the potential for becoming a genuine power base if the government continues separate development in earnest. As with the union movement, the impact of the bantustans on the liberation movements is apt to be most consequential to the degree that the new generation of African leaders choose political careers within the bantustans, rather than in exile politics.

Thus, on the whole, the external resistance movement remains in the stalemate it has been in for the past decade. They face overwhelming odds, lack secure staging areas, are internally divided, and cut off from their constituency within South Africa. A major issue remaining in this chapter is an evaluation of the degree to which the independence of Portuguese Africa will break this deadlock.

The Impact of Independence in Former Portuguese Africa

In the words of FRELIMO's publicity director, Jorge Robello, "bullets are beginning to flower" in what was Portuguese Africa. The military coup in Portugal on 25 April 1974 had, as one objective, disentanglement from the costly and endless holding actions in Angola and Mozambique. Both Angola and Mozambique have now achieved full autonomy.

Of the two, Mozambique is of far greater significance to South Africa. Because of the arid and featureless terrain along the southern border of Angola, and also because of the great distance to South Africa proper, Angolan independence does not pose any serious threat to South Africa.

Furthermore, the elaborate defenses in the Caprivi Strip, separating Angola from Botswana, additionally reduce the utility of Angola as a staging ground. At most, Angolan independence will serve to draw a certain number of South African troops away from the more crucial northeastern frontiers.

Mozambique is altogether another matter. Military strategists have long pointed out that a radical regime in Mozambique could well upset the balance of power in southern Africa. In a recent issue of *Objective: Justice*, a publication of the United Nations, it is stated flatly, "Once these buffer states [Rhodesia, Angola, and Mozambique] are liberated South Africa will be exposed and she, too, will eventually succumb." There are generally seen to be three new sources of peril for South Africa in Mozambique independence.

First, the border between Mozambique and South Africa provides ideal guerrilla cover. It is heavily forested and subject to severe seasonal rains. Defense of this border against infiltration supported by Mozambique would be very difficult.

Second, independence under FRELIMO control may place Rhodesia in jeopardy. In contrast to her border with Zambia, a large portion of which consists of formidable water barriers, the Mozambique border is likely to prove impossible to seal against determined guerrillas. In the event that the white regime in Salisbury were to fall, South Africa's defensive problems would increase. Because of the permeability of the Botswana-Rhodesia border, fully two-thirds of South Africa's now secure land borders would be subject to infiltration.

A third possibility is that Zambia's now restrained aid to South African partisans will be increased. As noted earlier, the bulk of Zambia's goods come and go through ports in Mozambique. Now that there is a sympathetic government in Mozambique, Zambia has secured transportation routes that are less dependent upon her remaining inoffensive to white Africa. It is therefore possible that Zambia will give much more overt support to the liberation of South Africa.

The eventual impact of Mozambique independence will be conditioned by two major factors. The first is the ultimate nature of the new government and the second is the reaction of this government to South African military and economic power. On the surface, the political future of Mozambique seems obvious: more or less complete control by FRELIMO leaders within a socialist framework and unqualified opposition to white rule in southern Africa. These are FRELIMO's stated goals. There is strong reason to believe, however, that an independent Mozambique may well pursue a moderate policy towards South Africa, at least in the short run. One push toward compromise is the national fatigue from the long war against colonial rule. The first orders of business of the new government are to heal the wounds of liberation conflict and to seek increased domestic prosperity. Radical action against South Africa would militate against both these goals.

As with existing black states, however, the ultimately decisive factor will be South Africa's economic and military power. During Portuguese domination, Mozambique has become economically dependent upon South Africa. The very symbol of this dependency is the Cabora Bassa dam on the Zambezi River in southern Mozambique. As one governor of Mozambique has put it, "to speak of the Mozambique economy is to speak of Cabora Bassa." Costing in excess of $400 million, the great bulk of its electrical output is to be purchased by South Africa. It does not seem likely that Mozambique, given her extreme poverty and lack of other resources to export, would lightly sever this vital economic link. To maintain the link, of course, Mozambique will have to be cautious in her dealings with South African resistance movements. Likewise, the flow of contract labor to South African mines is a crucial source of revenue and of foreign exchange. The importance of this arrangement is indicated by the fact that from 20 to 30 per cent of all persons employed in Mozambique's wage economy are contract workers in South Africa. Mozambique's economic problems, moreover, are apt to be intensified now that Portugal has ceased her massive military spending in the colonies, which will make the South African relationship of still greater importance.

Finally, the new Mozambique government is uncomfortably close to the most powerful accumulation of weapons and military manpower south of Egypt. A comparison of Mozambique's probable military strength to that of Zambia is enlightening in this regard, in that the larger and more powerful Zambia remains intimidated by the threat of South African force. Zambia's GNP, for example, is approximately 40 per cent larger than Mozambique's, and this difference will probably increase now that Portugal has completely withdrawn. It is unlikely, therefore, that Mozambique will be able to raise and maintain an army any larger than Zambia's fifteen thousand man force. South Africa has a GNP approximately fifteen times that of Mozambique and at least ten times as many troops as Mozambique is likely to be able to muster. Given these odds, it seems likely that even the ideologically radical Mozambique leadership will follow a very circumspect course towards South Africa.

In short, the South African external resistance movements are stalemated, and the withdrawal of Portugal from Africa does not promise to alter this situation in the forseeable future. Short of some unforseeable event, such as armed intervention by one of the superpowers, white South Africa seems destined, for a long time to come, to remain firmly in control of her nonwhite population and indeed of southern Africa.

Notes

1. Pierre van den Berghe, *South Africa: A Study in Conflict* (Berkeley: University of California Press, 1967).

2. Lewis H. Gann, "No Hope for Violent Liberation: A Strategic Assessment," *Africa Report* 17 (February 1972): 15-19.

3. This survey draws heavily upon factual materials presented in K. W. Grundy, *Confrontation and Accommodation in Southern Africa* (Berkeley: University of California Press, 1973).

4. Among the many excellent background sources on the South African opposition, see Edward Feit, *African Opposition in South Africa* (Stanford: Hoover Institute, 1967).

5. John Marcum, "The Exile Condition and Revolutionary Effectiveness: Southern Africa Liberation Movements" in *Southern Africa in Perspective* ed. Potholm and Dale (New York: Free Press, 1972).

Chapter 12

United States Policy Toward South Africa

Donald B. Easum

The decolonization process set in motion by the spectacular change of government in Lisbon in April 1974 produced a geopolitical earthquake across all of southern Africa. Its repercussions were deeply felt in the Republic of South Africa, where the government was forced to undertake a fundamental reassessment of South African relations with Mozambique, with Southern Rhodesia (Zimbabwe), and with Namibia (South West Africa).

The overthrow of the Caetano regime by a group of young Portuguese military leaders committed to giving up Portugal's African territories resulted little more than a year later in the emergence of an independent Mozambique dominated by the Mozambique Liberation Front (FRELIMO). This development poses difficult questions for the continuation of important economic relationships between South Africa and Mozambique. There are substantial mutual benefits from a labor force of more than 100,000 Mozambicans working in South African mines and factories, from South African commerce passing through the port of Lourenço Marques, and from potential South African purchases of electric power from the Cabora Bassa dam in central western Mozambique.

The rapid evolution to black rule on Southern Rhodesia's eastern frontier altered the military equation between the black Rhodesian nationalists and the white-controlled forces of Prime Minister Ian Smith, who declared the colony independent of Great Britain in 1965. FRELIMO is in a position to step up its material assistance to insurgents inside Rhodesia or apply economic sanctions by closing down Rhodesia's principal rail outlet to the sea at Beira. South Africa's already cautious para-military support of Smith's "anti-guerrilla" efforts will have to be reexamined in the light of FRELIMO's pro-Zimbabwe sympathies. Another consideration for South African policymakers is the increasing attention focussed by the Organization of African Unity and individual African states, particularly Zambia, Botswana, and Tanzania, on efforts for a negotiated solution of the Rhodesian problem.

Finally, with a unanimous Security Council vote in December 1974 demanding that South Africa take the necessary actions to transfer authority to the Namibian people, continued foot-dragging by South Africa regarding release of its one-time League of Nations mandate contrasts with the Republic's professed policy of "detente" with its black African neighbors.

South Africa's actions in each of these three problem areas will be conditioned by the implications that these actions can be expected to have on relations between the races inside the Republic. U.S. policy makers can be expected to assess these actions carefully in the formulation of U.S. policies toward the southern African region.

Apartheid: Setting for Policy

An examiniation of U.S. policy toward South Africa must proceed from an awareness of the special charcteristics of South African society and the nature of U.S. interests in South Africa.

Apartheid has conditioned U.S. policy toward the Republic of South Africa in ways that are unique to our relations with that country. Variously denominated by Pretoria as "separate development" "separate freedoms," "parallel development," "multi-national development," and "differentiation," *apartheid* is a carefully detailed blueprint for racial compartmentalization of South African society. Whereas racial discrimination and de facto separation of the races in South Africa go back some three centuries, *apartheid* has been official South African government policy only since the 1948 election victory of the Afrikaner-dominated Nationalist party. *Apartheid* constitutes the foundation of a political system through which four million whites have exercised deliberate control over the lives of eighteen million blacks, 2.3 million "coloureds" (mixed race) and 700,000 Asians.

The *apartheid* program offers blacks political and economic rights and "self-determination," including the option of independence, within the confines of "homelands" (or "bantustans"). Under the homeland concept the government has pared some twenty-six principal ethnic or "tribal" groups to nine. Every black person is officially classified as belonging to one of the nine. He is to have access to political and economic rights only in the geographic area or homeland set aside for his racial group.

For coloureds and Asians, who are without identifiable locus associated with racial origin, a somewhat different system of nongeographical "nationhoods" is envisaged.

The theory behind the elaborate institutionalization of segregation is that each South African racial group, whites included, must evolve separately in accordance with its own traditions and values. This means living apart as much as possible. Educational and other communal institutions must serve this separatist premise. Racial identities must be consciously preserved and protected in ways that will prevent frictions between racial groups or the domination of any one group by another or by combinations of others.

The nine homeland areas, to which nearly three fourths of the total population are officially assigned, constitute only thirteen percent of the total land area of the Republic. Much of this homeland area is of marginal economic value, without significant resources or infrastructure. Despite massive "relocations" of population, only about forty-five percent of all black South Africans reside in the homelands. Most of those outside the homelands are farm workers in rural white South Africa or laborers living in crowded segregated urban townships on the fringe of the major industrial centers. These ten million South African blacks outside their homelands can reside, work, associate, marry, use public facilities, be educated, carry on business, or engage in trade union or political activities only in the fashion and to the degree specifically allowed by the white minority.

The future of the urban blacks living far from their homelands has for long been one of the unresolved questions complicating the government's offer of eventual independence for the homelands. Another stumbling block is the homeland leaders' insistence on a fairer allocation of land and a consolidation of the bits and pieces that scatter two million Zulus, for example, across a Kwazulu homeland hodge-podge of forty-four "reserves" and some 144 noncontiguous "black spots." While the Transkei, the most geographically unified of the homelands, appears ready to accept independence in 1976, strong skepticism about the supposed benefits of homeland independence is evident on the part of other homeland leaders. The example of an independent Mozambique under black rule has stimulated them to ask themselves again whether independence for homelands would mean permanent eschewal of the benefits of black solidarity across the Republic and permanent loss of any chance of participating in the product and benefits of the entire South African society.

These racial policies have set the Republic of South Africa at odds with much of the rest of the world. The recognition that racial problems are by no means unique to South Africa has in no way diluted the conviction of black African leaders in particular that the African continent must one day be free of any system by which a white minority makes the determinative decisions affecting the daily lives of a black majority. This position was presented with eloquence and dignity in the "Manifesto on Southern Africa" issued by the heads of state of thirteen East and Central African states at Lusaka, Zambia in April 1969:

> We acknowledge that within our own states the struggle towards human brotherhood and unchallenged human dignity is only beginning. It is on the basis of our commitment to human equality and human dignity, not on the basis of achieved perfection, that we take our stand of hostility toward the colonialism and racial discrimination which is being practiced in southern Africa. It is on the basis of their commitment to these universal principles that we appeal to other members of the human race for support.

Black African governments view the attitudes and actions of other nations on the issues of decolonization and racial equality as barometers to guide African dealings with these nations. Any appearance of U.S. acquiescence in or indifference to *apartheid* exposes the U.S. to criticism from these African states, from a variety of "nonaligned," communist and other countries, and from numerous domestic groups within the U.S.

U.S. Interests

Interests determine policies. Policies appear confused or ambiguous, or evoke controversy, when the interests they are designed to serve are themselves in conflict. A policy that promotes one particular interest may threaten the condition of some other interest. This interrelationship of interests and policies is of unusual significance in the case of U.S. policies toward South Africa. These policies are judged in much of the rest of Africa by the single criterion of whether they buttress or weaken South Africa's racial policies. These judgments then become important elements affecting the environment for U.S. interests in those countries.

Political

The political interest of the U.S. in South Africa turns on South Africa's racial policies and on South Africa's relations with its immediate neighbors and the rest of Africa. This interest seeks nonviolent evolutionary progress toward political rights for nonwhites within South Africa. If sufficiently rapid and of sufficient substance, such progress might enable South Africa to be accepted in due course by its neighbors as a respected member of the African continental community. This interest also envisages a South African political environment that is not hostile to the U.S.

Apartheid will continue to be perhaps the major conditioner of the U.S. political interest. Repugnant to most Americans and branded by the U.S. government as abhorrent, *apartheid* has been of particularly deep concern to an articulate domestic constituency in the U.S. that is especially sensitive to human rights issues.

South Africa's external policies provide another dimension to the U.S. political interest in South Africa. To the extent that South Africa's policies toward its neighbors contribute to peaceful self-determination in the area, the U.S. believes that its objective of nonviolent change in South Africa and elsewhere in the region is well served. Prime Minister Vorster's pressure on Rhodesian Prime Minister Ian Smith to negotiate with his black nationalist adversaries is a singularly significant demonstration of the kind of political influence that South Africa can bring to bear on one of the most critical problem issues in southern Africa. The most difficult challenge yet to be met in South Africa's external political arena is the response it will make to the demands that it withdraw from Namibia.

Economic

The U.S. has substantial investment and trade interests in South Africa. Some three hundred American companies are established in the country. The most important include banks, pharmaceutical manufacturers, automobile manufacturers, and extractive industries. Direct U.S. investment is in excess of $1 billion, the largest amount in any African country south of the Sahara with the possible exception of Nigeria, where U.S. investment is growing faster than in South Africa. While U.S. investment in South Africa constitutes about one-fourth of total U.S. investment in sub-Saharan Africa and fifteen percent of total foreign investment in South Africa, it represents only approximately one percent of U.S. investment abroad and two percent of gross capital investment in South Africa from all sources, both foreign and domestic.

U.S. trade with South Africa in 1974, less than one-fourth of U.S. trade with all sub-Saharan Africa, was relatively much more important before the great increase in the values and amounts of oil purchased from Nigeria. Imports from South Africa in 1974 totalled $609 million. Exports to South Africa over the same period were $1,160 million, thus providing a favorable trade balance of more than half a billion dollars. These exports represented roughly one-half of all U.S. exports to sub-Saharan Africa in 1974. Imports of particular importance were asbestos, diamonds, platinum, chromium ore, and gold (by way of Europe). Principal exports to South Africa were machinery and electrical equipment, civilian vehicles and aircraft, chemicals, optical and photographic equiment, and paper and paper products.

The U.S. also has a collateral interest in the contribution that orderly marketing of South African gold makes to the world financial system.

Strategic

South Africa's geographic location astride the major line of communication between the Atlantic and Indian Oceans lends potential strategic importance to South African ports and airfields. Control of these facilities by unfriendly hands would be a complicating factor in the event of threat to U.S. and West European access to Middle Eastern oil and particularly that portion of the supply that is transported via the route around the Cape. Opening of the Suez Canal is not expected markedly to reduce these quantities, since most oil is carried in tankers which when loaded draw too much water to transit the canal even if anticipated dredgings are completed.

The Cape route is sometimes used by the U.S. Navy. While U.S. naval visits to South Africa have been suspended since 1967, South African ports have occasionally been useful to the Navy in cases of emergency. If Lourenço Marques and Angolan ports were to be closed to the Navy, the utility of calls at South African ports would become more attractive.

Scientific

For some years NASA maintained an earth satellite tracking facility near Johannesburg. It was scheduled to be phased out late in 1975. A deep space facility was closed down in mid 1974.

The U.S. scientific and industrial community is interested in the possibility of drawing upon South African experience in coal gasification and in extracting oil from coal.

South Africa controls 27 percent of the Western world's supply of uranium and in 1974 announced that it had completed construction of a pilot nuclear enrichment plant. South Africa claims to have invented a new process of nuclear enrichment. No information on the process has been released.

U.S. Policies: "Restraint" and "Communication"

Until the attention of the American public and of the Kennedy administration had been captured by the Sharpeville shootings in 1960 and by the full tide of African independence in the early years of that decade, U.S. relations with South Africa were shaped by a generally assumed commonality of interests and attitudes. South African forces fought with the Allies in World War II, South Africa participated in the Berlin airlift in 1948, and a South African air squadron operated with a wing of the U.S. Air Force under the United Nations Command in Korea from September 1950 until after the armistice in 1953. South Africa's credentials as a Cold War ally were impressive, in spite of growing concern among friends of South Africa about the increasing institutionalization of racial separation throughout the decade of the fifties.

Arms Embargo and Limitations on Military Contacts and Naval Visits

Fresh criticism of *apartheid* by new African nations and growing interest in the problem by an expanding black electorate and others in the U.S. culminated in the unilateral declaration by the U.S. in 1962 of an embargo on the sale to South Africa of arms and military equipment that could be used in the enforcement of *apartheid*. The following year the U.S. broadened its embargo by accepting the United Nations proscription on the sale and shipment of arms, ammunition, and military vehicles to South Africa, and on equipment and materials for the manufacture and maintenance of arms and ammunition in South Africa. The arms embargo has been accompanied by limitations on naval visits and on contacts with and visits to the U.S. by South African military officials.

The State Department has characterized U.S. policy toward South Africa as a composite of elements of "restraint" and elements of "communication without acceptance." This terminology, while admittedly imprecise, has proved useful to the State Department in describing the mix of policies the U.S. had devised for the conduct of relations with South Africa. The decisions restricting arms supply, military contacts and naval visits are important ingredients of the "restraint" dimension of that policy.

Trade Promotion

The "restraint" posture is also reflected in restrictions placed on Export-Import Bank facilities for trade with South Africa. No direct loans are permitted, and discount loans are available only in amounts of less than $2 million. Limitations are placed on insurance and guarantee coverage for U.S. exports. U.S. government agencies are enjoined from undertaking trade promotional activity that involves substantial and readily identifiable U.S. government participation and sponsorship.

Investments

The U.S. government neither encourages nor discourages U.S. investment in South Africa. It endeavors to alert U.S. firms to potential problems elsewhere in Africa and in the U.S. that may derive from investments in South Africa. The State Department encourages U.S. firms in South Africa to follow fair employment practices in employment of nonwhites, particularly with regard to improvement of pay, training, and fringe benefits. It published a booklet in February 1973 that gave examples of some of the progressive business practices already instituted by some U.S. companies. In mid 1974 it publicly called upon U.S. employers in South Africa to engage in collective bargaining with representatives of black trade unions even though the "unions" might not be recognized bargaining agents under South African law.

Nuclear Energy

In 1957 the U.S. and South Africa signed an agreement for cooperation in the civil uses of nuclear energy. This agreement and similar ones with twenty-eight other countries were made by the U.S. government under the Atoms for Peace Program, established in 1954, to provide an assured supply of nuclear equipment and material to foreign countries for peaceful purposes. By making the benefits of atomic energy available to other countries, the Atoms for Peace Program seeks to discourage the proliferation of nuclear enrichment installations around the world and to lessen the attendant risk of uncontrolled nuclear weapons development.

The 1957 U.S.-South African Agreement, as amended, authorizes the transfer of U.S.-supplied nuclear equipment and materials (enriched uranium) to South Africa for use in a research reactor and in two projected electric power generating reactors scheduled to come into operation in the early 1980s. The agreement stipulates that U.S.-supplied equipment and materials are not to be used for the development of atomic weapons or other military purposes. Bilateral safeguards and, since 1965, International Atomic Energy Agency safeguards ensure that nuclear equipment and material supplied under the bilateral agreement will not be diverted to unauthorized parties. In 1974, South Africa additionally agreed that U.S.-supplied nuclear materials would not be used to construct a nuclear device, even for peaceful purposes.

Cultural and Education Exchange

One of the principal vehicles for implementing the policy of "communication," this program's budget grew from $50,000 in 1970 to $200,000 in 1974. Since its inception in 1950, it has permitted some 375 South Africans to visit or study in the U.S. and has enabled a variety of U.S. leaders in various fields to visit South Africa. South African grantees come from all racial groups and are in rough proportion to their total numbers in South Africa.

U.S. Government Presence

The U.S. Embassy in Pretoria and the U.S. Consulates General in Capetown, Johannesburg, and Durban are essential instruments for the conduct of official business between the U.S. and South Africa. The substance and style of their activities, along with the information programs and cultural presentations of the United States Information Service, provide to all South Africans an exposure to the thought, life-style and policies of the U.S. Multiracial entertaining, the assignment of black American personnel, contact with South Africans of all races and political persuasions, and the facilitation of such contacts for American visitors bring individuals of different races together and encourage a better understanding by South Africans of U.S. policies and attitudes.

International Organization Membership

The U.S. has generally opposed actions to deprive South Africa of membership in international organizations when such actions would be in conflict with the organizations' constitutions. The joint U.S.-British-French veto in October 1974 of the Security Council resolution that recommended the expulsion of South Africa from the United Nations was precipitated by the U.S. belief that irreparable damage would be done to the world organization if a member were to be expelled because of disagreement with its politics. Further, the U.S. believed that ostracizing South Africa meant less chance of encouring change in South African actions and attitudes than continued pressure on South Africa within the world forum.

Humanitarian Activities

Many American religious, legal, and other private groups offer humanitarian and professional assistance to South Africans prosecuted under discriminatory legislation. The U.S. finances modest humanitarian and educational assistance through State Department programs for students and refugees, through the UN Educational and Training Program for Southern Africa, and through the UN Fund for Namibia.

Namibia

U.S. policy on Namibia has been frequently reiterated to South Africa through both public and official channels. The U.S. voted in favor of the 1966 UN General Assembly resolution terminating South Africa's mandate and bringing the territory under the direct responsibility of the United Nations. The U.S. similarly supported the UN Security Council resolution requesting the International Court of Justice to render an advisory opinion on the legal consequences of South Africa's continued administration of the territory. The U.S. accepted the court's conclusion in 1971 that South Africa's mandate was terminated and that her continued presence there was illegal. The U.S. has repeatedly called upon South Africa to implement UN decisions on Namibia by taking prompt action to permit self-determination for the area. The U.S. government endeavors to avoid actions that would tend to legitimize South Africa's presence in the territory.

Alone among major countries, the U.S. officially discourages any new investment in Namibia. No Export-Import Bank facilities are available, and investors are warned that the U.S. government will not intervene on behalf of investments made on the basis of rights granted by the South African government subsequent to the UN's termination of the mandate. Several American oil companies abandoned exploration leases in 1974-75 partly because of Namibia's "uncertain" status. Newmont Mining and American Metals Climax are the only large American investors in Namibia, with investments of some $50 million in the mining of copper, lead, and zinc.

Rhodesia

Although the U.S. itself breaks sanctions by importing Rhodesian chrome under the Byrd Amendment, the U.S. government has expressed the view that South Africa should accept UN decisions concerning Rhodesia, including the application of sanctions and the withdrawal of South African para-military personnel serving in Rhodesia.

The U.S. welcomed Prime Minister Vorster's efforts, initiated in late 1974, to persuade Prime Minister Smith to release jailed Rhodesian nationalist leaders and engage in negotiations with the Rhodesian African National Council. These efforts and South Africa's first steps early in 1975 to withdraw its para-military forces were seen in sharp contrast with the attitude epitomized by a South African cabinet minister's, oft quoted remark some years earlier that "good friends know what their duty is when their neighbor's house is on fire." Vorster told his parliament on 21 April 1975 that there should be no outside interference in Rhodesia's internal affairs and that continued presence of South African police there could be construed as interference. He said police had been placed there at a time when there were elements in guerrilla forces whose intention was to move against South Africa. There had been "an improvement" in this situation, he stated; moreover, the South African government had received certain "assurances" in this regard.

Mozambique

The U.S. views the South African government's willingness to accommodate to FRELIMO rule in Mozambique as evidence of pragmatic South African adjustment to new realities of political and economic interdependence. Without such adjustment South Africa's espousal of "detente" could hardly have been credible.

Criticism and Evaluation of the Policies

These various policies, programs, and activities form a posture that neither embraces nor isolates South Africa. This posture encounters a variety of criticisms from differing poles of opinion within the U.S.

U.S. policies on trade and investment, for example, are criticized by some as too restrictive. Those in favor of a more positive stance include businessmen and investors with interests in the prosperous South African market, persons who believe that the U.S. balance of payments deserves any additional boost that more active promotional efforts might produce, and others who see no utility in a policy that "neither encourages nor discourages" companies that could expect a yearly return of some 19 percent on their South African investments.

Other critics, on the other hand, urge tax disincentives and disinvestment, the termination of all Export-Import Bank support, termination of the foreign tax credit for U.S. corporations in Namibia that pay taxes to the South African Government (Senator Mondale's proposed amendment to the Trade Reform Act of 1973), and support for legislation proposed by Congressman Diggs obliging U.S. firms to follow U.S. fair employment practices in their South African establishments regardless of the dictates of South African law.

There are those who believe U.S. policies toward South Africa show insufficient regard for its strategic importance or its anticommunist convictions. Some proponents of these views, supported by U.S. manufacturers of aircraft and arms, maintain that the arms embargo should be relaxed or lifted. They would also remove the restrictions on military cooperation and naval visits and argue that the U.S. should acquire port facilities in South Africa.

Others hold that the importance of closer military collaboration with South Africa is exaggerated, that South African cooperation would probably be available in any event if needed, and that to seek it in absence of an obviously critical requirement would produce vehement backlash against the U.S. in black Africa and elsewhere in the Third World.

Particular controversy was aroused by charges in 1974 to the effect that NATO and the U.S. had been at work since 1973 drawing up "secret contingency plans for the air and naval defense of South Africa," and that NATO's Defense Planning Committee (DPC) had instructed the Supreme Allied Commander of the Atlantic (SACLANT) to prepare plans for an allied air naval task force "to stand ready to assist South Africa, should the need arise" (*Washington Post*, 2 May 1974). The departments of State and Defense responded that neither the U.S. nor NATO had any plans for the air naval defense of South Africa, and that SACLANT had been given no such instructions.

There were subsequently a variety of press reports of NATO contingency planning for the protection of shipping outside NATO's southern boundary, the Tropic of Cancer. The Department of Defense acknowledged that SACLANT had been directed by the DPC to engage in planning for the protection of oil supply routes through the Indian Ocean, around the Cape, and through the South Atlantic. The authorization from NATO specified that any resulting plan would require the approval of the Military Committee of NATO and would not be implemented or exercised without DPC approval. Furthermore, the DPC instructed that this contingency planning was not to be interpreted as extending NATO's southern boundary or as acceptance by the NATO nations of additional defense commitments. There was to be no contact with non-NATO countries in formulating this plan.

On 10 July 1974 the State Department gave the following response to a Congressional inquiry about this planning.

> We believe that the US and NATO must have an assured oil resupply to Europe in the event of hostilities. While the Department of State has had no active role in the development of the SACLANT plan, it has been aware of this effort and supports this NATO contingency planning in principle as authorized by the DPC.

Criticism of U.S.-South African "military collaboration" was fortified late in 1974 by press reports accusing the Nixon administration of having secretly "tilted" toward the white minority regimes of southern Africa. The supposed evidence for this charge appeared to have been drawn from a preliminary draft of a response to a 1969 National Security Study Memorandum (NSSM 39) that was leaked to the press in 1972. The stories in question revived a *New York Times* report of 2 April 1972 which claimed—on the basis of the same leaked document—that the Nixon administration in 1970 had quietly shifted from a policy of ostracizing the white governments of southern African to one of conscious attempts to improve relations with South Africa and Portugal.

At the outset of the Nixon administration in 1969, the National Security Council had indeed requested a review of U.S. policy toward southern Africa. Policies and actions toward that area during the decade of the sixties had been based in significant degree on ad hoc improvisation. Progress toward peaceful resolution of the problems of race and decolonization seemed to have stagnated despite U.S support of efforts in the United Nations and elsewhere. There were significant differences of view among the American public and in the government bureaucracy as to how much weight should be given to various U.S. interests in southern Africa. The time seemed therefore ripe for a rigorous reassessment of U.S. interests and policies in the area.

The review resulted in an options study submitted without recommendations to the National Security Council in December 1969. Six options were presented, which ranged from the spectrum from the one extreme of conducting fully normal relations with the white regimes to the other of isolating these regimes and applying increased measures of coercion, short of armed force. In accordance with the format used at the time by the NSC for scores of similar papers on other issues, each option was self-contained, opening with the statement of a premise, followed by the general policy posture which would result from the acceptance of that premise, illustrated by some specific operational examples which would flow from that general policy posture, and ending with a listing of the pros and cons of adopting the option under discussion.

The articles which revived the 1972 *New York Times* story contained verbatim quotes of extensive portions of what was then option 2. These quotes included the premises that "the whites are here to stay," "the only way that constructive change can come about is through them," and "there is no hope for the blacks to gain the political rights they seek through violence." Wide currency has since been given to the contention that the Nixon administration consciously adopted the premises of option 2 and that most of its "operational examples" were implemented.

None of the six options in the final paper was in fact adopted as such. A limited number of operational decisions were made. Most of them related to the Portuguese territories or Rhodesia. Helicopters were sold to South Africa for civilian commercial use, and Assistant Secretary for African Affairs David Newsom announced that the U.S. was prepared to license the export of small jet aircraft for VIP passenger transport by the South African Air Force. The important outcome of the policy review was to preserve the fundamental goals of the previous posture (i.e., support for peaceful self-determination and opposition to *apartheid*) while admitting that its efficacy in terms of results was open to question. U.S. policy makers were not alone in failing to predict the changes that were to come to Portugal and its African territories four years later.

Perhaps the major new element to result from the policy review was the concept of "communication." In a speech in Chicago in September 1970, Assistant Secretary Newsom described the policy, stating that "communication does not mean acceptance. . . .It means, in a sense, a greater challenge than isolation. . . .It could mean that greater hope could be given to both blacks and whites who seek another way [than violence]."

Appearing in the 25 July 1972 issue of *Newsday*, Newsom's response to a series of recent criticisms contained the following explanaton of U.S. policy goals in South Africa:

> US policy toward southern Africa has remained fundamentally unchanged since the late 1950s—support for the principle of self-determination for all peoples in Africa, opposition to the institution of apartheid, and favoring peaceful change in southern Africa by supporting constructive alternatives to the use of force. The objective of this administration toward South Africa is to encourage peaceful change. The major method of pursuing this objective is through communication without acceptance of apartheid. Our policy seeks to open up contacts between all elements of the South African population and those of all races in this country.

This policy has not pleased all Americans. Criticism, however, has been easier than the formulation of realistic recommendations for policy change. Arguments from "conservatives" against maintaining various elements of "restraint" in U.S. policy have faltered when confronted with the consequences of such changes for U.S. relations with black African states. On the other hand, proponents of more aggresive pressures against South Africa were reminded of the complications of the sovereignty principle when Newsom in the same *Newsday* article quoted South African Foreign Minister Muller's remarks about American policy of persuasion to promote change in South Africa: "In the practical application of such a policy the border line between persuasion and interference can be very flimsy." To those urging a stauncher anti*apartheid* voting record in the United Nations,

Newsome noted that UN resolutions on this question were becoming increasingly militant; the U.S. was not able to support unrealistic demands or agree in these circumstances to compulsory sanctions against a sovereign state.

Most options for applying greater pressures against South Africa, such as strictures on trade or investment, require legislation. There is little evidence that Congress will be amenable to passing laws prejudical to U.S. South African economic relations, especially in a period of economic contraction in the U.S.

Many of the critics watched the State Department with special interest after the change of regime in Lisbon in April 1974. They awaited evidence that the U.S. government would recognize the significance of this change for South Africa and its immediate neighbors and for U.S. relations with those countries. Public testimony that I presented to Congress before and after an extensive trip to southern Africa late in 1974 seemed to reassure many of these observers.

A Look to the Future

In April 1975 I was succeeded by Ambassador Nathanial Davis. Presiding over the ceremony at which Ambassador Davis took the oath of office, Secretary of State Kissinger said there were "problems in Southern Africa to which I believe a solution should be found and must be found rapidly and peacefully."

U.S. attitudes and policies toward South Africa will of course be influenced by the nature of the evolution of South African policies, both toward its neighbors and toward its internal racial equation.

South Africa's foreign policies appear to be moving in pragmatic and realistic directions, marked as they are by acceptance of black rule in Mozambique and by recognition that self-determination in Rhodesia contains less threat to South African interests than rising levels of violence. Meanwhile Vorster has reiterated his government's intent to seek "detente" by way of dialogue and economic collaboration with selected black African states. In the absence, however, of evidence that Pretoria intended to change its internal racial policies, the OAU has called for stronger pressures against South Africa on internal issues. The basic commitment to separate development and the belief in the need for its tenacious protection remain as central features of the South African social-political landscape, in spite of relaxations of some "petty *apartheid*" restrictions.

Among the most difficult issues requiring address by the secretary of state's advisors on policy toward South Africa will be Namibia and homeland independence, although continuing controversy can be expected to surround the question of the arms embargo, alleged NATO interest in the security of the Cape route, and U.S.-South African cooperation in nuclear energy matters.

Foreign Minister Muller's statement in late 1974 that "all options are open" in Namibia was initially seen by many as suggesting a major retreat from previous obstinacy. In April 1975 Zambian Foreign Minister Mwaanga was able to inform a special OAU Council of Ministers meeting in Dar-es-Salaam that the South African government had made clear it was ready to grant independence to Namibia as soon as the inhabitants had decided what form this independence should take. Delegates to the Dar-es-Salaam meeting endorsed continued African contacts with the South African government aimed at bringing majority rule to Rhodesia and independence to Namibia.

African countries made no secret of their unhappiness with Foreign Minister Muller's letter of 27 May 1975 to UN Secretary General Waldheim, making public South Africa's latest position on Namibia. The letter constituted in effect the South African response to the Security Council's resolution of December 1974, which called upon South Africa to take a series of actions by 31 May 1975 to transfer authority to the Namibian people. On 6 June the Security Council voted on a resolution presented by the African and Nonaligned Group in the Council, setting an October deadline for South African compliance with previous resolutions and demanding an arms embargo if South Africa failed to comply. The vote was ten in favor, three against (the U.S., the United Kingdom and France), and two abstentions (Japan and Italy).

The U.S. veto was cast "with grave reluctance and concern." The U.S. was disappointed by the slow movement toward genuine self-determination in Namibia and continued to believe that South Africa should act quickly and decisively to end its illegal occupation of the region. However, the U.S. could not concur in a mandatory arms embargo. The U.S. did not share the view that the situation in Namibia constituted a "threat to international peace and security" under the terms of Chapter VII of the UN Charter. As U.S. Ambassador John Scali explained, "we cannot accept the view that there exists a genuine threat to peace in Namibia in a situation where the wrongdoer, South Africa, has offered, even if on terms not entirely to our liking, to enter into discussions with the organized international community on the objective of self-determination of Namibia."

In the aftermath of the UN vote, some sectors of U.S. opinion will seek a more active U.S. stance on the Namibian question. There will be new interest in U.S. government pressure on South Africa to allow prompt self-determination in the territory. Fresh attention can be expected to be drawn to the role of the UN Council of Namibia; there will be calls for reexamination of the utility of possible U.S. membership on the Council. New legislation may be proposed to deny credit for taxes that U.S. companies in Namibia pay to the South African government.

The Namibian future is clouded by such questions as how to determine the criteria for measuring self-determination and whether the South West African Peoples Organization (SWAPO) will be accepted as spokesman for the nonwhite populations. The form of governmental structure that may evolve is similarly unclear. U.S. policy holds that (1) all Namibians should, within a short time, be given the opportunity to express their views freely and under UN supervision on the political future and constitutional structure of the territory; (2) all Namibian political groups should be allowed to campaign for their views and to participate without hindrance in peaceful political activities in the course of the process of self-determination; (3) the territory should not be split up in accordance with *apartheid* policy; and (4) the future of Namibia should be determined by the freely expressed choice of its inhabitants.

The homelands issue will also pose important questions for U.S. policymakers. How will the U.S. respond to those homelands which, like the Transkei, accept the South African government's offer of independence? Will the U.S. support their admission to the UN if other homeland leaders and the Organization of African Unity continue to oppose this step? Investment and aid policies toward the homelands also require careful study.

The overarching problem will continue to be how to weight the several important U.S. interests that compete in uneasy interrelationship in the formulation of U.S. policies toward South Africa. There is no easy way to avoid the effect of *apartheid* on this interrelationship. There is general agreement in the U.S. and between the U.S. and black Africa, on the moral issues that *apartheid* poses. Differences of view exist, however, on the merits of U.S. pressures and on the effect that such pressures might produce on other U.S. interests. These will not be easy judgments. They will be seen throughout Africa as indicators of America's attachment to fundamental principles of human dignity and individual rights.

EDITORIAL NOTE:

This chapter was written before Henry Kissinger's African initiatives in 1976 and before the presidential election that brought a changed administration—and perhaps a markedly changed foreign policy—to the White House. Until the demise of Portuguese colonial rule in Angola and Mozambique, Kissinger had acted in the belief that the problems of Southern Africa were of relatively minor import to the United States and could best be handled by applying gentle persuasion to the obstinant white regimes. By doing virtually nothing to disturb the status quo in the region, the United States in effect helped to preserve it.

The Angolan civil war produced a swift change in U.S. policy. Cuban troops not only secured a victory for the Marxist faction in the civil war, but also remained in Angola, posing a potential military threat to white rule in Rhodesia, Namibia, and perhaps South Africa itself. Southern Africa suddenly become a focal point in the ideological and strategic struggle of the United States and the Soviet Union. Recognizing that the apparent tolerance of the United States for the white regimes was seriously damaging America's long-term interest in Southern Africa, Kissinger visited several countries in the region, and in Zambia he declared that the United States "unequivocally" supported the movement to majority rule within Rhodesia and South Africa. Kissinger was also able to persuade Mr. Vorster to apply strong pressure to the Smith government to accept the principle of majority rule in Rhodesia. The exact details of this "pressure" are still undisclosed, but they probably involved a threat by South Africa to reduce both military and economic assistance to its neighbor. The Rhodesian government declared a willingness to move toward majority rule within two years, and representatives of the government and the black liberation movements met in Geneva to work out the details of the transition. The talks collapsed, and the Smith government is now apparently intent on sharing power with the more pliable black conservatives inside Rhodesia.

The early gestures of the Carter administration suggest a much stronger policy against Rhodesia and South Africa, and it is clear that the president and the State Department now regard Southern Africa as a priority in foreign policy. The new U.S. ambassador to the United Nations, Andrew Young, is a black civil rights activist and a close confidant of the president; one of his first official acts was to visit Southern Africa and to reaffirm U.S. support for majority rule in the immediate future. The new administration also lobbied intensively and successfully for the repeal of the Byrd Amendment, which permitted the United States to break UN sanctions by importing Rhodesian chrome—a key foreign exchange earner for Rhodesia. Perhaps most important, the Carter administration has given every indication that it intends to make a concern for human rights a cornerstone of foreign policy. The decades-old U.S. policy of shoring up any anticommunist regime, however reactionary and brutal, is finally coming to be seen by policymakers as both immoral and counterproductive for U.S. interests. If the Carter administration can maintain its new course—and there will be many pressures on it not to do so—American policy in Southern Africa may become more enlightened, more effective, and more popular in Africa and elsewhere than it has been in the past.

PART IV
LOOKING AHEAD

Chapter 13

Prognosis: Evolution

Laurence Gandar

There is a widely held view that South Africa's white minority cannot indefinitely exercise total power over five times as many black people,[1] that history provides no precedent for such a ruling group willingly surrendering its power and privileges, and that change in South Africa will come about only by revolution, violence, and bloodshed.

It is a sombre scenario and the assumptions on which it is constructed are formidable. Certainly the first two decades of Afrikaner Nationalist rule produced little evidence that change might be brought about effectively enough to avoid the predicted bloodbath.

In the closing years of the sixties, however, and increasingly in the seventies, there have been indications, merely intriguing at first but unmistakable now, that the South African situation is beginning to respond to the forces of change and that at last there are grounds for hope, cautious and qualified though this must be, that the country may yet manage to edge its way into the future in a tolerably orderly fashion. This is the proposition I intend to argue here.

I will start by listing some of the changes that I regard as significant:

•South Africans are now generally agreed, in theory if not in practice, that a political system based on race discrimination is untenable in the long term and that the existing order must be adapted to take account of this.

•For the first time since unification in 1910, the hazy outlines of a political consensus are emerging. This takes the form of concepts of federalism and confederalism ranging from a loose constellation of sovereign independent white and black states as visualized by the Nationalists to a classical geographic federation propounded by the Progressive-Reform party. It is particularly significant that the bantustan leaders have also endorsed the federal idea, making the embryonic consensus truly national in scope.

•There is rising concern among whites, including traditional government supporters, about the hardships and injustices involved in such aspects of *apartheid* as the migrant labor system, the pass laws, and the gross disparities in education, housing, and public amenities between the races. It is acknowledged that these hurts must be eliminated in the course of time, though a sense of urgency about this is as yet not widespread.

•There is also growing recognition of the need to consult with the black peoples in matters affecting them. Leaders of these groups have lately addressed congresses of the opposition parties and the prime minister has followed up meetings with individual black leaders with a full summit meeting. Further such comprehensive meetings are in prospect. In short, interracial consultation is becoming a fairly regular practice.

•A new mood of self-awareness and self-confidence is spreading among the country's black peoples and with it a fresh determination to struggle for their own advancement. This is a welcome development after a long spell of resigned listlessness.

•The bantustan policy has provided the homelands leaders with platforms which they are using with skill, courage, and tenacity to articulate the grievances and aspirations of their peoples. And their words receive the attention of many whites.

•There is wide agreement, in government circles too, that the whole question of black labor—wages, working conditions, training, and opportunities for collective bargaining—must be extensively reviewed.

•The churches have become much more outspoken on national issues and some have begun to elect blacks to leadership positions. Fully multiracial congresses, with all delegates staying at the same hotels, are becoming commonplace.

•Several major sporting events have been successfully staged on a multiracial (or "multinational") basis and a recent opinion poll has shown a clear majority of whites in favor of more multiracial sport.

•Blacks are slowly being absorbed into the armed forces, including combat units—hitherto a closed preserve of the whites.

•Numerous city and town councils have begun phasing out *apartheid* in the use of such civic amenities as parks, libraries, theaters, transport services, and so on. There are also moves in the direction of multiracial governing or consultative bodies at municipal and provincial levels.

Of particular importance are the changes that have taken place within the realm of Afrikaner Nationalism, since this is where political power resides. Not only is there much more open and vigorous debate among Afrikaners than ever before, but the terms in which this is conducted are more educated and civilized than has been the case in the past, though there are occasional regrettable lapses.

Furthermore, the influential Dutch Reformed Churches, normally solidly behind the government, are beginning to question aspects of national policy and also to associate themselves, albeit hesitantly, with enlightened statements of race principle at international church assemblies.

Among the youth, too, there are signs of fresh thinking and impatience with outmoded doctrines, while a new spirit of independence is evident among Afrikaner businessmen, more and more of whom are speaking out on matters where *apartheid* policies clash with economic commonsense.

The Afrikaans press, also, is gradually freeing itself from its slavish adherence to the National party line and is subjecting government policy and cabinet decisions to a much more critical scrutiny, something unimaginable a few years ago.

What all this demonstrates is the impossibility of one part of the world isolating itself completely from the rest. With the growth of world trade, travel and instant communications, differences of outlook peculiar to South Africa are becoming blurred within the wider mass culture of our industralized "global village."

Urbanization and secularization, to both of which influences the Afrikaner is increasingly exposed, are part of this process of deculturizing him as a local phenomenon and acculturizing him as a man of the world, with all this means in terms of more easy-going, pragmatic, and sophisticated attitudes. In this sense, what one is seeing is the westernization of the Afrikaner Nationalist.

It will no doubt be asserted that these changes are mainly cosmetic in character, they they are minor adjustments of no deeper import. It is undoubtedly true that the main structure of *apartheid* remains intact, that the crushing disabilities suffered by the ordinary black person under the system have not as yet been conspicuously diminished and that there is a wide gap between rhetoric and action in bringing about changes of substance. It is true, also, that there have been retrogressive developments as well, notably a tightening of censorship, a tougher line on demonstrations and student dissidence, threatened legislation against the press, and a proposed revision of court procedures designed to tilt the balance in favor of the state.

However, on any dispassionate auditing of positive and negative, I believe it would be held that progress has been and is being made overall—an assessment shared by almost every diplomatic observer in South Africa. It should be borne in mind, too, that human advancement is usually a matter of two steps forward and one step back, and that it takes time for changes in public attitudes to be reflected in official policies.

It is already noticeable that the governing National party is less rigidly doctrinaire than it used to be and has made several shifts of grounds towards more moderate positions, notably on the key issue of the urban blacks, for whom it has lately introduced aid centers to reduce the number of arrests under the pass laws, allowed greater freedom of movement in job-seeking, and made provision for greater security of home tenure.

The government even seems close to accepting the permanence of blacks in the white urban areas and is now in the process of examining the whole cumbersome machinery of influx control to see where it can be simplified and humanized. It is also adopting a more flexible approach to the question of interracial contact in hotels, restaurants, and other public places.

Best of all, an unexpectedly sharp upsurge of support for the Progressive party in the general election of April 1974 and in a by-election almost immediately after saw it return to Parliament with a respectable power base of seven seats instead of the one seat held for the past thirteen years by its distinguished but lonely representative, Mrs. Helen Suzman. Since then the United party has disintegrated and its Reform wing has joined the Progressives, further strengthening the progressive forces in Parliament. What this means is that the liberal point of view has at last established an authentic and viable place for itself in South African politics through the ballot box. This is an advance of major significance and one which will make its impact on the character and quality of the country's political life.

Indeed the election revealed a marked spirit in favor of reform, renewal and reconciliation, and not only among opposition supporters either. *Verligtheid* (enlightenment) has become an insistent theme of national politics and all parties except the lunatic right are responding to it. The outlook for South African politics is thus more favorable than it has been for a long time.

With its large majority increased even further, the Nationalist government will feel that much freer to maneuver, to make bolder adjustments and more far-reaching concessions. The United party, for so long equivocal and evasive on issues of civil liberties and race relations, has disappeared from the scene. The Progressive-Reform party, heartened by its new-found strength, it going all out to extend its bridgehead in Parliament and broaden its electoral support.

But of course a political system representative of and responsive to the interests of white people exclusively is inherently unsuited to resolving a conflict between a different set of interests—between white and black in fact—and it would probably to be too much to expect the fundamental changes that are necessary in the country's way of life to come about as a result of party political activity alone. Indeed, the tendency in South Africa, as in many other countries, is for the major parties to follow public opinion rather than lead it.

Fortunately, apart from the social influences mentioned earlier which are helping to modernize the attitudes and outlooks of South African whites in general and the recently urbanized Afrikaners in particular, there are other favorable factors worth noting.

The first of these is the altogether healthy tendency now under way for individuals and organizations to work for change outside the confines of formal politics. Examples of this are the channels of communication being established between white and black community leaders in a wide variety of spheres—cultural, sporting, professional, and commerical—as well as the increasing attendances of whites and blacks at gatherings of all kinds. The emphasis these days is on contact and dialogue between the races—a development from which only good can come.

Second, the homelands leaders themselves are initiating valuable forms of contact that are having an impact on white attitudes—a conscious effort on their part to "liberate" whites from the prison of prejudice in which the history has enclosed them for so long.

Third, the continued absorption of blacks into the economy at a steadily increasing pace and at higher levels of skills not only emphasizes the interdependence of the races in South Africa, but provides these workers with the leverage to improve their standards of living and, indirectly, their stake in society.

The inescapable fact is that 75 per cent of South Africa's total work force is black, and the black component is growing three per cent faster than the white component. Several basic industries such as mining, manufacturing, construction, transport, and communications are already predominantly black, while the textile, clothing, and footwear industries are almost entirely black. Furthermore, it has been authoritatively estimated that before the end of the century, blacks will be filling half of all jobs in the country's skilled occupations. The engineering industry provides an example of what is happening, with blacks taking over more and more skilled and semiskilled work with the approval, however grudging, of the hitherto notoriously recalcitrant white trade unions.

For the blacks, this is economic power, real power, and a realization of what it signifies is slowly dawning on them following the lightning strike of Ovambo tribesmen in South West Africa in 1972, the rolling strikes in Natal during 1973, and the sporadic strikes in various parts of the country since then. For although black trade unions are not officially recognized and strikes by blacks are technically illegal, the blacks used their economic muscle nevertheless, winning for themselves the de facto right to strike and substantial wages increases as well.

It is thus in the economic sphere rather than the political sphere that the greatest hope of peaceful change in South Africa is to be found. It is not only here that the black people have their best opportunity to exert pressure in support of their interests; moreover, studies of human conflict suggest that the most powerful agent in resolving differences between groups of people is the existence of some shared activity, some common purpose of palpable importance to both sides. In economic cooperation and the pursuit of economic growth, South Africans of all races do have such a common goal, a real mutuality of interests. This is especially so now that it is coming to be accepted that the fruits of economic endeavor must be shared far more equitably between whites and blacks.

There remains for discussion the perennial question of external pressure as a factor of change in South Africa. This is a large and complex subject, some aspects of which have been dealt with in earlier chapters. Generally speaking, external pressure is conducive to change when it is perceived and felt to be effective, when it strikes an answering chord of inner guilt, and when its aim falls within the range of tolerable adjustment. Pressure for multiracial sporting teams is a case in point and real progress is being made in this area. Pressure exercised on and through foreign companies operating in South Africa for improved wage scales and conditions of employment for their black workers is also yielding beneficial results. On the other hand, attempts at economic sanctions, although warily watched in South Africa, are considered ineffectual, while sweeping moral condemnation is dismissed with resentment as repetitive, unconstructive, and displaying double standards of judgment.

Threats of military intervention, as posed by the African liberation movements, have in the past been counterproductive in that they have tended to evoke gut responses and reinforce reactionary attitudes.

However, Portugal's bloodless revolution of April 1974, the dismantling of that country's African empire, and the consequent danger of guerilla warfare along South Africa's own borders have had a profound impact on thinking in the Republic, as has the white Rhodesian leadership's recognition of the inevitability of majority rule.

Politically, these events have given a sharp, new impetus to the country's "outward" policy of detente with black Africa and have also heightened awareness of the pressing need for change in race policies at home. Militarily, with the loss of two key buffer states in Mozambique and Angola to the forces of African nationalism, the strategic importance of the third, Rhodesia, has been seriously diminished. Indeed, the Rhodesian issue, and that of South West Africa, have come to be seen in South Africa as the principal obstacles to detente and thus as liabilities rather than assets in South Africa's overall security system.

Accordingly, the prime minister, Mr. Vorster, aided by a small group of cabinet ministers and officials, has plunged himself into the task of "normalizing" South Africa's relations with as many African states as possible. In this endeavor, he has been helped by four developments.

First, South Africa's own responses to the decolonization of Mozambique and Angola (if not to the aftermath of Angolan decolonization) have been scrupulously correct, while behind the scenes every effort has been made to be helpful to the emerging new regimes in those territories—for example, in sending wheat consignments to Mozambique during a spell of severe grain shortage and in helping to restore rail links to, and harbor facilities at, Lourenço Marques after early disruption caused by the panic departure of so many Portuguese workers.

Second, South African initiatives in getting negotiations on the "Kissinger package" started between the Rhodesian government and the African nationalist groups have helped to establish South Africa's sincerity in seeking detente with black Africa, especially in the minds of Presidents Kaunda and Nyerere and of the Frelimo leader, Samora Machel.

Third, the increasing Soviet naval presence in the Indian Ocean and the spreading Russian and Chinese influence in African countries along the eastern seaboard, from Ethiopia in the north to Mozambique in the south, have alarmed some of the Western powers sufficiently to have induced them to give discrete support in black Africa to the idea of detente. For the last thing the Western powers want is a major race war in Africa in which the communist powers would side with the blacks, with the Western powers finding themselves reluctantly driven to supporting the whites in order to protect their investments, sources of essential raw materials, and strategic interests related to the Cape sea route.

Finally, this is a particularly unpropitious time for black Africa to have to contemplate a resumption and escalation of warfare in the subcontinent. The disastrous droughts in the Sahelian states, the crippling burden of quadrupled oil costs, the collapse of other commodity prices on which so many African countries depend, the shrinking of economic aid available in a recession-hit world, the secessionist uprising in Eritrea, internal dissention in Zaire and Kenya, and the early political and economic difficulties in the former Portuguese colonies—all these circumstances are giving rise to a new mood of what has been called economic realism in many countries of black Africa. The result is that South Africa's tempting offers of cooperation and aid, coupled with an apparently genuine anxiety to be rid of the Rhodesian and South West African problems and a new readiness to introduce reforms at home, however modest and cautious, are making a discernible impression in various parts of Africa.

Detente, in short, has become a distinct possibility though there are some acute difficulties still to be overcome—notably that of Rhodesia, where the whites, resentful and confused by South Africa's change of attitude towards their predicament, seem to be seizing on every obstacle to, rather than opportunity for, meaningful negotiations with the African nationalist leaders.

Within South Africa, the relationship between the chances of detente abroad and the progress made at home in eradicating race discrimination, which the government has now officially pledged itself to bring about, is more and more coming to be perceived.

Such progress will doubtless be slow and faltering and there will be setbacks and disappointments. But if a settlement in Rhodesia can be achieved and the South West Africa issue disposed of—and certainly the government regards these things as its two top priorities—there seems a reasonable chance that a breathing space can be won for the work of modernizing South African society. Much then will depend on whether the pace of white concessions can match the rise of black expectations.

To many people abroad this will seem wildly improbable but, long-time pessimist that I have been, I am now not without a modicum of hope that this troubled country is on the long road back to sanity and a place once more in the community of nations.

Notes

1. The term "black" is used throughout this chapter to refer not only to Africans but to South Africa's colored races generally.

Chapter 14

Prognosis: Conflict

Russell Warren Howe

In political analysis, wishful thinking is the thief of objectivity. The bane is widespread: Marxists tend to predict revolution everywhere, even in places where it is more possible than probable; unrevolutionary thinkers tend to predict virtually anything else—even when the smoke is already rising. Those who foresee urban terror as the pattern of conflict diplomacy in the decades to come are often categorized as *partisans* of violence, much as reporters get letters from readers complaining not of what they have said, but of what they have quoted a senator as saying. In a situation like South Africa's it is tempting a choose a "best" solution—and a scenario to fit—and to assume that common sense and reality are one; but since ideology is to journalism what a club foot is to athletics, reporters who turn to history have at least the unconcerned amoralist's advantage.

The revolution in South Africa will not be pleasant. It will almost certainly lead to a painful aftermath, fraught with internecine conflict among the victors. To avoid it would require a whirlwind of reforms that would make revolution redundant; but at this juncture it is far from sure that a revolution can be avoided merely because it is no longer needed. The Ethiopian events that began in 1974, and the aproaching Kenyan conflict illustrate the point that revolutions have a momentum of their own which surpasses their redundancy.

The *ideal* solution in South Africa would be evolution. This would require a massive change in white thinking, a continuation of black patience,

exceptional prosperity, and the ability of white reformers to avoid overthrow by the armed forces of what is probably the world's second most
militaristic noncommunist society after Israel. Evolution implies not only
that a powerful minority with voting rights will surrender power peacefully,
but will do so at a pace that the majority finds acceptable, that a settler
society, most of whose members believe that they have no other *par-
tria*—will decolonize at least as rapidly as European governments giving up
exotic conquests in which their only interests were economic and
peripheral.

Separate development, as envisaged in the homelands policy, would
also be a possible solution—if it were acceptable to the African majority;
(much as, for instance, continued Israeli occupation of East Jerusalem,
and controlled access to it by Muslim and Christian Arabs and other Christians, would be a feasible solution to one aspect of the Mid-East conflict, if
this were all the Arab powers wanted, or all they felt they had the power to
achieve.) What is true is that separatism (a euphemism for segregation)
corresponds to a current Third World reaction to the problems of adapting
preindustrial societies to independence in an industrial age. But the sensible acceptance of the "band-aid" homelands solution to South Africa's ills
by such hard-nosed leaders as Matanzima and Buthelezi is principally
motivated by the knowledge that the Transkei and KwaZulu provide an
unprecedented political base, and administrative training, for Africans.
This writer's belief is that separate development in South Africa is probable
and possibly inevitable—but on exactly opposite lines to those of the
homelands policy. My assumption is that there will be eventually be only
one "homeland"—for Europeans—and that the bulk of the country will
have representative government; in other words, that the political forces
opposed to this development, no longer have the power to control events.

The prognosis of revolution must be based in part on finding the other
two prognoses unworkable. The homelands policy implies that the country's most numerous, and potentially active, political forces will accept the
white, minority view that they (the majority) are incapable of governing
South Africa as a whole, and will be satisfied with 13 per cent or so of the
country. To put it no more strongly, such a theory would seem to
misconstrue the balance of potential political power in South Africa.

Achieving an egalitarian society by evolution would mean, in essence,
ensuring that black truck drivers earn as much as white ones. This might
well be impossible, even in a time of prosperity, since white salaries in
South Africa are drawn *above* the value of the task performed, and sub-
sidized by the "race tax"—the amount by which Africans, Eurafricans and

Asians are underpaid to subsidize "Western" living standards in a country with a per capita income of under $1,000. To equalize wages—especially in the current era of recession—would require cutting back white wages to realistic levels (the levels of their productive worth). It is hard to see how an elected government could move its electors' wage scales downward to meet those of nonvoters.

It is equally hard to see a dour, Afrikaner government extending the vote to the black equivalents of the white truck driver. The alternative to a universal franchise would be a merit voting system that would not give the vote to all, and would therefore also disenfranchise some whites who already vote. Could an elected government win support for disenfranchising some of its electors, especially when the party in power derives its main support from the poorest whites?

To the hard core economic and political arguments against evolution must be added psychological ones. The Afrikaner power caste among whites sees itself as a chosen people brought to South Africa by God's will; the Dutch Reformed Church, in a parallel, teaches that Africans are divinely ordained inferiors. In South Africa as elsewhere, the dimunition in the political and societal significance of sophisticated religions has not blunted the strength of fundamentalism.

The temptation for the optimists has been to point to recent reforms in the American South. But the South is not a separate country, nor did its racism have the same character as South Africa's: racism in the American South, even when violent, was counterbalanced by contact. The Mississippi cracker knew and knows his black neighbors intimately, from the days when he grew up playing with his black neighbors. Most white South Africans know as little of African culture as do Finns or Swedes. The assumption that Johannesburg currently has the cultural capability to become another Atlanta is rooted in unreality.

Evolutionists correctly attribute importance to the Nixonian advantage of having Johannes Vorster as prime minister. Mr. Nixon could embrace Mao-tse-Tung without being scored for being soft on communism (in a way that, for instance, President Kennedy could not have done.) Mr. Vorster, with a background that includes two years in the penitentiary for Nazi activities during World War II, could make concessions without risking the accusation of being soft on race. Indeed, Mr. Nixon, by making ideological flexibility in foreign affairs respectable, has facilitated this approach elsewhere: he has given a cachet of absurdity to rigid inflexibility between hostile political forces. In Mr. Vorster's case, this trend exemplified itself in his February 1975 meeting with African leaders on the Rhodesian question, his decision to junk the Smith regime, and his general *appertura* to black Africa, including his visits to West African capitals. But

Mr. Vorster's radicalism, like Mr. Nixon's, is limited to foreign affairs, and only emphasizes his lack of a radical approach at home.

Domestically, Mr. Vorster is politically able to go further along the path of reform than virtually anyone else in South African politics. But there are pragmatic limits to what even a Vorster could impose, and strong emotional limits to what he or his party would want to propose. Helping give Rhodesia black government—and thus acquiring tens of thousands of white refugees to boost South Africa's European population—has clear advantages, both in terms of detente with countries outside South Africa, and in terms of more white strength within. Nothing, however, indicates that South Africa's Afrikaner leadership is prepared to show its own country's majority leaders the same realistic "Nixon-Mao" appearance of respect that it offers foreign black leaders. Indeed, the trend of Nationalist party thinking seems now to reemphasize separate development—rather than that integration which the promised "racial justice" would make necessary. Where domestic and foreign affairs commingle, in Namibia, the ambivalence is most evident: assuming that Premier Vorster's promises to UN Commissioner Sean McBride mean independence for the former League of Nations territory, the intention seems to be to divide up even that country of less than one million inhabitants to perpetuate a sophisticated form of *baasskap*. An independent, agricultural Ovamboland will apparently be "free" (read: encouraged) to join Angola, leaving the rest of Namibia whiter, richer and more under the continued influence of Pretoria.

In short, while dividing foreign African opinion, and easing its pancontinental foreign relations task, there seems no way that the Nationalist party can avoid racial conflict at home—and no way that political rivals can displace them from office. The United party, after losing ground for years, has disintegrated. Despite recent electoral successes, neither the Progressive-Reformists nor the Democrats—even in coalition—seem likely to form the government in the near future. Burgeoning black discontent now exists as a challenge to Pretoria, which has never hesitated to choose the weapons of force and terror to defend itself—practising what Alan Paton once called a "policy of stamping out nonviolence." This means that activists for change in South Africa, buoyed by global and especially regional trends, have little option but to use terror and other force to achieve their aims.

What happens next? What seems probable is a wave of petty reform in such areas as salaries and employment (including promotion and job reservation), but without full equality; the acceptance of black officers in the armed forces and police; the integration of public facilities; and so on. Such trivia will be front page in South Africa—and foreigners should not underestimate their temporary anesthetic effect. But the South African government's willingness to walk will emphasize its unwillingness to trot, in a galloping age. Integration of housing, education, and family life, except perhaps for a privileged few blacks, seems unlikely in the foreseeable future. The reality is that both the black and white working classes desire separation. Black urban terrorists will demand the whole country, and hard core whites will make a similar counter-claim; but separation seems the inevitable sequel of powerful, competing nationalisms. Where the partition line will come will depend on the power and skill of the revolutionary leadership, and the relative weakness and isolation of the regime in its hour of conditional surrender. Prediction here would be difficult; all that it seems safe to say is first, that whites will end up with less than half the country, and second, that the only zone to which they have historic claim is the western cape.

The only comparable precedent in recent history for South Africa is Algeria, where one million Europeans were not enough to justify the retention of any territory. Whereas white settlement in Rhodesia is recent (mostly post-World War II), native white South Africans have the same quasi-secular commitment to the country of their birth as Algeria's *pied-noirs*. But although the *pieds-noirs* knew little of France, the existence of French government in the *département* and the proximity of France itself made the largely Italian and Maltese "Frenchmen" of Algeria feel some bonds to Paris. The dilemma of the white South African, and particularly the Afrikaner, is undoubtedly greater. English-speaking South Africans have a wide choice of the world for resettlement: the Afrikaner cannot even speak enough Dutch to avoid derision in Holland. White South Africans can be expected to move, with regret, to Australia, North America, Europe, and Israel, but—except in the latter case—without emotional motivation. Portuguese and Italian South Africans may resettle in Latin America, Asians either in the "Europstan" or in North America.

This writer's assumption is that the predominantly rural, rump territory which whites will probably retain will be inadequate for the size of the present white population—at all costs for its unskilled and semiskilled urban mass. The managerial, entrepreneurial, and technological white middle class would have more motivation for staying in the white "homeland"—but some of these, especially of the younger generation, may also expatriate themselves. Even though a truncated white South Africa may well survive, geographically and politically, it can only be an anachronism, offering little future for ambitious youth.

How will the Western powers react to developments in South Africa? The United States, like most great powers, tends to support a status quo which is not hostile. It opposes *apartheid,* but not the existence of white control. Yet several factors would encourage American inaction, in a period of revolution. A 1973 report of the International Institute of Strategic Studies, mostly based on American data, noted that southern Africa had little or no strategic global significance. Economic considerations are marginal: the U.S. has less investment in South Africa than it had in pre-Castro Cuba—and in any case opposing reform would only invite seizure later, while supporting reform would not risk seizure now. Add in the congressional trend toward isolationism. The American inclination would probably be to let the conflict fester: the status quo, though squalid, is harmless in global terms; urban warfare, though regrettable, would be quarantined within one remote peninsula, pointed at the Antarctic icecap.

Washington's view would probably set the pattern for most of the Western nations—although the U.S. could well have a mediatory role to play in any final negotiations about partition, and in helping finance the ensuing redevelopment. France alone might be prepared to continue overt support of Pretoria, notably in terms of sophisticated arms and military cooperation. But even France would probably help the South African government resist an urban revolution only for so long as Paris believed that there was a chance that it could be successfully resisted.

South Africa's principle Western leverage comes from its mineral resources: the world could do without its gold and diamonds, but not without, say, its lignite or titanium. This, however, is a double-edged weapon, and the blade facing Pretoria is the sharper of the two: it is unlikely that South Africa would "boycott" the West—but possible that a future black government might do so if it took umbrage at the West's attitude to the black revolution. Nor is Western inaction—evenhandedness—in the coming phase entirely certain. The West might opportunistically back the revolution in measured form. Finally, it is hard to see how the communist powers, and particularly China, could fail to provide support for that revolution.

The austral African effects of the revolution in Lisbon have, as we have seen, sparked a promise of eye-dropper reforms in the Republic, and have authorized the Vorster *appertura a sinistra* in South Africa's relations with other African states. Ironically but understandably, these complementary developments have already emboldened official Western strictures on the *apartheid* state. Western support for the UN majority's desire for economic sanctions against the Pretoria regime is now conceivable. Such proposals have been rejected in the past as unworkable; they might well, of course, be rejected now by Western powers, as likely to encourage opposition in South Africa, increasing the risks of revolutionary violence, which the West abhors. (The weaker and more isolated the South African govern-

ment becomes, the more it would be a natural target for terrorism.) Nevertheless, the possibility of sanctions can no longer be ruled out.

The use of sanctions against Rhodesia, although largely unsuccessful,
set a useful historical precedent—and it would take a cynic to believe that
those sanctions were voted only because it was known that they would not
work. In South Africa's case, such measures would be immensely easier to
apply, since only oil sanctions would be necessary. Over a leisurely
period—giving Pretoria time for reassessment, while it depleted its extensive reserves—oil sanctions would literally grind the country to a halt.

But the major Western nations would only go along with sanctions of
any type if the African countries wanted them—and if these were prepared
to pay some sort of realistic political price. At present pan-African interest
in the problem of *apartheid* seems limited—but it remains part of the
rhetoric, and the rhetoric is sincere. Real outside pressure for reform seems
more likely to come from the United States, and from an increasingly
socialistic Europe—provided of course that there is some continued *pro-
forma* pressure from Africa.

Like major weapons in general, oil sanctions would be almost frighten-
ingly simple. The high visibility of tankers at sea, and the concentration of
the industry in the hands of a small number of corporation would facilitate
implementation. The major requirement would be U.S./Soviet cooperation, under the UN flag—a prospect no longer so difficult to imagine. Persistent South African sabotage of UN sanctions against Rhodesia would
help greatly in validating UN sanctions against South Africa itself. Pretoria
is further in "contempt of court" at UN because of its continued, illicit occupation of Namibia. As Peck's bad boy of the global scene, no nation
seems more likely to attract an international scourging, when the time is
right.

Moreover, the probable development of urban guerilla warfare on the
Ulster pattern already presaged in the urban riots of the late seventies,
could in turn provoke the kind of repression (similar to France's in In-
dochina and Algeria) which would lose the South African government its
last hope of being given "time" by the international community; it would
also rekindle pan-African sentiment on the South African issue. This in
turn could lead to a greater involvement by the communist powers,
especially the astutely opportunistic Chinese government, and even to the
introduction of IRBM's—for instance, at the old NATO base at Kamina in
southern Zaire. South Africa is armed to respond to such a threat, but it is
immensely more vulnerable to this kind of confrontation than are its more
rural neighbors to the north.

If confrontation is involved, the position of Zambia will be crucial. The
Vorsterian backstage diplomacy of early 1975 created apparently har-

monious relations between Pretoria and Lusaka. But Zambia's impending (and total) rail, road, electric power and pipeline independence from its white-ruled southern neighbors will enable it to resume its natural role as a base for southern African resistance activities, should it need to do so.

When the question of a wider conflict is raised, Pretoria habitually points optimistically to its virtually all-white forces, presumably impervious to subversion, and notes that guerillas, both from within and without, could not permanently occupy state machinery, key cities, or the means of production. But as urban guerilla warfare from Belfast to Montevideo amply demonstrates, the urban guerilla does not covet these objectives: he or she seeks only to demoralize and intimidate, to create a climate conducive to political surrender. Resistance movements kill more quislings than enemies.

In an age when large-scale nuclear warfare is nearly unthinkable, and conventional conflicts like those of the Middle East and Southeast Asia more and more restricted by great power authority, urban terror has probably become the main instrument of the weak against the strong or relatively strong. It has also become the most successful. Dr. Kissinger has put it well: "The guerilla wins when he does not lose. The conventional soldier loses when he does not win." There seems no reason to think that South Africa will be an exception to the trend.

Chapter 15

Prognosis: The United States of South Africa

Edwin S. Munger

No observer is sapient enough to essay the thin ice of prophecy without occasionally falling through, and South Africa is a most parlous place for predictions. John Buchan did predict in 1903 that the future South African society "must grow up on the soil, and it must borrow from the Dutch race, else it is not true growth but a frail exotic." He warned that any attempt to import alien institutions and values would be a waste of time and money. The prophecy was not heeded and British forms were too slavishly duplicated. The attempt to Anglicize the Dutch led directly to the growth of Afrikaner nationalism.

In the penumbra of World War II the South African historian Arthur Keppel Jones wrote a famous book called *When Smuts Goes*, in which he depicted the rise of a Nazi nationalism in South Africa and the triumph of a fascist state. His prophecy bears little resemblance to events as they developed. For example, Keppel Jones predicted that 1956 would be the year of the greatest pogrom, when in fact it was the year that the Jewish community presented Prime Minister Malan with a silver plate, terming him "The Moses of the Afrikaner people."

Buchan prophesied well because he understood the character of the Afrikaner; Keppel Jones failed because, in common with so many critics, he did not grasp the essence of the Afrikaner character. The accuracy of my attempt at prediction will be determined primarily by whether it is correct in its analysis of the Afrikaner. Too many critics base their predictions on what they would like to see happen, rather than on a realistic assessment of the forces that are directing change in South Africa. The salient feature of the South African policy is that it is dominated by the Afrikaner, that there is no plausible prospect of this situation ending in the forseeble future, and that the direction of policies will therefore be primarily determined by the Afrikaner. As is well appreciated, the Afrikaner has no present intent of surrendering control of that part of the country to which he claims a historical right. As is less well appreciated, the Afrikaner has no intrinsic interest in denying self-determination to others—provided that doing so does not involve the sacrifice of what he has fought so long and bitterly to gain. I believe that the homelands concept, which envisions separate and ultimately fully independent territories for each of the African ethnic groups in South Africa offers a solution to the dilemma.

The goal is justice in South Africa, and not a particular ideologically predetermined way of achieving it. This is perhaps much easier to appreciate in the United States of the seventies—where South Boston has become the Little Rock of the North, and where the emergence of racial and ethnic pride among blacks, Indians, Mexican Americans, and the various "white ethnics" has laid to rest the simplistic image of America as a melting pot. In making predictions, is not always instructive to compare black Africans in the Republic with black Americans. A better analogy to Africans in South Africa is the American Indians. The growth of Red Power and its demands not only for a place within American society, but also for a place apart where traditional languages and cultures can continue their present renaissance, is one ethnic development that will contribute to an understanding of South African complexities and erode the facile notion that all efforts at mother tongue instruction and cultural diversity are based on malevolent racism. Only an ideological obtuseness can prevent us from recognizing the validity of the Afrikaner's own self-identity and his desire for its preservation; and one's moral outrage must be very selective indeed if one cannot countenance the possibility that territorial separation, whatever its drawbacks, may prove the most viable long-term solution to an otherwise intransigent problem. This is not to say that separate homelands are, as originally envisioned by Dr. Verwoerd and his supporters, the sole answer to racial injustice. But they do offer a means through which a multiethnic country will move, relatively peacefully, to a just society.

Separate homelands will in fact play a vital part in achieving such a society. They permit the granting of authority to many Africans over much of their daily activities without at the same time immediately threatening the white power structure. Unfortunately, nearly all critics of South Africa in the Western countries have retarded the achievement of a nonracist polity in Southern Africa by their purblind ideological opposition to the homelands concept. In doing so they have encouraged initial opposition on the part of already understandably suspicious urban Africans. The United Nations has been particularly blind, because it has coupled its ideological opposition toward separatism in South Africa with a massive disregard of racial injustice in independent Africa and an apparent unconcern with genocide when the executioners as well as the victims are black. Such double standards have undermined the potential prestige and influence of the world organization in South Africa.

Among the whites, too, there are signs of growing support for separate development. The Nationalist party, of course, has been committed to the homelands concept for decades. But light has also dawned in the policies of the Progressive-Federal party, which has finally recognized that the homelands have achieved a political viability and must be considered a permanent feature of the political geography of the region. Mrs. Helen Suzman, long the lone Progressive in parliament, takes a pragmatic approach. She does not tell the African leaders in South Africa what they should want. She listens to them. Soon after the Transkei achieved a measure of autonomy in 1963, the Progressives realized that Matanzima, and later other homeland leaders such as Buthelezi, Mangope, Nsantwisi, Phatudi, and Sebe, are right in affirming that you do not begin the process of achieving political justice by depriving ethnic groups of what modest power they have been given.

This does not mean that they support the entrenched racial policies of the National party. They oppose them with the utmost vigor. But they are far ahead of Western critics, and especially of the United Nations, in perceiving the potentially constructive role of the homelands. The United party, notably unable to provide any alternative to the homelands policy other than the unacceptable one of continued white domination and racial segregation, and unwilling to follow the Progressive lead in acknowledging the existence of the homelands, has predictably disintegrated.

I do not see a political threat in this development to the Nationalist party, since the opening up of the political left by the Progressives and breakaway elements from the United party will create a new middle ground in white South African politics, into which the National party will move with its usual adroitness. The new alignment will mean that, strange bedfellows though it makes, almost all the parties from the Herstigtes on the far right to the Progressives and new groupings on the left will be in favor, enthusiastically or otherwise, of some kind of separate development. Support for separate development, then, is not restricted to the Nationalist party, or even to the whites. This is what so many overseas observers of South Africa have failed to recognize, and consequently their views lose whatever impact they might have had within the Republic.

How will the homelands evolve? First, let us disabuse ourselves of some unreasonable criticism by the outside world. At present the territory allocated to Africans is not at all a fair proportion of the land in South Africa, considering the relative sizes of the various populations. But it is not inferior land. It excludes the desert-like Karoo and contains some of the better agricultural land in a general dry country. On average, the homelands have better agricultural land than the tracts held by whites.

Second, there can be no objection in principle to the territorial separation of competing or hostile groups, and indeed such geographical separation has won international approval in the past. India and Pakistan are prime examples of how the "stan" principle was accepted as the best way out of a bad situation in which millions had died as a result of ethnic hatred and anarchy. Bangladesh provides further, if even more tragic, evidence that even bonds as strong as those as Islam are inadequate to bind up all ethnic wounds. There is considerable international support at present for the suggestion that an independent Arab state be created in Palestine. Separatism, like any other solution, is never the perfect answer to situations of intense intergroup rivalry, but it may offer more hopeful prospects than the alternatives.

Third, we must recognize that the fragmentation of the land held by individual homelands, though not politically desirable, is not ipso facto evil. Many nations have much further-flung noncontiguous land units. Indonesia is spread out across thousands of miles. West Berlin is as much an outlier of the Federal Republic as the Thaba Nchu area is of BophuthaTswana. KwaZulu is now in five pieces, but so is the United States if you consider Alaska, Puerto Rico, Hawaii, and the Virgin Islands. Having noncontiguous units is no wicked thing in itself, although it does make administration more difficult.

Despite the common market aspects of the South African economy, however, almost insurperable difficulties will obstruct the functioning of the homelands as effective poltical units if they proceed to full independence as presently constituted. Further geographical consolidation is clearly required, but how? The most difficult approach is the one the South African government first adopted and still follows in theory—that is, buying out white landowners in areas designed as African. Blacks can be moved from white areas with political impunity; but whites have votes and in most instances where whites are moved to permit consolidation of homelands, they are Afrikaners and supporters of the government. It is not the cost, admittedly high, of expropriating Afrikaans farmers, but rather their emotional attachment to the land—a salient feature of Afrikaner character—that renders the movement of Afrikaners to make way for Africans the most politically explosive problem the government faces in its homelands policy.

What will happen is a major modification of government policy. The solution that will be adopted for the consolidation of the homelands, and also for their expansion to encompass a more equitable share of the land surface of South Africa, will be some provision whereby whites will retain ownership rights while the homelands consolidate and expand around them. A logical way for such whites in consolidated African homelands to express their political wishes would be voting in so-called "white South Africa." This would be the same approach that the government takes to Africans in "white" urban areas who vote in their respective homelands. It is not a permanent solution, any more than voting in their countries of origin is for permanent migrants in Europe, but it has interim advantages. In the long run, it is likely that the African leadership of the homelands will allow political expression to whites on a basis of equality and that it will be accepted. Chief Minister Cedric Phatudi has made it clear to this author that he envisions the Lebowa homeland as having no racial distinctions at all among its citizens.

Such a solution may not come easily, because it cuts against previous government pronouncements. Moreover, it will offer a powerful precedent for Africans who live and work in the "white homeland" to have a reasonable claim to excercise a franchise there. It is a Gordian knot that must be cut if the homelands are to consolidate. The government will find it easier to change its theories than move its farmers. It will do so.

Along similar lines, there will be significant steps to give urban Africans far greater autonomy over their affairs. Soweto, the great sprawling black annex of Johannesburg with a population of over a million, will be granted a large measure of self-government. In the second largest city, Cape Town, much of African work force is still essentially migratory and there is no real analog to Soweto. In the third city, Durban, the boundaries of KwaZulu come right into the urban conurbation and offer a modus vivendi for ensuring that most Africans live in a homeland.

It is conceivable that there will emerge in South Africa a "multistan," which is to say a part of the country delineated for people of all races, not just a particular race. The most likely regional expression of such a philosophy is the KwaZulu bantustan. Chief Gatsha Buthelezi has been the most prominent homelands leader calling for the nonracial society. He has stressed that under his leadership in KwaZulu, all white and colored citizens would be of equal status to Zulus. In principle but less vocally, he has said the same for the Indians. This is a politically courageous stance to take, since the worst race riots in South African history were those between

Zulus and Indians in Durban in 1948. The right of Indians to use their present superior financial status to by land in what has always been Zulu territory could well produce violent reactions from some KwaZulu citizens. Eventually, however, multistan pattern could well spread from KwaZulu to other homelands—and in the very long run to "white" to South Africa itself, once separate development is fully under way and whites no longer fear black hegemony in their areas.

If the homelands are to be more economically viable, further modifications of government policy will be necessary. It was only a decade ago that Prime Minister Verwoerd absolutely insisted that no "white" capital be allowed into the Transkei and other potential homelands. One afternoon in Cape Town he argued with me for an hour on this point alone. He had sound reasons for his intransigent attitude. If white, Asian, or foreign speculators and developers were to buy out a major part of his so-called African homelands, it would make a travesty of his program. Do New Zealanders allow rich Texans or even their own white citizens to buy Maori-owned land? Or do Americans allow anyone to purchase parts of the Navajo Reservation holdings? American regulations regarding alienation of a few acres of Samoan land to establish a factory to create jobs are far tighter than restrictions in the Transkei or other homelands.

Nevertheless, the South African government, under John Vorster, wisely modified its policy once the political status of Africans in the homelands was better established. Investments of so-called "white" or "foreign" capital are now permitted in the homelands under increasingly generous terms. But this investment will always be controlled—and not just by the South African government—because of the strongly expressed wishes of the individual homelands governments concerned. The new policy will provide a better basis for the future economic viability of the homelands, ensuring that their ultimate political independence will be a meaningful one.

As the homelands develop and the political aspirations of Africans find a genuine outlet, there will be an easing of discriminatory practices within "white" South Africa. Prime Minister Vorster denies, for general consumption that there is such an animal as "petty *apartheid*," preferring to focus on the grand *apartheid* of territorial separation. But however you describe it, there is considerable discrimination in public facilities against individuals on the basis of color in South Africa. This apparatus of discrimination is already being dismantled and its manifestations will rapidly decline in South Africa in the future. It does not take a particularly sensitive observer to detect that the new skyscrapers proliferating in South African cities do not have racially separate elevators, or that the signs with racial overtones in industrial plants, parks, public buildings, and elsewhere are disappearing. The handsome new Nico Malan theatre in Cape Town was initially barred to the colored community, but the prime minister himself intervened directly in the issue in favor of open facilities. It has become commonplace to forecast the rapid growth in interracial sports activities, and equally common to deride such changes as unimportant.

Those nations that prevent a South African team, chosen entirely on merit and traveling and living without racial discrimination, from competing at the Olympic Games shortsightedly overlook the patriotism of all South Africans, who are drawn into a common support of "their" athletes regardless of race. Only more perceptive individuals, including some such as Arthur Ashe, who have the greatest concern over discrimination and who participate in integrated events in South Africa before integrated audiences, realize how important a positive involvement in South Africa can be as opposed to a blind negativism. In this field as elsewhere, supposedly well-intentioned critics of South African policies impede rather than hasten the process of change toward a just and nondiscriminatory society.

The pattern of change in South Africa in the future will depend to a great extent on the wisdom of the leaders of the black and white communities. A peaceful transition will require that the African leaders adopt a flexible and pragmatic approach, and that the Afrikaner leaders recognize the necessity of change and persuade their followers to accept it.

South Africa, unlike most African countries in their colonial period, has a great reservoir of well-educated and able black leaders. Consequently, it is all but impossible for the leadership of political movements in South Africa to be retained by the radicals in exile. When a leader departs, there emerge new local African leaders of talent and energy. Fifteen years of attempted subversion and guerilla warfare have led nowhere, and the prestige of the exiled revolutionaries is dwindling in proportion to the increase in popularity of the homelands leaders. This means that as South Africa advances toward a just society, the sometimes extreme and highly ideological views of exile groups will not act as hindrances to reasonable compromise within South Africa as power devolves from white to black. In the history of political change, it has usually been far easier to adopt intransigent positions from the security of a safe and comfortable foreign country. The sense of grievance is no less among the Africans within the Republic, who continue to suffer indignities day by day, but they have a stronger pragmatism that seeks a step-by-step advance and does not have a vested interest in a *Götterdamerung* scenario.

A leadership element strong in the past, that of the radicals, is now missing. But the better-educated, better-off urban Africans will shortly shift their present divided allegiance (to imprisoned leaders of the sixties, to exile organizations, and to the more charismatic homelands politicians) to a new

African leadership in the cities. Coming changes in African homeowner-
ship in urban areas, greater opportunities to engage in many business activities, new financial institutions such as African banks, and the rise of a
stronger professional and business middle class with greater security will
provide the foundation for a new breed of African leaders.

They will be militant in their criticism of the existing order but will not
cast themselves in the role of urban guerrillas. Unlike many of the African
leaders of the sixties, they will not be manipulated by white communists.
The new generation of black college students, both in and out of the
African Students Organization—whose isolation from the whites the
government has encouraged—have gone another step in their conscious
rejection of liberal white students who were their self-appointed mentors in
the past. The day when whites—communists, liberals, or Afrikaner Nationalist officials—could speak for urban Africans is over.

The emergent urban leaders, more secure in their tenure, will be less
suspicious of and more cooperative with homelands leaders, while at the
same time challenging their positions as African spokesmen. Inevitably,
there will be impassioned speeches and physical confrontations with white
authority in urban areas. Violence will break out again. Hundreds more
may be killed. It will appear at such times that the chances for peaceful
change have vanished in the violence. But calm and reason will return and
progress to a just society will resume, with pragmatic adjustments by both
black and white. These urban leaders will not accept separate development as a principle. It is a framework forced on them. But they will seek to
use it. What will remain significantly different in South Africa as compared
to other areas of ethnic partition is that the South African decision was
made by whites without consulation with or approval by blacks. Tribal
areas have been kept separate with African approval, but this is not the
case with the urban areas and it will continue to rancor Africans in these
centers.

The continual strengthening of a practical African leadership—not one
whit less idealistic than that of the Africans abroad or imprisoned—will prove critical to a steady change on the part of the white oligarchy. If a prognosis of relatively peaceful change is to be borne out by events, it is the
rate and degree of change, by whites that will be crucial. It is therefore vital
that the whites are not scared off, that they are willing to accede to
peaceful change and are not driven into the *laager*—the Afrikaner's traditional defensive formation of ox-wagons.

When we talk of the whites we talk primarily of the Afrikaners, both
those behind the government and those opposing it on the right. The
Afrikaners are critical to the process of peaceful change because power is
held by Afrikaners. The most pervasive reason to be optimistic about white

accommodation to reasonable African aspirations lies in the nature of the Afrikaner and his nationalism. As I described in a book in 1967,[1] a great deal of African nationalism follows patterns against the Afrikaners similar to those the Afrikaner followed against the dominance of the British. The Afrikaner's fight was against this dominance—in his case against political control from overseas—just as the black African's has been. Afrikaners like John Vorster, when they were forbidden to speak their own native language in the school playground and were beaten if they did, fought with great intensity for equal rights for their language. A harder and more subtle struggle developed against the economic domination of British.

But Afrikaners have not been imperialists. They have not suppressed the English language in South Africa. Quite the opposite. Most of them are more fluent in English than Engish speakers are in Afrikaans. The government has strongly encouraged African languages in African schools. The Afrikaner sought political power over the whole country not to dominate others but to free himself. As a people, the Afrikaners want security for their language and their religion, and freedom for their children to live and prosper in southern Africa. Such generalized goals do not depend on oppressing any group. In fact, a substantial number of Afrikaans leaders have come to realize that Afrikaner survival is dependent on oppressing *no* group in South Africa, whether in the homelands or in what is presently (but not for always) thought of as "white South Africa." The Afrikaner need not dominate to survive and thus need not fight to the last man for what he now posesses.

Change will not take place without upheavals in Afrikanerdom, or without the necessity for some strong-arm tactics by the government. There may be serious trouble and even armed resistance from the extremist Herstigtes. They will gain adherents from the right wing of the Nationalists, but not enough to seriously undermine the government. Violent reactions by the ultra-right wing Scorpio organization and similar clandestine groups will increase, but without becoming a dominant factor. There will be assassinations of Afrikaner *"veraaiers,"* or traitors, who are perceived as active symbols of change. But no military coup will come from the right to stop a peaceful resolution of South Africa's political problems. Indeed, leading officers in all services, a majority of them Afrikaners, have themselves expressed the need for flexibility and change. Cultural changes within Afrikanerdom—particularly those generated by the impact of television, only recently introduced, and the rapid urbanization of the Afrikaner population—will serve to condition political accommodation.

What evidence is there, the reader may ask, of Afrikaner flexibility? The dark events of 1977, which increased international pressure on South

Africa and elicited the sharp reaction from the Praetorian guard, led many critics to the conclusion that South African racial policies are set in concrete.

Perhaps the changes within South Africa, such as the abolition of some forms of "petty" *apartheid*, are cosmetic. Even the post-1977 election promises to the citizens of Soweto for a degree of autonomy are more symbolic than significant.

But changes are far more than cosmetic in Namibia, where the South African government holds de facto power. The appointment of a new Suffragan bishop for the "Episcopal" Church there is absolutely unprecedented when one realizes that he is a black Namibian and has a "white" wife. The repeal of the Mixed Marriages Act is basic, as is the repeal of the Immorality Act. The barring of discrimination in major hotels on the basis of race is fundamental. The deep philosophical shift in Namibia from the concept that people should vote and should express their views within the framework of their ethnic groups to the broad concept that each person counts as an individual is, of course, directly contrary to the National party philosophy for South Africa.

Much has been made of the snags in the way of true Namibian independence. But the issue of Walvis Bay (legally part of South Africa's Cape Province but clearly essential as the port of Namibia) is more likely a bargaining chip than a boulder on the path of change. The sharp reduction in the size of the South African military force in Namibia (to be further reduced contingent on peaceful conditions in the Angola interface with external SWAPO) suggests that policing the territory during and after the election is not an insoluble problem.

This Afrikaner flexibility and adaptibility in both principle and practice in Namibia is conclusive evidence that all Nationalist thought is not set in concrete. True, South Africa is the heartland and not a mandated territory. Relatively peaceful changes in Namibia may have come more easily and as a result of greater pressure than will be possible in the Republic of South Africa.

Alan Paton succinctly summed up the dilemma of the English South African to me as follows: if he is a pessimist, he should leave; if he is an optimist, he should see a psychiatrist; and if he has a gram of hope, he should keep working for a peaceful and just solution.

But this advice applies to few Afrikaners. If the Afrikaner is to do his share in bringing about peaceful change—and this statement recognizes that forces may develop that do not allow peaceful change—then it will be Afrikaner institutions that provide the framework for an adaptation in thinking. From the perspective of 1978, and without going into the supporting details, this observer judges Afrikaner institutions as follows. The intellectuals, including the universities, emerged as a force for peaceful change in the 1950s. However, they have not been important in traditional Afrikaans society. The Fourth Estate, which slavishly echoed the whole "party line" from 1948 to 1970, has unshackled itself and is playing a critical role in communicating the need for change. The judiciary, whose members, thought by no means all Afrikaners, are now almost entirely appointed by Afrikaners, has been a consistent bastion of fair judgment. Many decisions by Afrikaner judges have been against the government's case. The judiciary remains steadfast, though its importance has been seriously diminished by a shift in legislation to administrative law beyond the purview of the courts.

Perhaps most disappointing has been the failure, with few exceptions, of the leadership of the three "Dutch Reform" churches to play the significant role that I expected from them. This reflects, among other factors, the decline of religion as a major factor in Afrikaner thinking outside of Sundays. It also reflects the growing secularization of the Afrikaner since 1948 as he moved from being a Boer on the platteland to being a businessman in the city, where most Afrikaners now live and where the National party holds two-thirds of its parliamentary seats.

A relatively peaceful solution to South Africans' problems is complicated by the emergence of a whole new black spirit. The situation has not reached the point anticipated by Alan Paton decades ago that by the time the whites turn to loving, the blacks will have turned to hating. But that is the trend. Despite what the Nationalists say, without pressure for change, change would take a century.

Perhaps no individual has personified the new black consciousness, free of the communist trappings of the African National Congress, more than the late and onetime leader of the South African Students Association, Steve Biko. As far back as 1971 Biko said, inter alia:

> The Progs have never been a black man's real hope. They have always been a white party at heart fighting for a more lasting way of preserving white values in this Southern tip of Africa. It will not be long before the Blacks relate their poverty to their Blackness in concrete terms. A new breed of black leaders was beginning to take a dim view of the involvement of the liberals in a struggle that they regarded as essentially theirs, when political movements of the Blacks were either banned or harassed into non-existence. This left the stage once more open to the liberals to continue their work of "fighting for the blacks. . . ." The myth of integration as propounded under the banner of the liberal ideology must be cracked and killed because it makes people believe that something is being done when in actual fact the artificial integrated circles are a soporific on the Blacks and provide a satisfaction for the guilt ridden whites.[2]

Biko was farsighted. The negotiations will be between the Afrikaner Nationalists and the black Nationalists without white liberals or communist ideologues assigning themselves a surrogate role. Afrikaners will understand this better than most English-speaking whites and better than the world outside South Africa.

The significance of the 1977 election is not that Prime Minister Vorster ran so successfully against interference in South African affairs by the Carter administration, or in an approving reaction by white voters to Minister Jimmy Kruger's crackdown on moderate Africans, or in constitutional changes regarding coloureds and Asians. The significance is that the real white opposition within South Africa lies within the National party. Ever since its electoral victory in 1948, the party has stood for broad principles. There have always been those who today are characterized as more *verlig* (enlightened) or more *verkramp* (ultraconservative). But now in 1978, we have a National party that is far more polarized. Dr. Jan Marais, former head of the South African Foundation, put it candidly when he said that his ideas were progressive, but that with so little time left, the only effective action within the white sphere is within the National party. His election to parliament along with other strongly *verlig* MP means that the battle for enlightened change to avoid bloodshed does have its leaders within the governing oligarchy. What overseas newspapers failed to underscore in analyzing the election is the utter failure—really more disastrous than in previous efforts—of right-wing Herstigtes.

Finally, the contribution of the homelands to political change must be reemphasized. Never will they be *the* answer. But they will continue to be a factor. Prime Minister Matanzima failed in his battle to let the Xhosa choose their citizenship. Prime Minister Lukas Mangope of BophutaTswana succeeded in obtaining this choice for the Tswanas against tough opposition in Pretoria. If and when Chief Gatsha Buthelezi moves to accept "independence" for KwaZulu, it will only be, I predict, on the basis of another major concession by the South African government. That concession will be full consolidation of the five major Zulu blocks into a political whole. Without these fundamental changes, but no more startling than changes already made in Nabimia, KwaZulu will never accept independence.

It was not inevitable but always likely that the stage would be set as we now find it for direct negotiations between Afrikaner and African without foreign and/or white liberal intermediaries. Gatsha Buthelezi's comment on the significance of the 1977 election was that the blacks' political salvation lies in their own hands. And the massive assault on black leadership, including the jailing of such a voice of reason as Percy Qoboza and the banning of his newspaper, *The World*, creates a greater sense of black unity without eliminating ethnicity.

In my opinion, the Afrikaners will find it easier to make *their* "trip to Jerusalem" if they go directly to African leadership. African nationalism has paralleled Afrikaner nationalism through the early and middle stages. In the next few years we will discover how well the Afrikaners know their own emotions and their own history. The results are likely to surprise some of their more vociferous critics and doomsayers.

John Vorster, if he is to lead South Africa through great changes, will be successful only if the whites do not sense the rate of change sufficiently to offer strong resistance and if the Africans also do not sense the change and reach out too far and too fast. To prevent this, the Afrikaner leader will almost certainly move against both friend and foe in the press, in politics, and among student groups who perceive his strategies. In fact, much of the thrust of security police activity in recent years has been directed against the right-wing Herstigtes and others who oppose his new policies. The newspaper that will probably feel the heaviest of Mr. Vorster's lashes, however, is the liberal *Rand Daily Mail,* for Vorster will attack precisely those papers that praise his efforts to effect change. Prime Minister Vorster is likely to rationalize that some freedom of the press will have to be sacrificed, paradoxical as it may seem, to bring about rapid political and social change in South Africa. An associate of the prime minister put it another way: to win the war of rapid change one may have to adopt the kind of draconian measures that most democratic societies have adopted in wartime, when their goal was also freedom

Mankind often believes that destiny is shaped by virtues and not by vices. Yet it is to the vices of the Afrikaner that most critics look in judging their character and future. But a great strength of the Afrikaner is that he has not suffered from the lack of will so commonly found of late in America and Europe. In the Toynbean sense, Afrikaners will respond to the challenge to their culture by being flexible.

Only a fool would predict political change in southern Africa without recognizing how fallible such an excercise may prove to be. But the changes that are foreseen in this prognosis have their roots in the history of the Afrikaner and of South Africa. Much of the world believes that the Afrikaner thinks he must dominate to live. If that belief is true, he will die. But the real thrust of Afrikaner history is not to dominate but to avoid domination. Hence there are excellent opportunities for a relatively peaceful transformation of the present divided and multiethnic society into a just society and, in time, into a United States of South Africa.

Notes

1. Edwin S. Munger, *Afrikaner and African Nationalism: South African Parallels and Parameters* (London and New York: Oxford University Press, 1967).

2. The quotations are taken from the paper by S. B. Biko on "White Racism and Black Consciousness" at the First Inter-University Research Workshop on Students and Youth in South Africa at the Abe Bailey Institute in 1971.

CONTRIBUTORS

HERIBERT ADAM is professor of sociology at Simon Fraser University in Vancouver. He has taught at the University of Natal and has also been visiting professor of sociology at the American University in Cairo. He is author of *Modernizing Racial Domination: The Dynamics of South African Politics* and editor of *South Africa: Sociological Perspectives.*

KENNETH CARSTENS, an ordained minister, was born in South Africa and educated at Rhodes and Harvard. He is executive director of the American branch of the International Defence and Aid Fund for Southern Africa and has been a consultant on South Africa for the United Nations, the National Council of Churches, and the International Court of Justice.

JOHN DANIEL was educated at the University of Natal, Michigan State, and the State University of New York at Buffalo. He is a former president of the National Union of South African Students and is now a political scientist specializing in southern African affairs. His South African citizenship has been revoked, and he is currently teaching political science at the University of Swaziland.

DONALD EASUM is a former U.S. under secretary of state for Africa and is currently U.S. ambassador to Nigeria. He was educated at Wisconsin, Princeton, and London, and worked as a journalist and teacher until he joined the foreign service in 1953. He has served in several African countries, including Gambia, Senegal, and Upper Volta.

LAURENCE GANDAR is former editor of the *Rand Daily Mail*, where his editorials and exposures of South African prison conditions won him the World Press Achievement Award. He was successfully prosecuted by the South African government for the prison articles, and subsequently

271

worked for Amnesty International in London. He is now retired and is living in Natal.

RUSSELL WARREN HOWE is a former dean of the American press corps in Africa; he covered the continent for several major newspapers between 1954 and 1972. He has published numerous articles and six books on Africa, including *Along the Afric Shore,* a history of American-African relations. He is now a free-lance writer in Washington, D.C.

COLIN LEGUM was born in South Africa, but has spent much of his career in London as the African and Commonwealth correspondent of the *Observer* (London). He has lectured and broadcasted on African affairs in many parts of the world, and has been a UN consultant on race relations. He is author or editor of several books, including *South Africa: Crisis for the West.*

MARGARET LEGUM is an economist by training. She has coauthored several books with her husband, Colin Legum, and is a regular broadcaster for the BBC in London. She is author of *The Coming Struggle for South Africa* and of many articles on South Africa and Namibia. For several years she has been involved in the problems of South African refugees living abroad.

REINIER LOCK was born in Rhodesia. He was educated at Rhodes, Oxford, and the University of California at Berkeley, and is a member of the Rhodesian, London, and California bars. He has worked as economics correspondent for the *Financial Mail* (Johannesburg) and the *Financial Times,* (London) and currently practices law in San Francisco.

DAVID MECHANIC was educated at Stanford and is currently professor of sociology at the University of Wisconsin Center for Medical Sociology and Health Services Research. He has published extensively in the areas of social psychology and medical sociology, and has studied health services in South Africa.

EDWIN S. MUNGER was educated at the University of Chicago and is now professor of political geography at the California Institute of Technology. He has made over thirty field visits to South Africa since 1947 and is author or over 240 articles and seven books on the continent, including *Afrikaner and African Nationalism.*

IAN ROBERTSON was banned under the Suppression of Communism Act in 1966 while president of the National Union of South African Students. He subsequently studied at Oxford, Harvard, and Cambridge, where he has taught social sciences. He has published a number of articles on South Africa and is author or editor of several books in the fields of sociology and social psychology.

ALBIE SACHS was born in South Africa and educated at the University of Cape Town. He practiced at the bar for many years, specializing in political cases. He was twice detained without trial and was banned under the Suppression of Communism Act. His books include *Justice in South Africa* and *Jail Diary*. He now lectures in law at the University of Southampton in England.

RANDALL STOKES was educated at the University of California at San Diego and at Duke University, and is now assistant professor of sociology at the University of Massachusetts in Amherst. He has done field work on nationalism and social change in several southern African countries, and has published a number or articles on these topics.

PIERRE VAN DEN BERGHE was educated at Harvard and is now proessor at sociology at the University of Washington; he has also taught in France, Kenya, Nigeria, and South Africa. He has written several books, including *South Africa: A Study in Conflict,* and has published numerous articles on race relations in South Africa and elsewhere.

RANDOLPH VIGNE was born in South Africa and educated at Oxford University. He was a leading member of the South African Liberal party and edited two journals, *Contact* and *New African,* until they were banned. He subsequently joined an underground organization, the African Resistance Movement, and narrowly escaped from the country in 1963. He is now a publisher in London.

PHILLIP WHITTEN was educated at San Jose State University and Harvard University. He has worked for some time in the publishing industry, and is now a free-lance publisher and writer in Marblehead, Massasschusetts. He has written several articles on African affairs and has authored and edited a number of books in the social sciences.